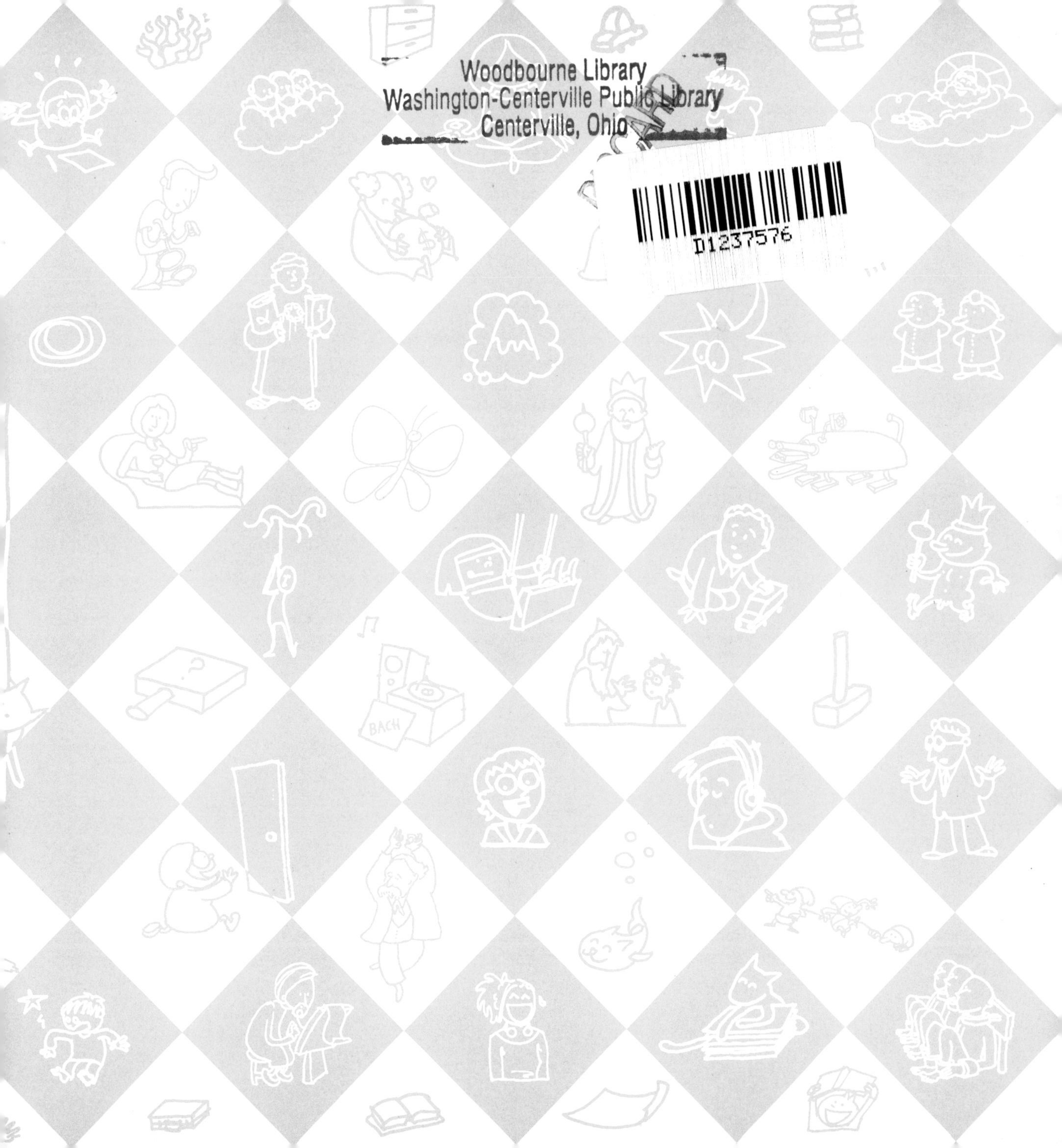

Margreet de Heer

PHILOSOPHY
A DISCOVERY IN COMICS

NANTIER · BEALL · MINOUSTCHINE
Publishing inc.
new york

Copyright @ 2010 Uitgeverij Meinema, Zoetermeer, The Netherlands
Copyright English translation © 2012 Margreet de Heer & Yiri T. Kohl

Original title: Filosofie in Beeld
Published originally in Dutch by Uitgeverij Meinema, 2010

Publication in the U.S.: NBM Publishing, 2012
Printed in China
1st printing September 2012

ISBN 978-1-56163-698-3
Library of Congress Control Number 2012938931

Text & drawings: Margreet de Heer
Colors: Yiri T. Kohl
Translation & lettering assistance: Emma Ringelberg & Dan Schiff

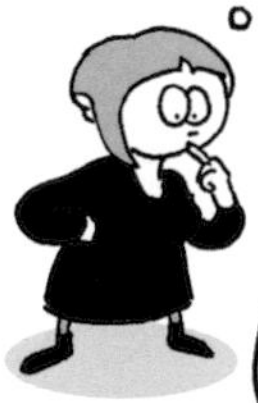

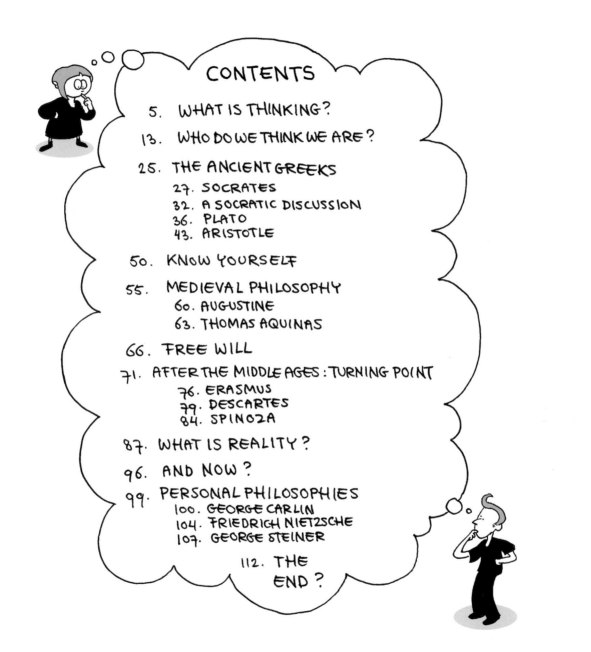

CONTENTS

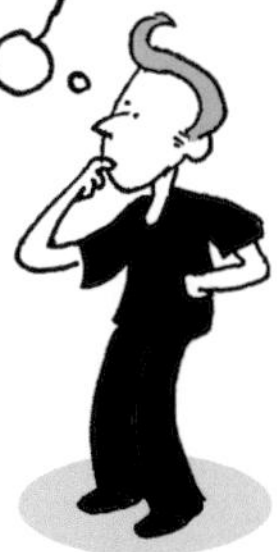

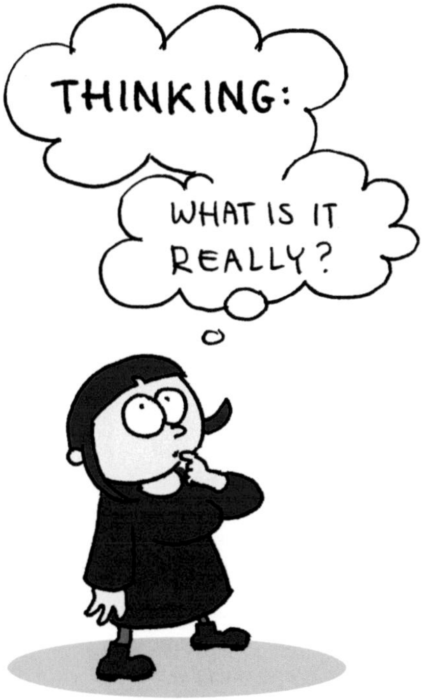
THINKING:
WHAT IS IT
REALLY?

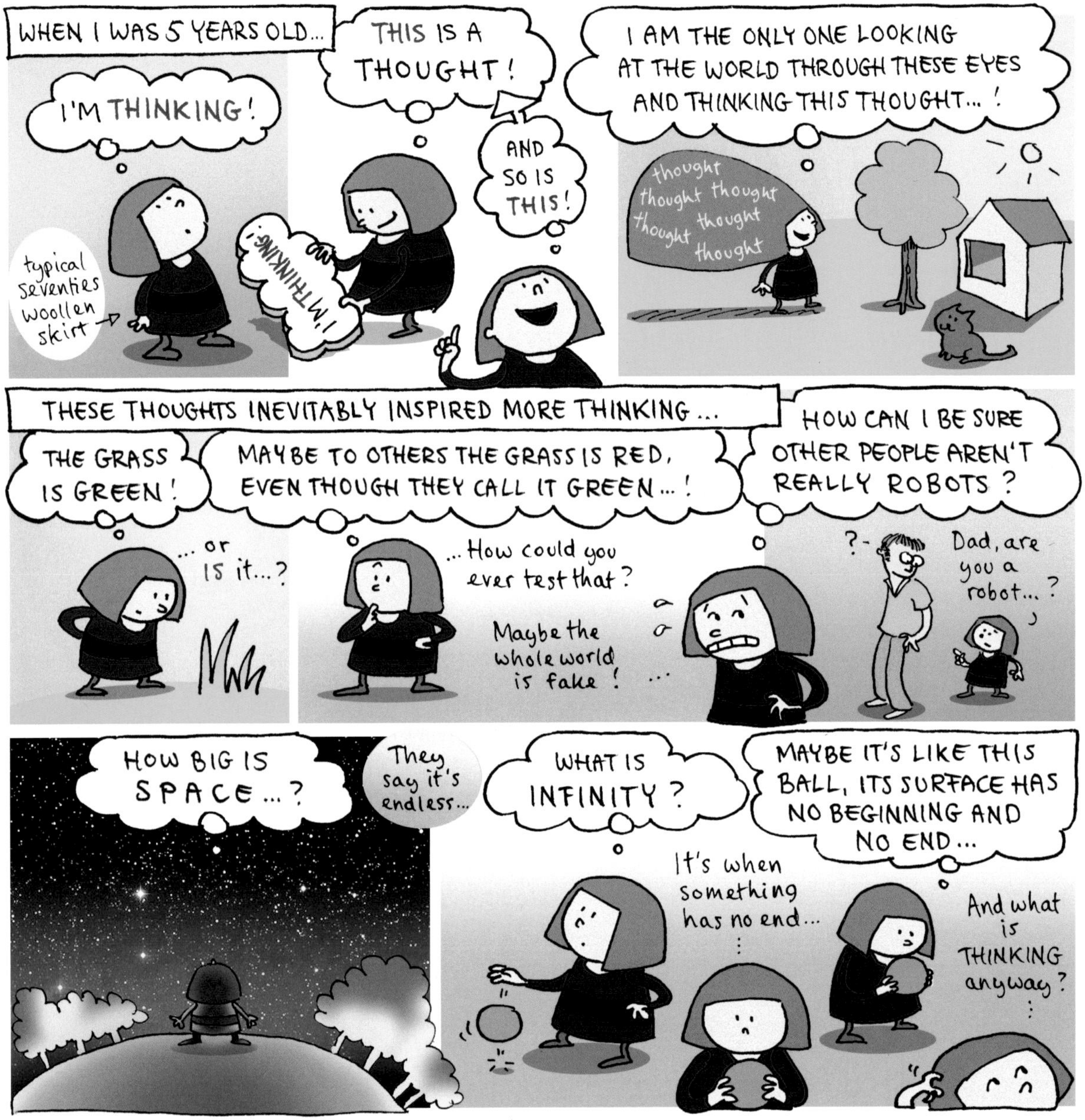
WHEN I WAS 5 YEARS OLD...
I'M THINKING!
typical seventies woollen skirt
THIS IS A THOUGHT!
I'M THINKING!
AND SO IS THIS!
I AM THE ONLY ONE LOOKING AT THE WORLD THROUGH THESE EYES AND THINKING THIS THOUGHT... !
thought thought thought thought thought thought
THESE THOUGHTS INEVITABLY INSPIRED MORE THINKING...
THE GRASS IS GREEN!
... or is it...?
MAYBE TO OTHERS THE GRASS IS RED, EVEN THOUGH THEY CALL IT GREEN... !
... How could you ever test that?
Maybe the whole world is fake! ...
HOW CAN I BE SURE OTHER PEOPLE AREN'T REALLY ROBOTS?
?-
Dad, are you a robot...?
HOW BIG IS SPACE...?
They say it's endless...
WHAT IS INFINITY?
It's when something has no end...
MAYBE IT'S LIKE THIS BALL, ITS SURFACE HAS NO BEGINNING AND NO END...
And what is THINKING anyway?

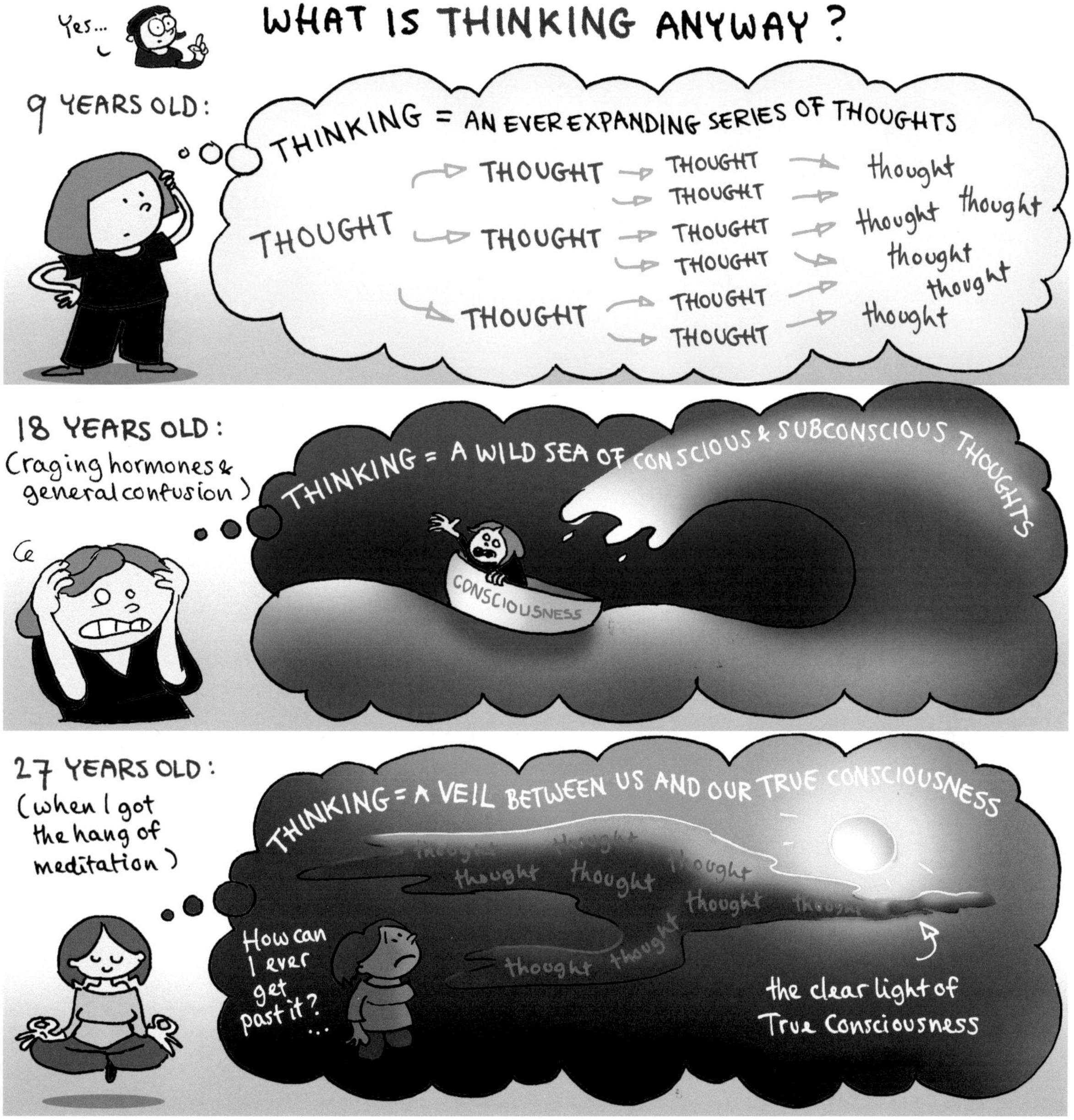
Yes...
WHAT IS THINKING ANYWAY?
9 YEARS OLD:
THINKING = AN EVER EXPANDING SERIES OF THOUGHTS
THOUGHT
THOUGHT
THOUGHT
THOUGHT
THOUGHT
THOUGHT
THOUGHT
THOUGHT
THOUGHT
THOUGHT
thought
thought
thought
thought
thought
thought
18 YEARS OLD:
(raging hormones & general confusion)
THINKING = A WILD SEA OF CONSCIOUS & SUBCONSCIOUS THOUGHTS
CONSCIOUSNESS
27 YEARS OLD:
(when I got the hang of meditation)
THINKING = A VEIL BETWEEN US AND OUR TRUE CONSCIOUSNESS
thought
thought
thought
thought
thought
thought
thought
thought
How can I ever get past it? ...
the clear light of True Consciousness

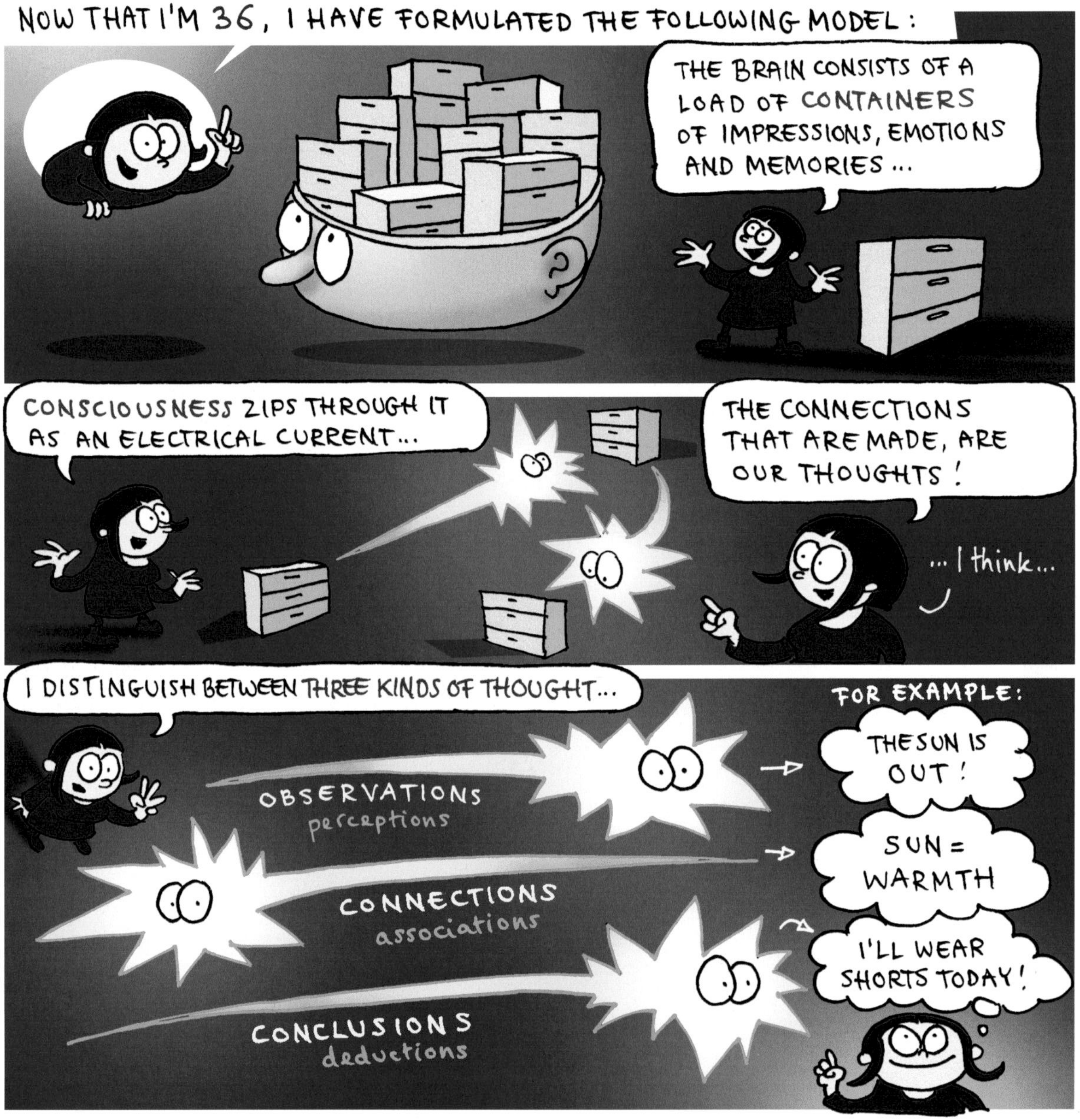
NOW THAT I'M 36, I HAVE FORMULATED THE FOLLOWING MODEL:
THE BRAIN CONSISTS OF A LOAD OF CONTAINERS OF IMPRESSIONS, EMOTIONS AND MEMORIES...
CONSCIOUSNESS ZIPS THROUGH IT AS AN ELECTRICAL CURRENT...
THE CONNECTIONS THAT ARE MADE, ARE OUR THOUGHTS!
...I think...
I DISTINGUISH BETWEEN THREE KINDS OF THOUGHT...
FOR EXAMPLE:
OBSERVATIONS
perceptions
THE SUN IS OUT!
CONNECTIONS
associations
SUN = WARMTH
CONCLUSIONS
deductions
I'LL WEAR SHORTS TODAY!

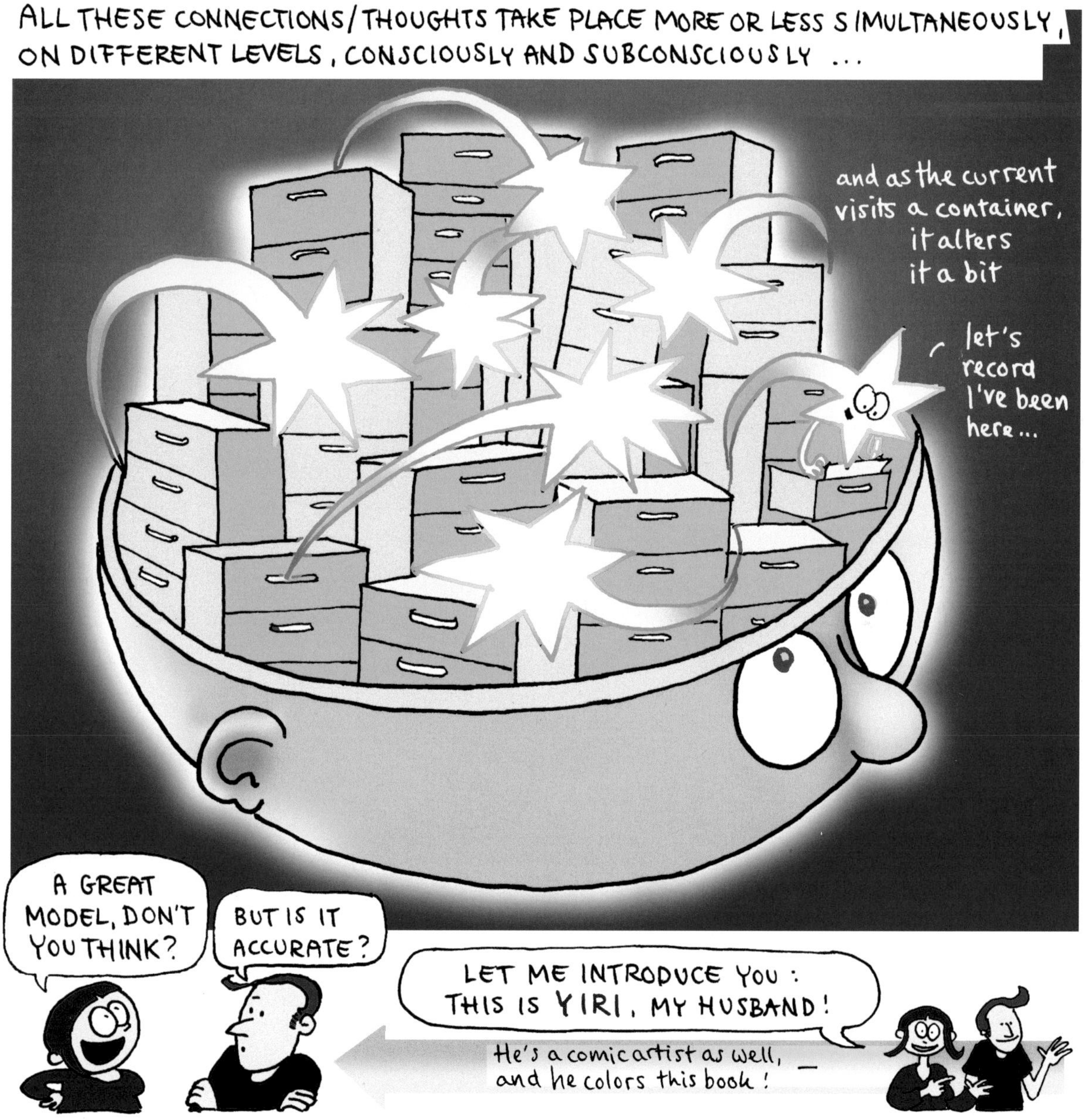
ALL THESE CONNECTIONS/THOUGHTS TAKE PLACE MORE OR LESS SIMULTANEOUSLY, ON DIFFERENT LEVELS, CONSCIOUSLY AND SUBCONSCIOUSLY ...
and as the current visits a container, it alters it a bit
let's record I've been here...
A GREAT MODEL, DON'T YOU THINK?
BUT IS IT ACCURATE?
LET ME INTRODUCE YOU: THIS IS YIRI, MY HUSBAND!
He's a comic artist as well, and he colors this book!

THINKING ON YOUR OWN IS ALL WELL AND GOOD ...
... BUT NEW THOUGHTS ONLY REALLY THRIVE ON A BIT OF INPUT AND REPARTEE!
knock knock
HAVE YOU TRIED THIS THOUGHT YET?
THINKING BY YOURSELF IS LIKE RIDING THE FREEWAY:
QUICK & EASY
THE TRODDEN PATH
ELSEWHERE
- This way!
... BUT YOU CAN ONLY REACH YOUR DESTINATION BY PULLING OFF THE ROAD AT SOME POINT!

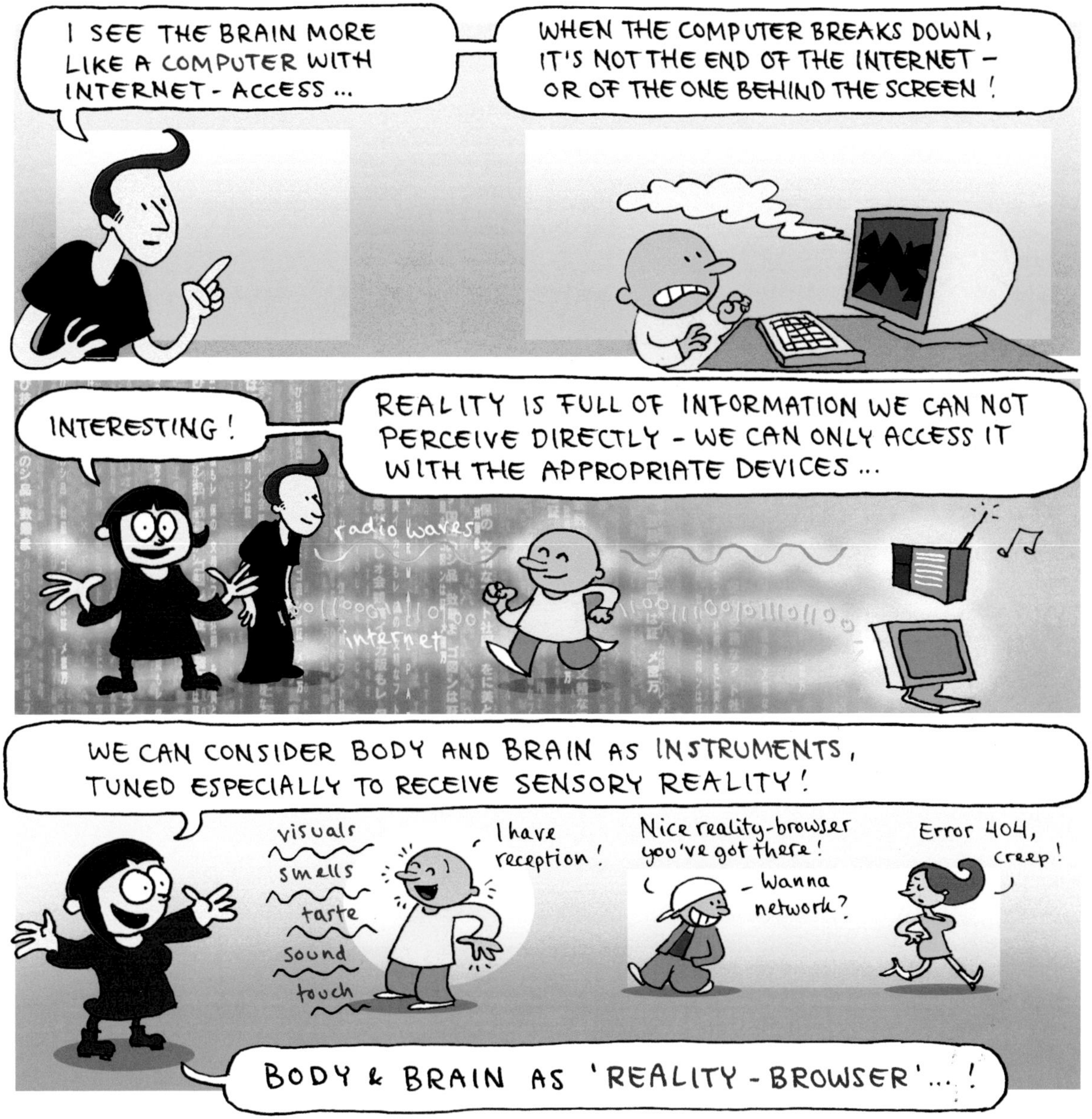
I SEE THE BRAIN MORE LIKE A COMPUTER WITH INTERNET-ACCESS ...
WHEN THE COMPUTER BREAKS DOWN, IT'S NOT THE END OF THE INTERNET - OR OF THE ONE BEHIND THE SCREEN!
INTERESTING!
REALITY IS FULL OF INFORMATION WE CAN NOT PERCEIVE DIRECTLY - WE CAN ONLY ACCESS IT WITH THE APPROPRIATE DEVICES ...
radio waves
internet
WE CAN CONSIDER BODY AND BRAIN AS INSTRUMENTS, TUNED ESPECIALLY TO RECEIVE SENSORY REALITY!
visuals
smells
taste
sound
touch
I have reception!
Nice reality-browser you've got there!
- Wanna network?
Error 404, creep!
BODY & BRAIN AS 'REALITY-BROWSER'...!

THEN THINKING IS THE METHOD BY WHICH OUR INSTRUMENT (body + brain) PROCESSES THE INFORMATION WE RECEIVE.

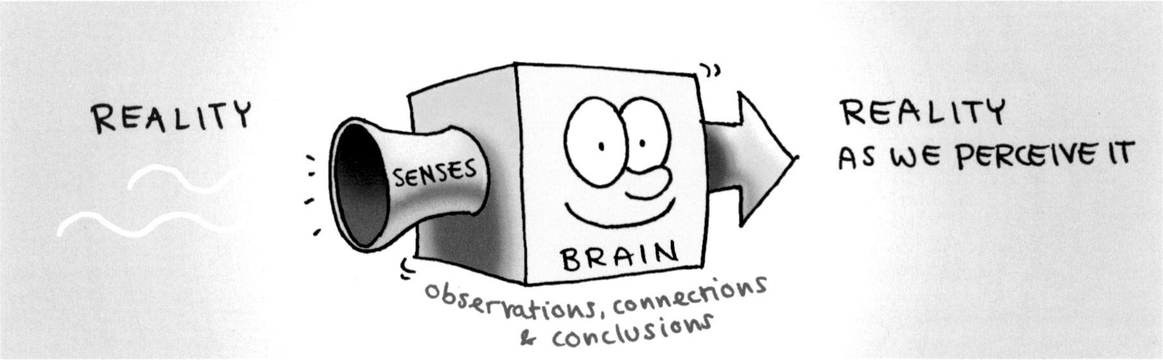
REALITY
SENSES
BRAIN
observations, connections & conclusions
REALITY AS WE PERCEIVE IT

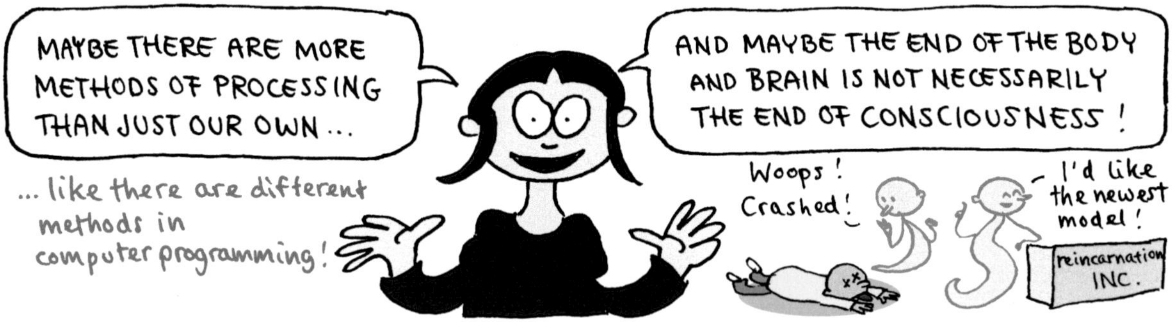
MAYBE THERE ARE MORE METHODS OF PROCESSING THAN JUST OUR OWN ...
... like there are different methods in computer programming!
AND MAYBE THE END OF THE BODY AND BRAIN IS NOT NECESSARILY THE END OF CONSCIOUSNESS!
Woops! Crashed!
- I'd like the newest model!
reincarnation INC.

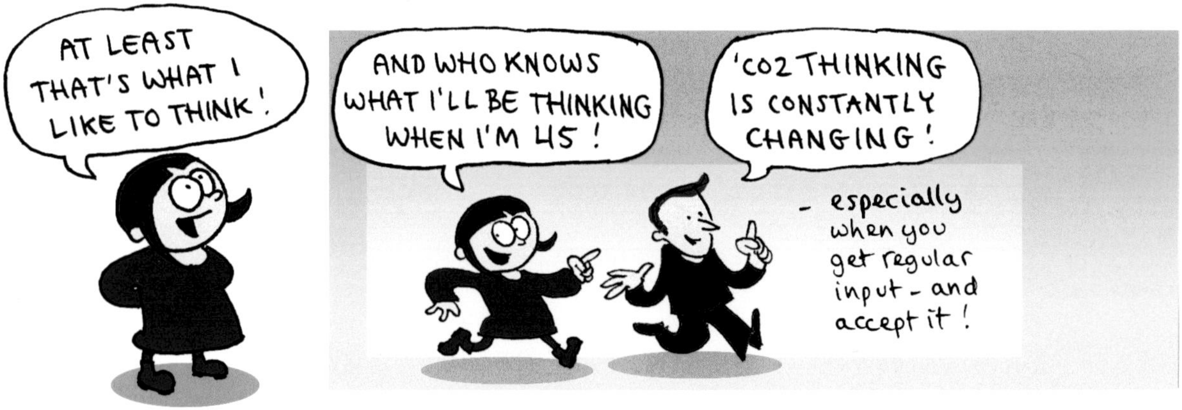
AT LEAST THAT'S WHAT I LIKE TO THINK!
AND WHO KNOWS WHAT I'LL BE THINKING WHEN I'M 45!
'COZ THINKING IS CONSTANTLY CHANGING!
- especially when you get regular input - and accept it!

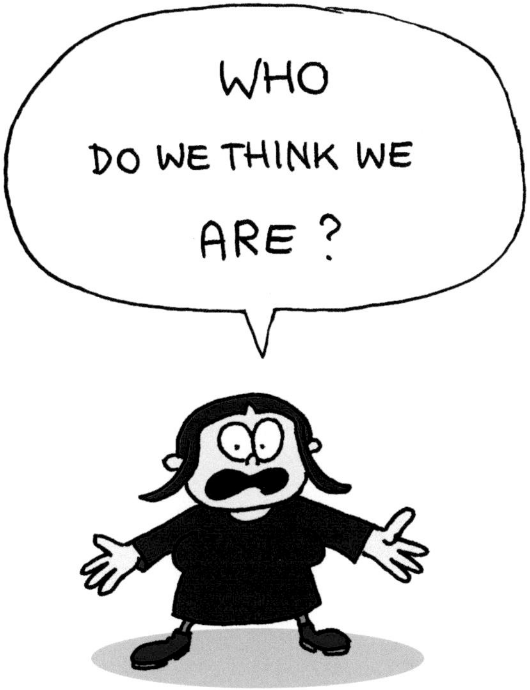
WHO
DO WE THINK WE
ARE ?

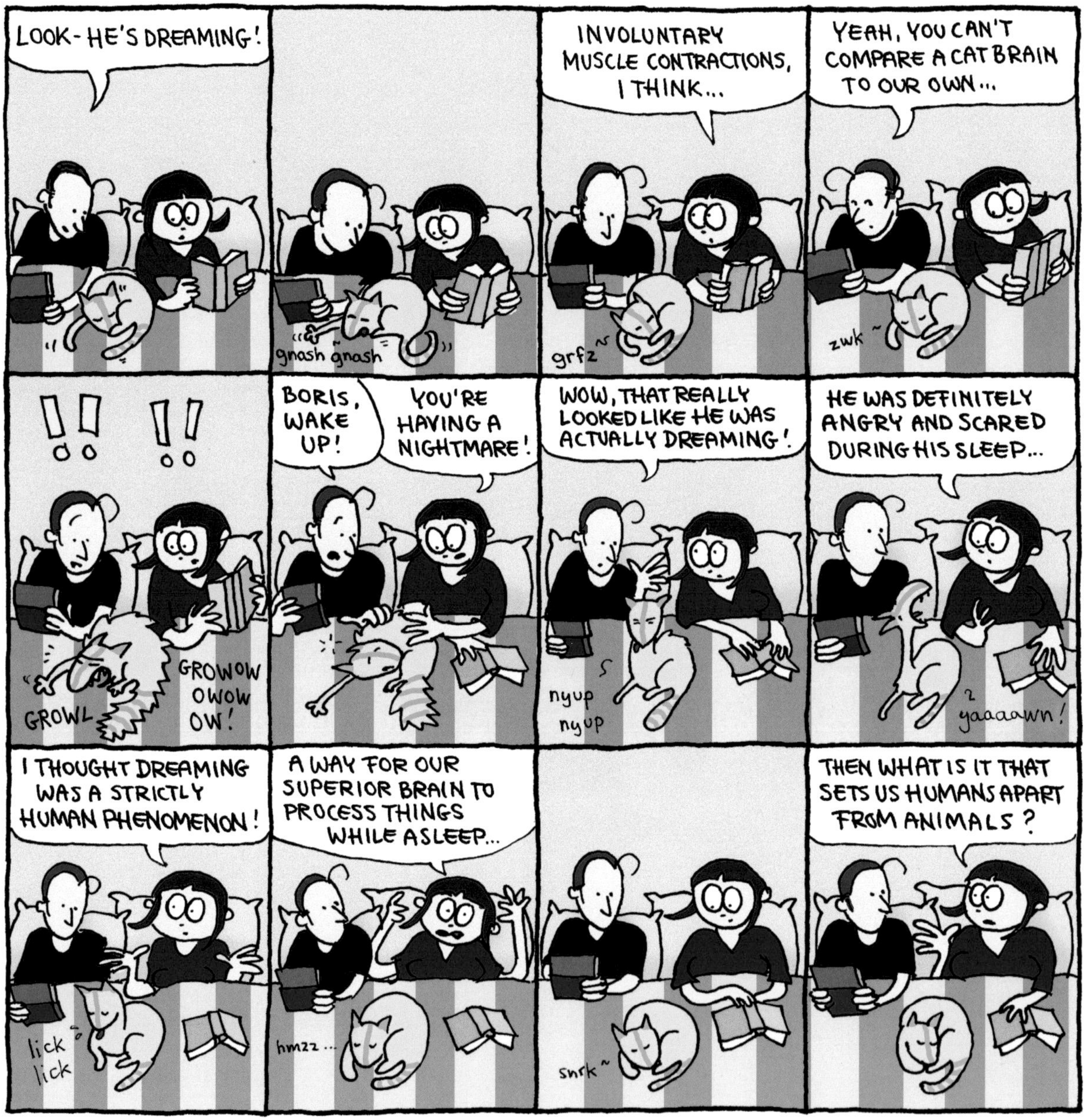
LOOK- HE'S DREAMING!
gnash gnash
INVOLUNTARY MUSCLE CONTRACTIONS, I THINK...
grfz
YEAH, YOU CAN'T COMPARE A CAT BRAIN TO OUR OWN...
zwk
!! !!
GROWL
GROWOW OWOW OW!
BORIS, WAKE UP!
YOU'RE HAVING A NIGHTMARE!
WOW, THAT REALLY LOOKED LIKE HE WAS ACTUALLY DREAMING!
nyup nyup
HE WAS DEFINITELY ANGRY AND SCARED DURING HIS SLEEP...
yaaaawn!
I THOUGHT DREAMING WAS A STRICTLY HUMAN PHENOMENON!
lick lick
A WAY FOR OUR SUPERIOR BRAIN TO PROCESS THINGS WHILE ASLEEP...
hmzz...
snrk
THEN WHAT IS IT THAT SETS US HUMANS APART FROM ANIMALS?

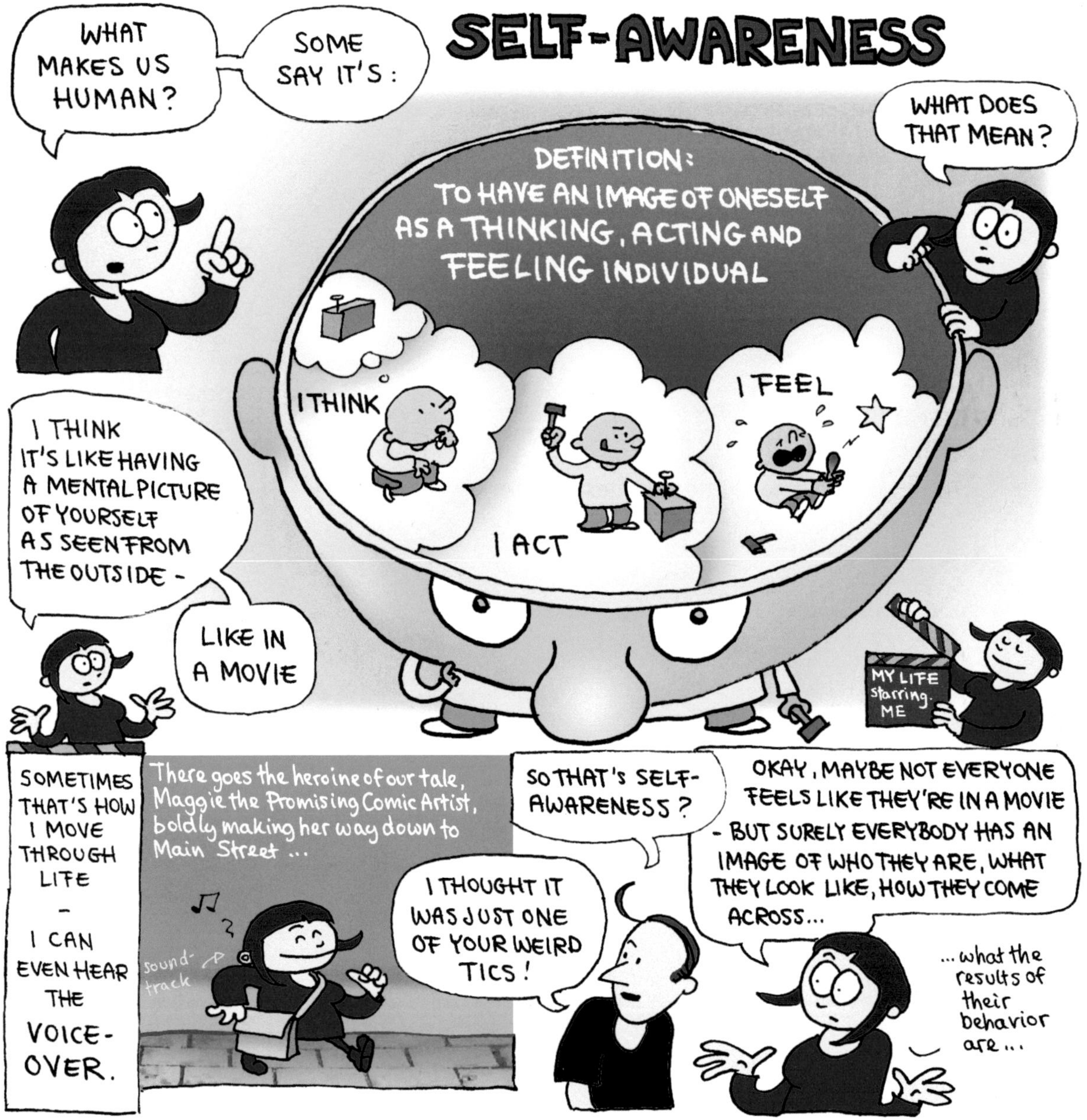

SELF-AWARENESS
WHAT MAKES US HUMAN?
SOME SAY IT'S:
WHAT DOES THAT MEAN?
DEFINITION: TO HAVE AN IMAGE OF ONESELF AS A THINKING, ACTING AND FEELING INDIVIDUAL
I THINK
I ACT
I FEEL
I THINK IT'S LIKE HAVING A MENTAL PICTURE OF YOURSELF AS SEEN FROM THE OUTSIDE -
LIKE IN A MOVIE
MY LIFE starring ME
SOMETIMES THAT'S HOW I MOVE THROUGH LIFE - I CAN EVEN HEAR THE VOICE-OVER.
There goes the heroine of our tale, Maggie the Promising Comic Artist, boldly making her way down to Main Street ...
sound-track
SO THAT'S SELF-AWARENESS?
I THOUGHT IT WAS JUST ONE OF YOUR WEIRD TICS!
OKAY, MAYBE NOT EVERYONE FEELS LIKE THEY'RE IN A MOVIE - BUT SURELY EVERYBODY HAS AN IMAGE OF WHO THEY ARE, WHAT THEY LOOK LIKE, HOW THEY COME ACROSS...
...what the results of their behavior are...

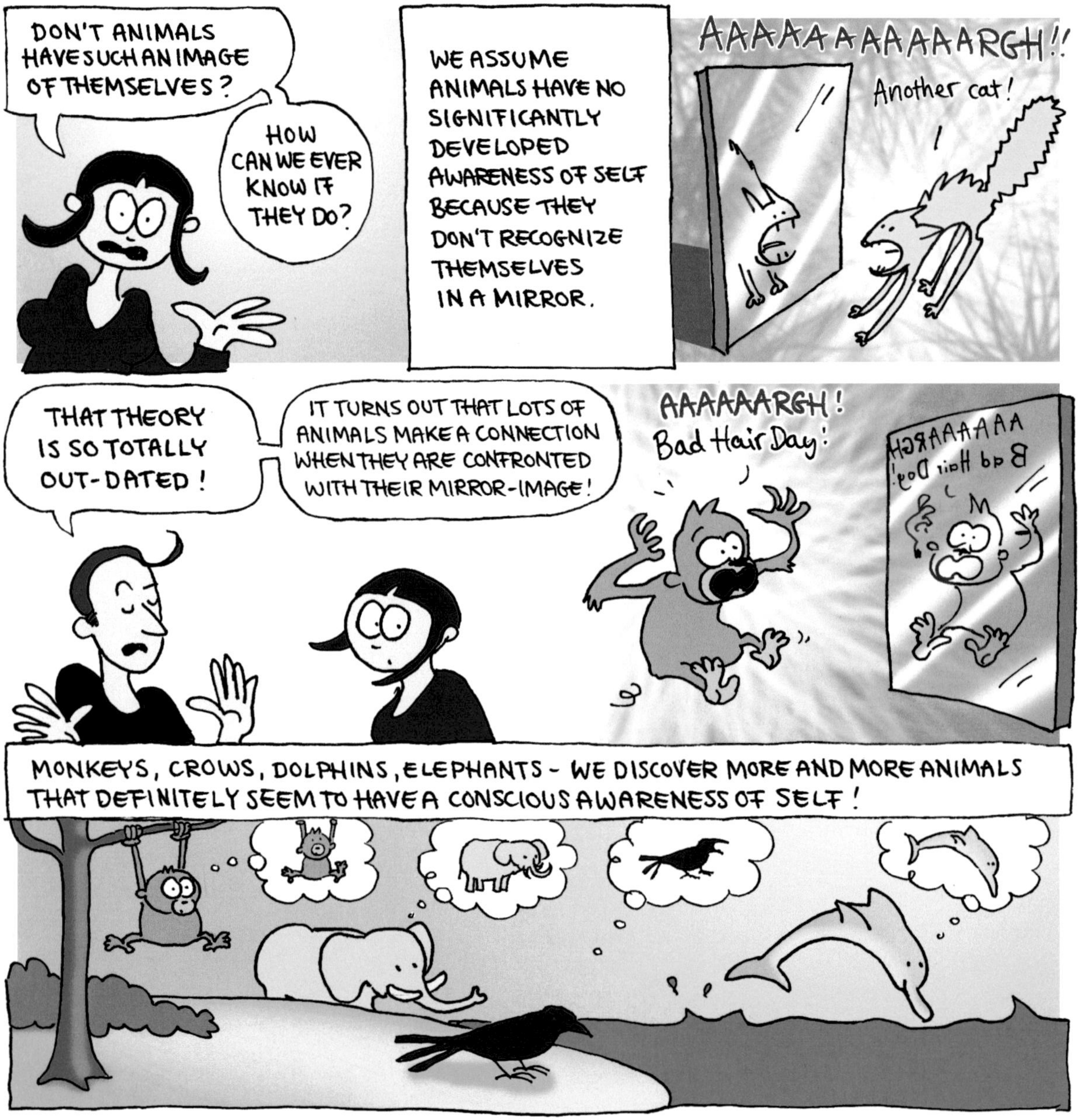
DON'T ANIMALS HAVE SUCH AN IMAGE OF THEMSELVES?
HOW CAN WE EVER KNOW IF THEY DO?
WE ASSUME ANIMALS HAVE NO SIGNIFICANTLY DEVELOPED AWARENESS OF SELF BECAUSE THEY DON'T RECOGNIZE THEMSELVES IN A MIRROR.
AAAAAAAAAAAARGH!!
Another cat!
THAT THEORY IS SO TOTALLY OUT-DATED!
IT TURNS OUT THAT LOTS OF ANIMALS MAKE A CONNECTION WHEN THEY ARE CONFRONTED WITH THEIR MIRROR-IMAGE!
AAAAAARGH!
Bad Hair Day!
MONKEYS, CROWS, DOLPHINS, ELEPHANTS - WE DISCOVER MORE AND MORE ANIMALS THAT DEFINITELY SEEM TO HAVE A CONSCIOUS AWARENESS OF SELF!

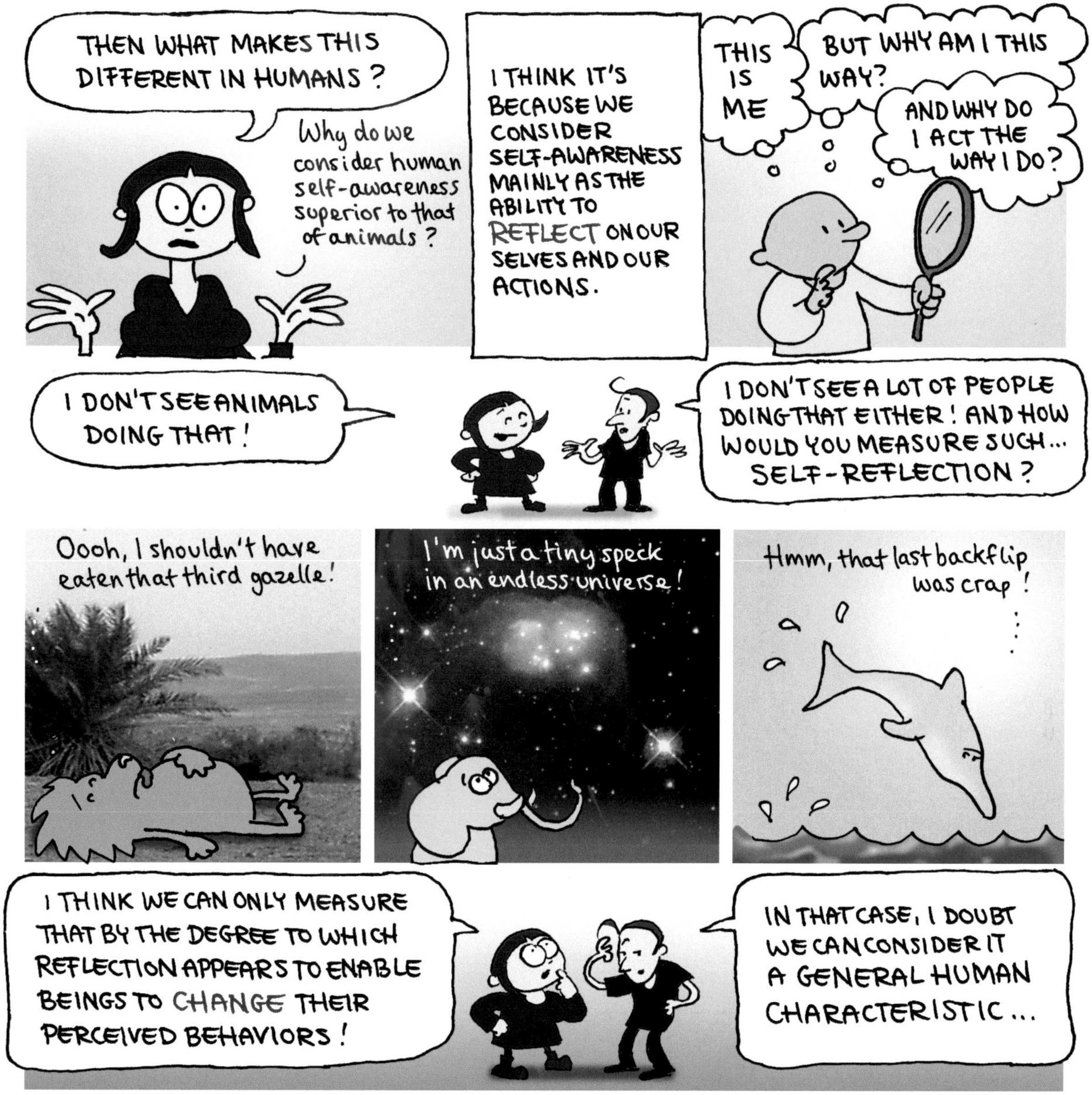
THEN WHAT MAKES THIS DIFFERENT IN HUMANS ?
Why do we consider human self-awareness superior to that of animals ?
I THINK IT'S BECAUSE WE CONSIDER SELF-AWARENESS MAINLY AS THE ABILITY TO REFLECT ON OUR SELVES AND OUR ACTIONS.
THIS IS ME
BUT WHY AM I THIS WAY?
AND WHY DO I ACT THE WAY I DO?
I DON'T SEE ANIMALS DOING THAT!
I DON'T SEE A LOT OF PEOPLE DOING THAT EITHER! AND HOW WOULD YOU MEASURE SUCH... SELF-REFLECTION?
Oooh, I shouldn't have eaten that third gazelle!
I'm just a tiny speck in an endless universe!
Hmm, that last backflip was crap!
I THINK WE CAN ONLY MEASURE THAT BY THE DEGREE TO WHICH REFLECTION APPEARS TO ENABLE BEINGS TO CHANGE THEIR PERCEIVED BEHAVIORS!
IN THAT CASE, I DOUBT WE CAN CONSIDER IT A GENERAL HUMAN CHARACTERISTIC...

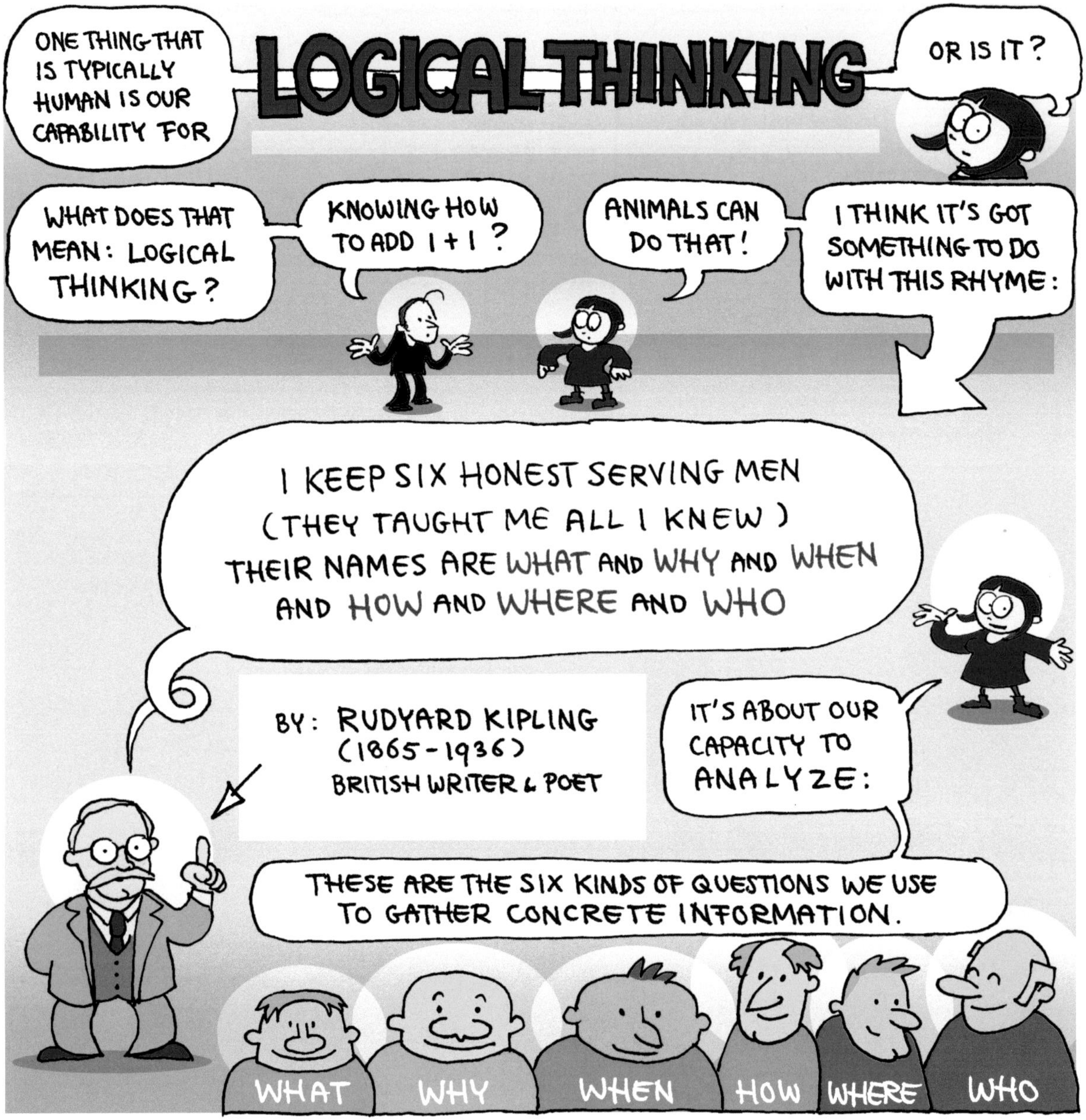
ONE THING THAT IS TYPICALLY HUMAN IS OUR CAPABILITY FOR
LOGICAL THINKING
OR IS IT?
WHAT DOES THAT MEAN: LOGICAL THINKING?
KNOWING HOW TO ADD 1+1?
ANIMALS CAN DO THAT!
I THINK IT'S GOT SOMETHING TO DO WITH THIS RHYME:
I KEEP SIX HONEST SERVING MEN (THEY TAUGHT ME ALL I KNEW) THEIR NAMES ARE WHAT AND WHY AND WHEN AND HOW AND WHERE AND WHO
BY: RUDYARD KIPLING (1865-1936) BRITISH WRITER & POET
IT'S ABOUT OUR CAPACITY TO ANALYZE:
THESE ARE THE SIX KINDS OF QUESTIONS WE USE TO GATHER CONCRETE INFORMATION.
WHAT
WHY
WHEN
HOW
WHERE
WHO

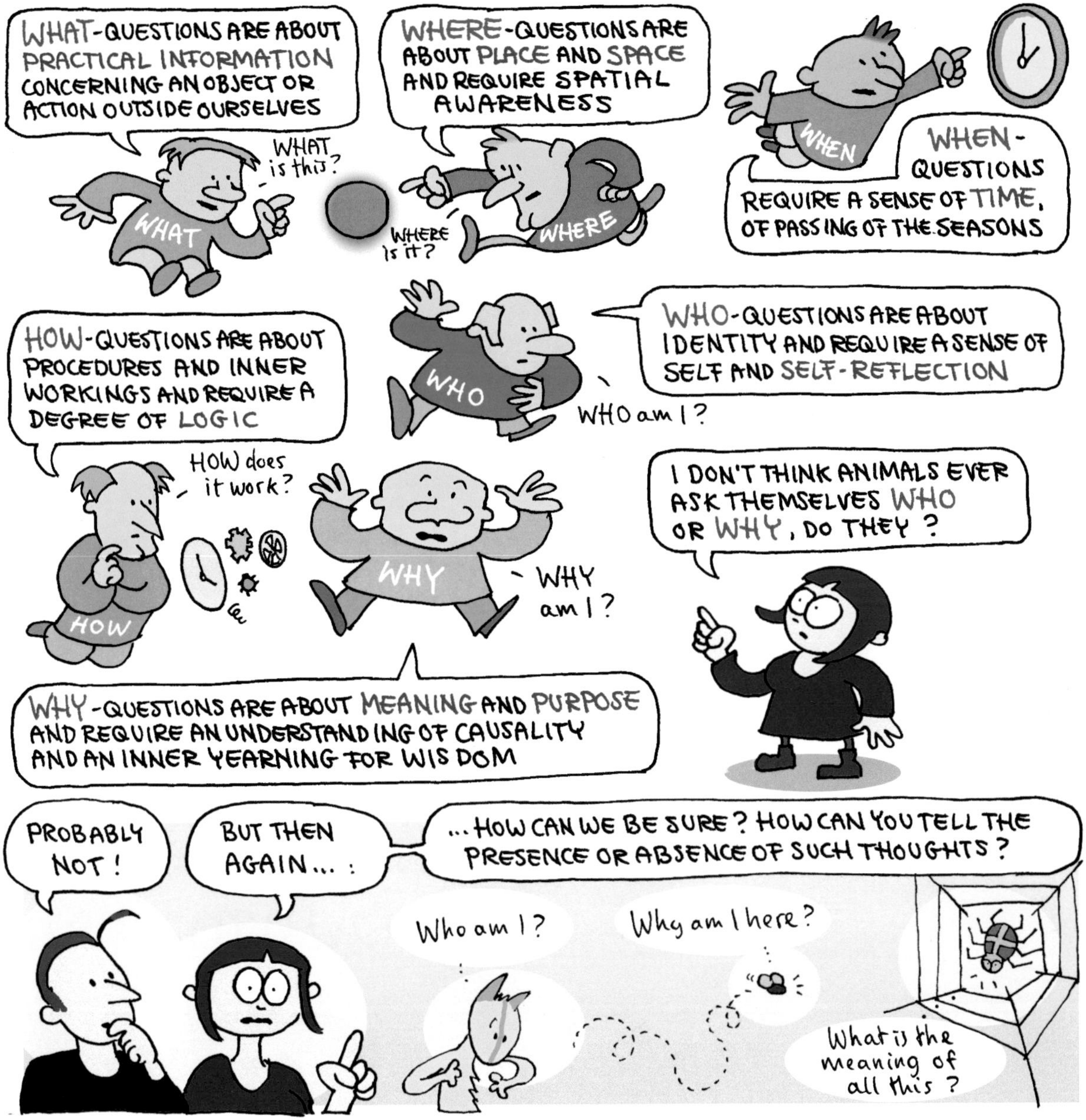
WHAT-QUESTIONS ARE ABOUT PRACTICAL INFORMATION CONCERNING AN OBJECT OR ACTION OUTSIDE OURSELVES
WHAT is this?
WHAT
WHERE-QUESTIONS ARE ABOUT PLACE AND SPACE AND REQUIRE SPATIAL AWARENESS
WHERE is it?
WHERE
WHEN
WHEN-QUESTIONS REQUIRE A SENSE OF TIME, OF PASSING OF THE SEASONS
HOW-QUESTIONS ARE ABOUT PROCEDURES AND INNER WORKINGS AND REQUIRE A DEGREE OF LOGIC
WHO
WHO-QUESTIONS ARE ABOUT IDENTITY AND REQUIRE A SENSE OF SELF AND SELF-REFLECTION
WHO am I?
HOW does it work?
HOW
WHY
WHY am I?
I DON'T THINK ANIMALS EVER ASK THEMSELVES WHO OR WHY, DO THEY?
WHY-QUESTIONS ARE ABOUT MEANING AND PURPOSE AND REQUIRE AN UNDERSTANDING OF CAUSALITY AND AN INNER YEARNING FOR WISDOM
PROBABLY NOT!
BUT THEN AGAIN...
...HOW CAN WE BE SURE? HOW CAN YOU TELL THE PRESENCE OR ABSENCE OF SUCH THOUGHTS?
Who am I?
Why am I here?
What is the meaning of all this?

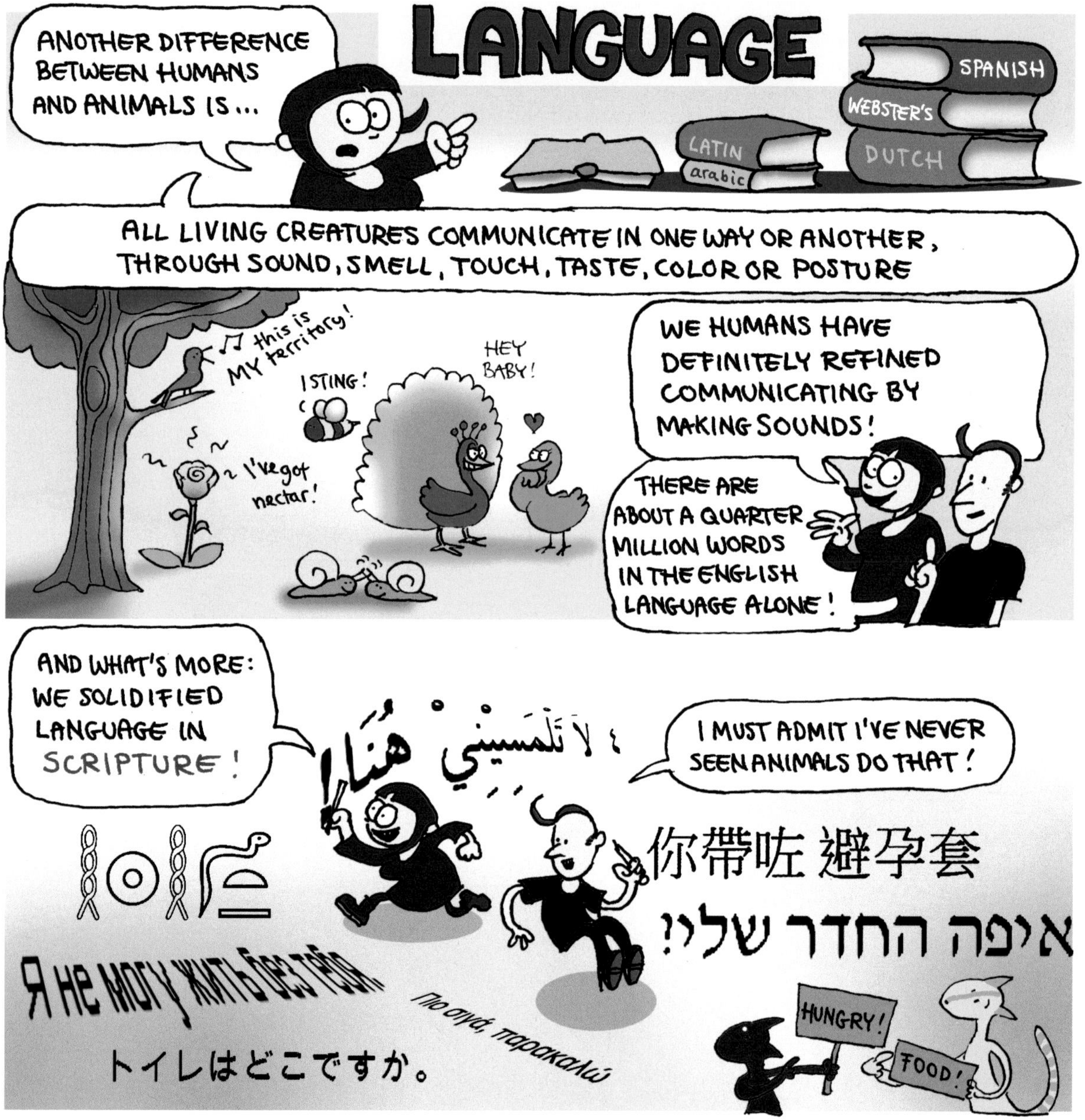
ANOTHER DIFFERENCE BETWEEN HUMANS AND ANIMALS IS...
LANGUAGE
SPANISH
WEBSTER'S
DUTCH
LATIN
arabic
ALL LIVING CREATURES COMMUNICATE IN ONE WAY OR ANOTHER, THROUGH SOUND, SMELL, TOUCH, TASTE, COLOR OR POSTURE
this is MY territory!
I STING!
HEY BABY!
I've got nectar!
WE HUMANS HAVE DEFINITELY REFINED COMMUNICATING BY MAKING SOUNDS!
THERE ARE ABOUT A QUARTER MILLION WORDS IN THE ENGLISH LANGUAGE ALONE!
AND WHAT'S MORE: WE SOLIDIFIED LANGUAGE IN SCRIPTURE!
لا تلمسيني هنا!
I MUST ADMIT I'VE NEVER SEEN ANIMALS DO THAT!
你帶咗 避孕套
איפה החדר שלי?!
Я не могу жить без тебя.
Πιο σιγά, παρακαλώ
トイレはどこですか。
HUNGRY!
FOOD!

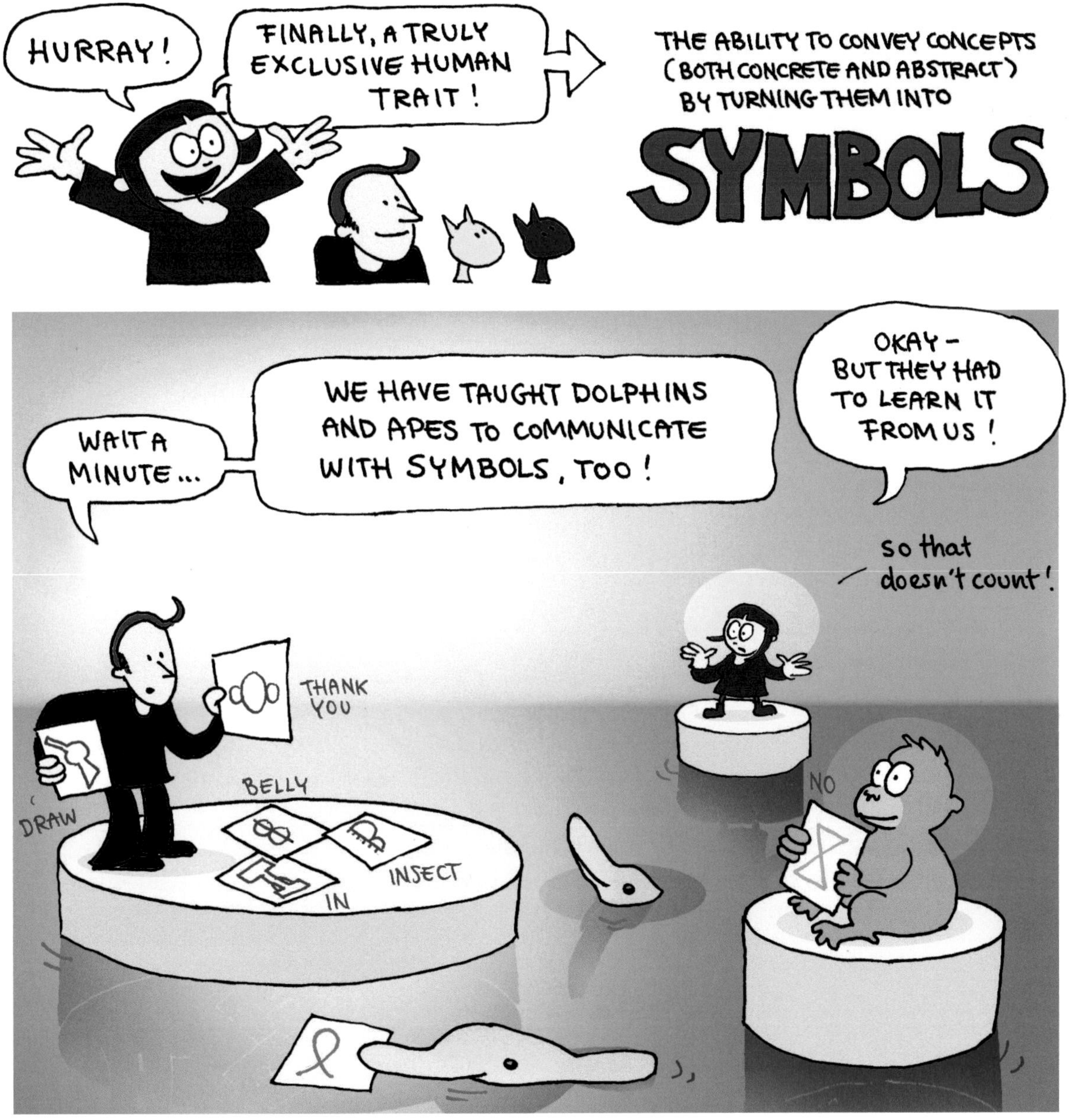
HURRAY!
FINALLY, A TRULY EXCLUSIVE HUMAN TRAIT!
THE ABILITY TO CONVEY CONCEPTS (BOTH CONCRETE AND ABSTRACT) BY TURNING THEM INTO
SYMBOLS
WAIT A MINUTE...
WE HAVE TAUGHT DOLPHINS AND APES TO COMMUNICATE WITH SYMBOLS, TOO!
OKAY - BUT THEY HAD TO LEARN IT FROM US!
so that doesn't count!
THANK YOU
DRAW
BELLY
INSECT
IN
NO

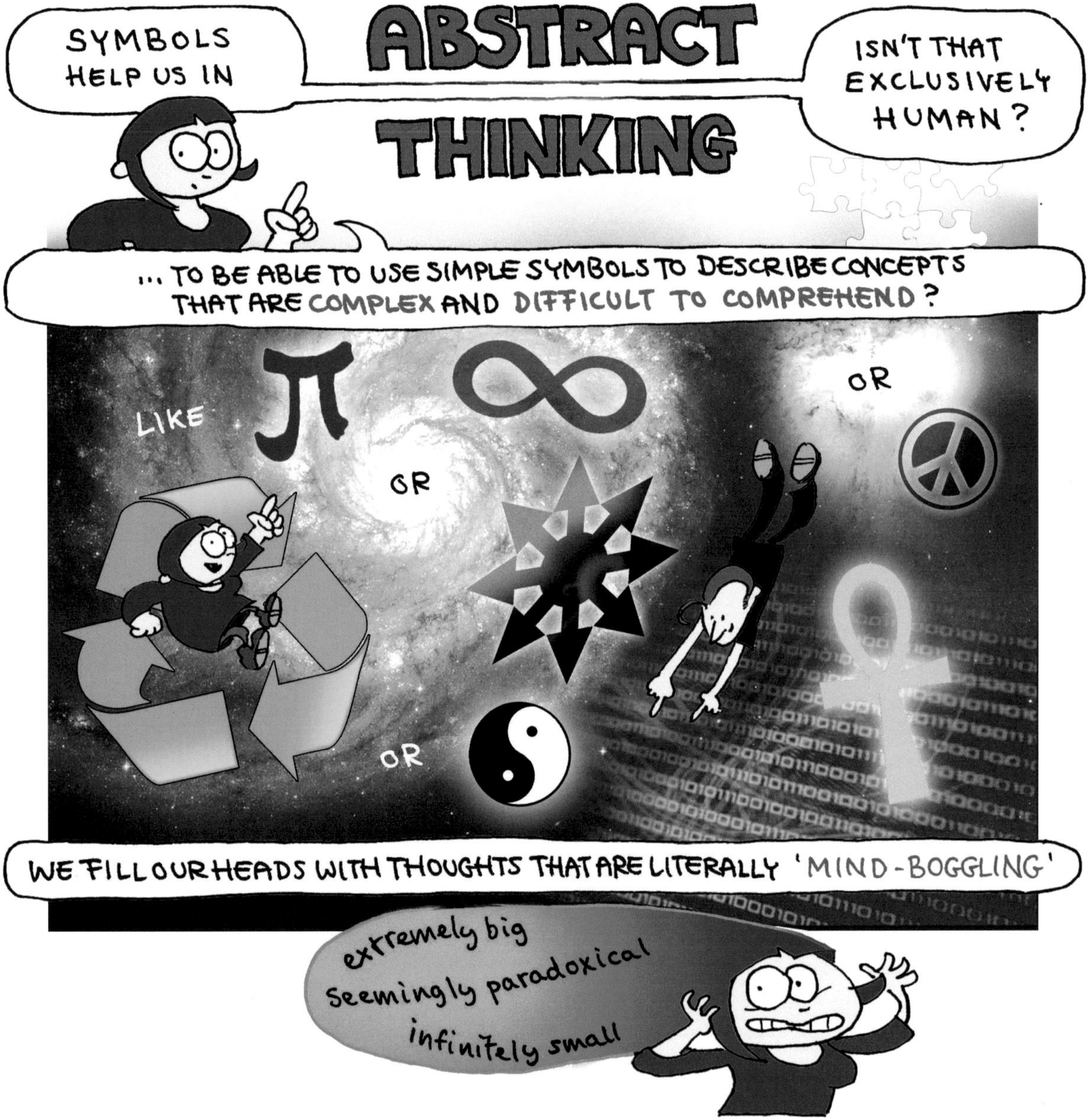

ABSTRACT THINKING
SYMBOLS HELP US IN
ISN'T THAT EXCLUSIVELY HUMAN?
... TO BE ABLE TO USE SIMPLE SYMBOLS TO DESCRIBE CONCEPTS THAT ARE COMPLEX AND DIFFICULT TO COMPREHEND?
LIKE
OR
OR
OR
WE FILL OUR HEADS WITH THOUGHTS THAT ARE LITERALLY 'MIND-BOGGLING'
extremely big
seemingly paradoxical
infinitely small

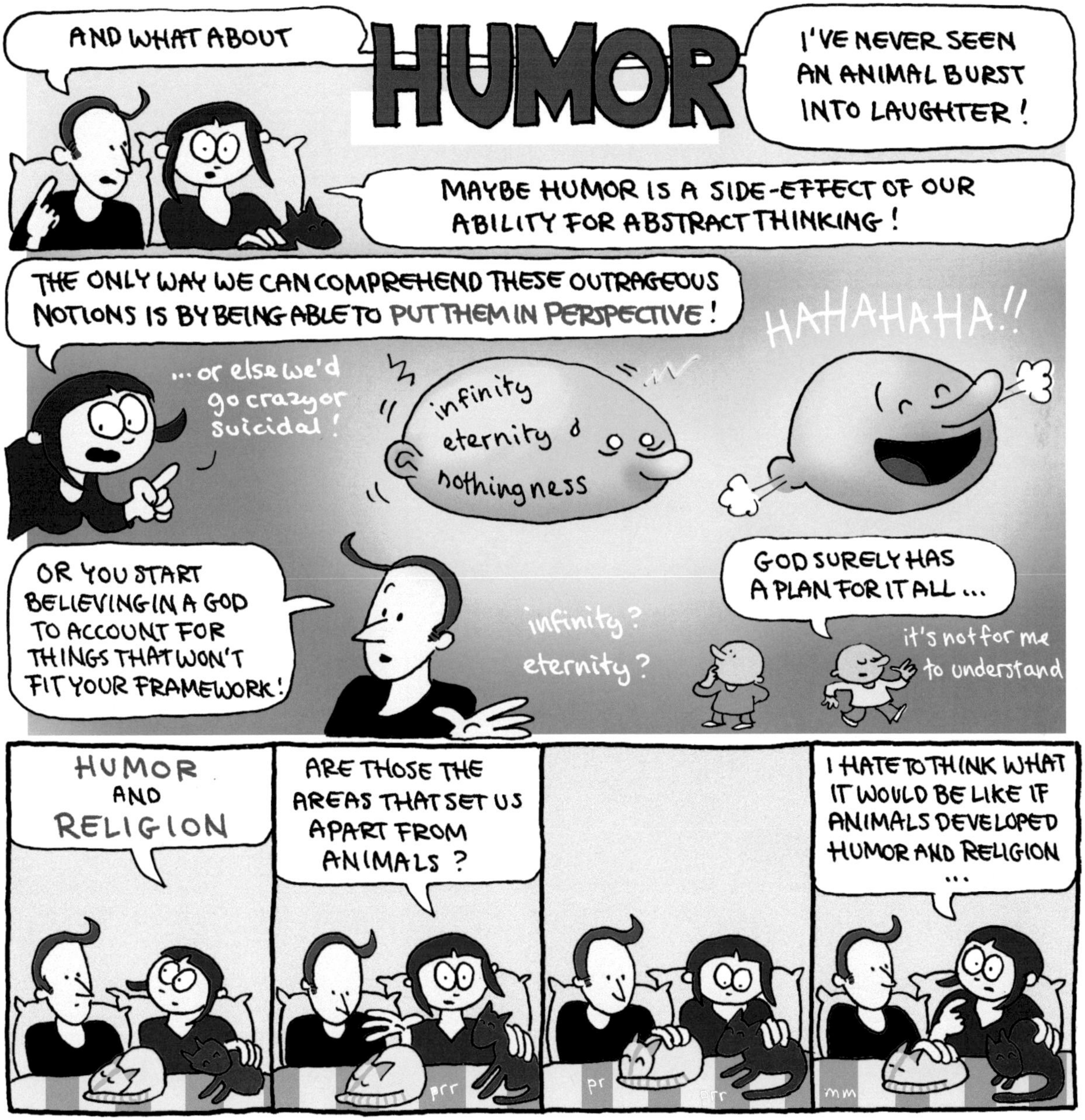
AND WHAT ABOUT
HUMOR
I'VE NEVER SEEN AN ANIMAL BURST INTO LAUGHTER!
MAYBE HUMOR IS A SIDE-EFFECT OF OUR ABILITY FOR ABSTRACT THINKING!
THE ONLY WAY WE CAN COMPREHEND THESE OUTRAGEOUS NOTIONS IS BY BEING ABLE TO PUT THEM IN PERSPECTIVE!
... or else we'd go crazy or suicidal!
infinity eternity & nothingness
HAHAHAHA!!
OR YOU START BELIEVING IN A GOD TO ACCOUNT FOR THINGS THAT WON'T FIT YOUR FRAMEWORK!
infinity? eternity?
GOD SURELY HAS A PLAN FOR IT ALL...
it's not for me to understand
HUMOR AND RELIGION
ARE THOSE THE AREAS THAT SET US APART FROM ANIMALS?
prr
pr
prr
I HATE TO THINK WHAT IT WOULD BE LIKE IF ANIMALS DEVELOPED HUMOR AND RELIGION...
mm

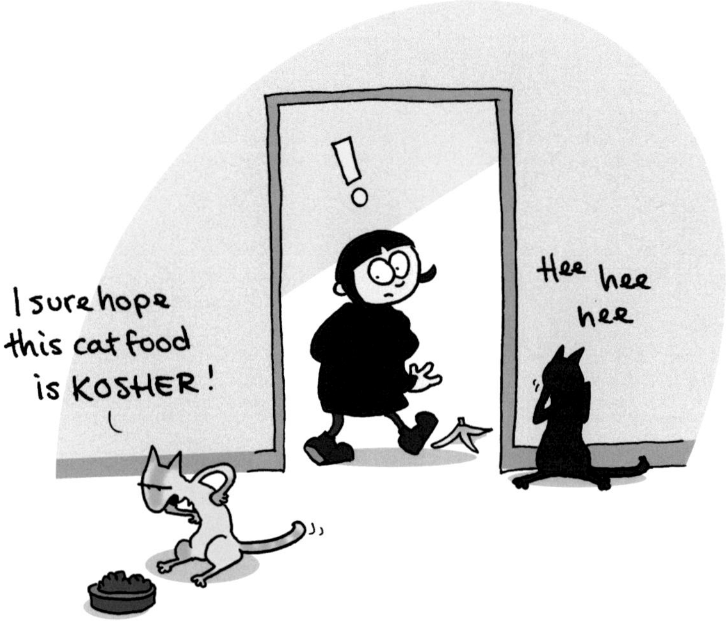
!
I sure hope this cat food is KOSHER!
Hee hee hee

THE FOUNDATION OF WESTERN PHILOSOPHY

SOCRATES
PLATO
ARISTOTLE
IDEAS
CRITICAL THINKING
GOAL
WESTERN PHILOSOPHY

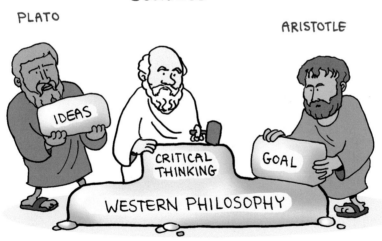

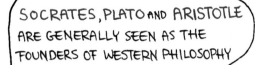

SOCRATES, PLATO AND ARISTOTLE ARE GENERALLY SEEN AS THE FOUNDERS OF WESTERN PHILOSOPHY

WHAT DOES THAT MEAN: "WESTERN PHILOSOPHY"?

WHAT ARE ITS CHARACTERISTICS?

AND THEN WHAT IS "EASTERN PHILOSOPHY"?

AND WHAT IS THE DIFFERENCE?

HMM, I THINK EASTERN PHILOSOPHY IS BASED ON:

WHEREAS WESTERN PHILOSOPHY IS ABOUT:

UNITY

the essence of things is in their relationship to the WHOLE

EVERYTHING IS ONE

CONNECTING

SEEMING OPPOSITES

DUALITY

the essence of things can only be revealed by examining them on their OWN

EVERYTHING IS a collection of PARTS

DE-COMPOSE

REDUCE & DEDUCE

THE FOUNDATIONS OF OUR THINKING ARE SO DEEP WE TEND TO FORGET THAT THERE ARE ALTERNATIVES ...

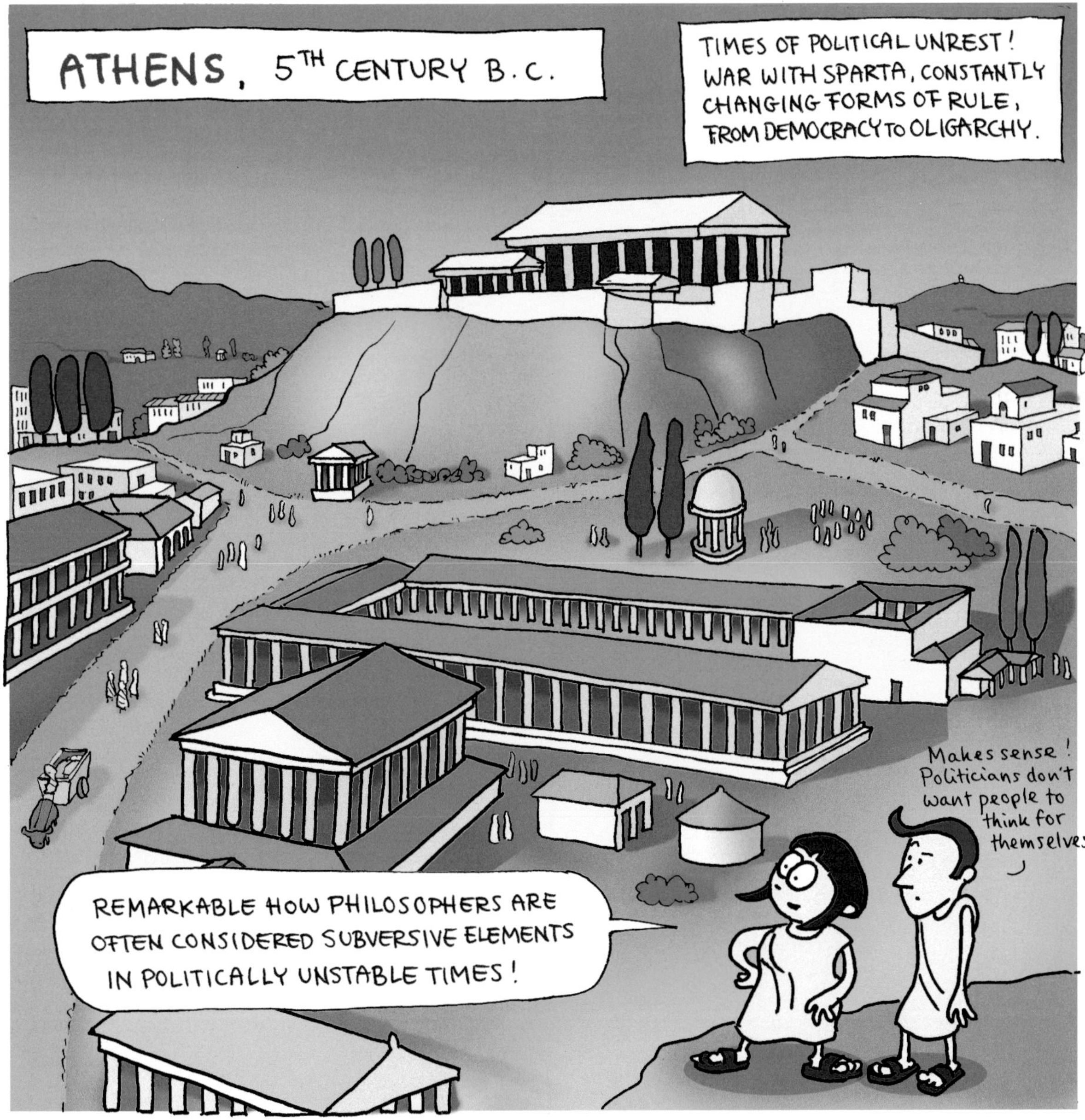
ATHENS, 5TH CENTURY B.C.
TIMES OF POLITICAL UNREST! WAR WITH SPARTA, CONSTANTLY CHANGING FORMS OF RULE, FROM DEMOCRACY TO OLIGARCHY.
REMARKABLE HOW PHILOSOPHERS ARE OFTEN CONSIDERED SUBVERSIVE ELEMENTS IN POLITICALLY UNSTABLE TIMES!
Makes sense! Politicians don't want people to think for themselves!

THE LIFE OF SOCRATES

469 - 399 B.C.

SOCRATES WAS BORN IN ATHENS, 469 B.C.

father Sophronicus

mother Phaenarete

HIS FATHER WAS A STONEMASON, HIS MOTHER A MIDWIFE. SHE MAY HAVE BEEN HIS INSPIRATION FOR THE DISCUSSION TECHNIQUE HE LATER CALLED THE MIDWIFE TECHNIQUE.

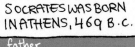

KNOWLEDGE MUST BE BROUGHT FORTH IN THE SAME WAY A MIDWIFE ASSISTS IN BIRTHING!

PUSH! PUSH!

THINK HARDER!

KEEP BREATHING!

Bring it on!

Thinking hurts!

SOCRATES GREW UP DURING ATHENS' HEYDAY. IN 431 B.C., WHEN HE WAS 38, THE PELOPONNESIAN WAR BROKE OUT, WHICH LASTED 27 YEARS. BY THE END OF THE WAR, SOCRATES WAS 65, ATHENS WAS DEFEATED BY SPARTA AND GREATLY IMPOVERISHED.

Socrates took part in three campaigns against Sparta:

- at Potidaea (432 B.C.)
- at Amphipolis (424 B.C.)
- at Delium (424 B.C.)

HE SPREAD HIS IDEAS IN THE MARKETPLACE:

WHAT IS KNOWLEDGE?

OUR GOVERNORS THINK THEY ARE WISE, BUT ARE THEY REALLY?

MAKE HIM SHUT UP!

Don't we have enough problems as it is?!

SOCRATES MARRIED XANTHIPPE, WHO WAS MUCH YOUNGER. THEY HAD THREE SONS.

A feisty wife, but she keeps me on my toes!

SOCRATES' IDEAS WERE WRITTEN DOWN BY HIS PUPIL PLATO.

ABOUT THE IDEAL STATE

ABOUT VIRTUE

IN 399 B.C., WHEN HE WAS 70, HE WAS PROSECUTED & SENTENCED.

He's corrupting our youth! He doesn't abide by the law! He laughs at the gods!

SOCRATES CHOSE POISON OVER EXILE AND DIED AMONG HIS FRIENDS.

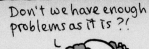

A SOLDIER DOES NOT RUN AWAY IN THE FACE OF DEATH!

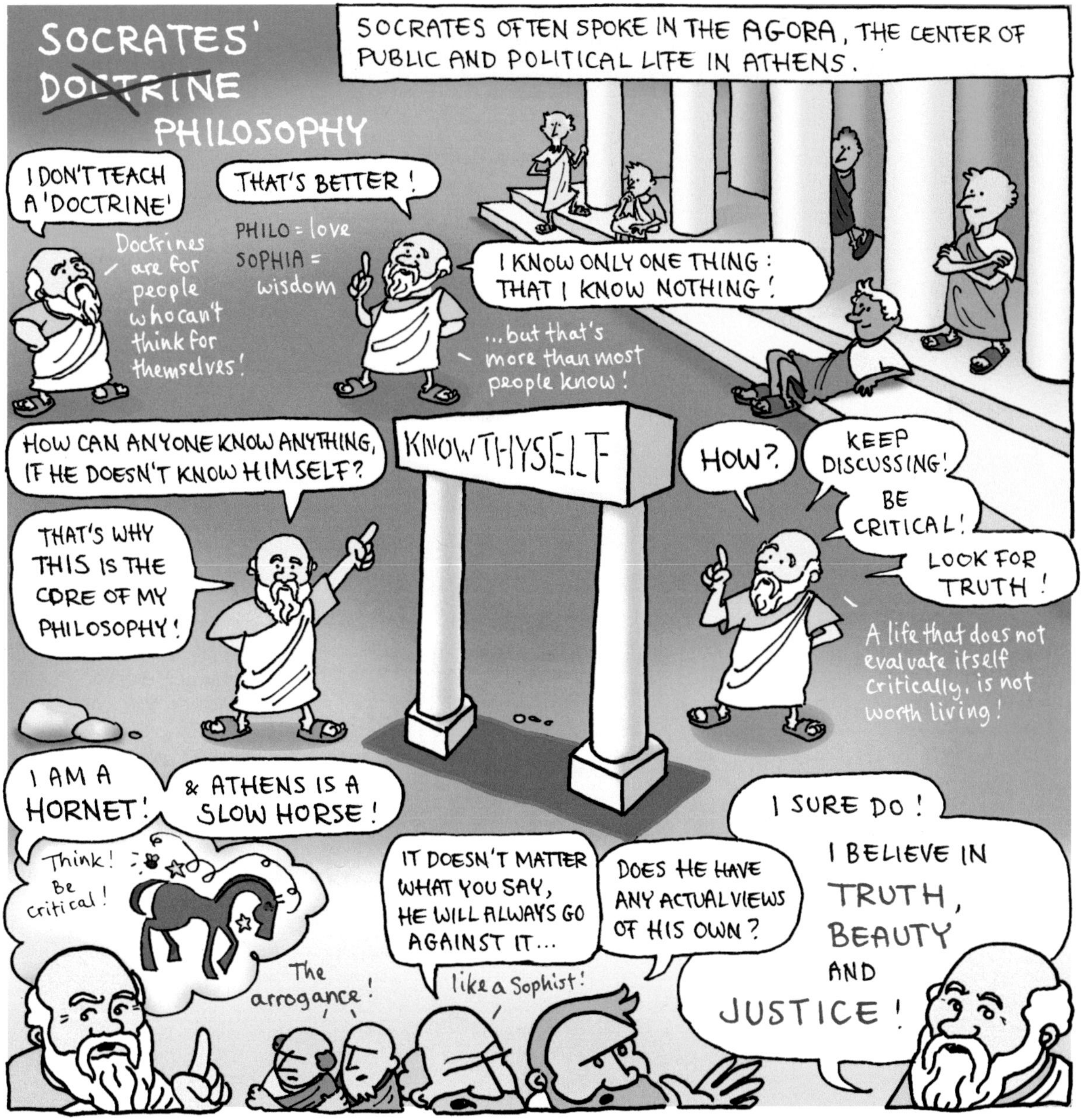
SOCRATES' DOCTRINE PHILOSOPHY
SOCRATES OFTEN SPOKE IN THE AGORA, THE CENTER OF PUBLIC AND POLITICAL LIFE IN ATHENS.
I DON'T TEACH A 'DOCTRINE'
Doctrines are for people who can't think for themselves!
THAT'S BETTER!
PHILO = love
SOPHIA = wisdom
I KNOW ONLY ONE THING: THAT I KNOW NOTHING!
...but that's more than most people know!
HOW CAN ANYONE KNOW ANYTHING, IF HE DOESN'T KNOW HIMSELF?
KNOW THYSELF
THAT'S WHY THIS IS THE CORE OF MY PHILOSOPHY!
HOW?
KEEP DISCUSSING!
BE CRITICAL!
LOOK FOR TRUTH!
A life that does not evaluate itself critically, is not worth living!
I AM A HORNET!
& ATHENS IS A SLOW HORSE!
Think! Be critical!
The arrogance!
IT DOESN'T MATTER WHAT YOU SAY, HE WILL ALWAYS GO AGAINST IT...
like a Sophist!
DOES HE HAVE ANY ACTUAL VIEWS OF HIS OWN?
I SURE DO!
I BELIEVE IN TRUTH, BEAUTY AND JUSTICE!

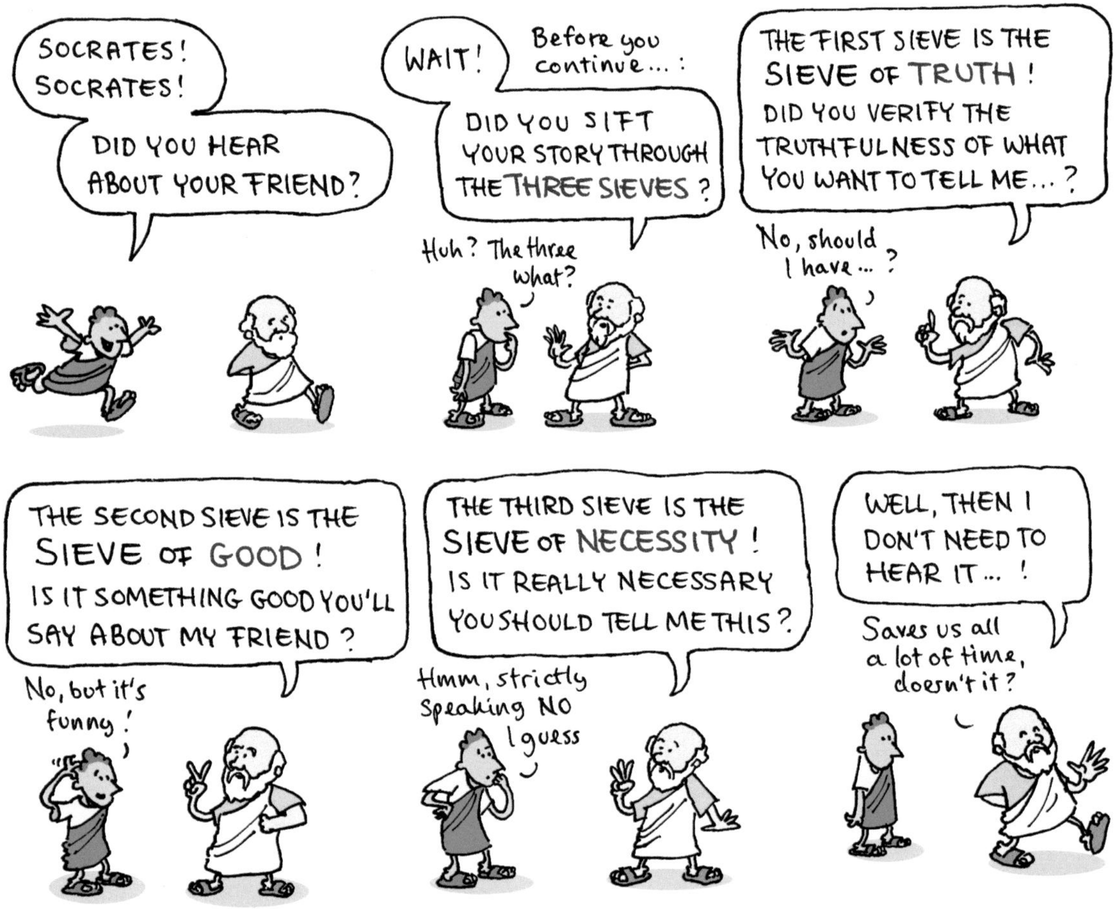
SOCRATES! SOCRATES!
DID YOU HEAR ABOUT YOUR FRIEND?
WAIT!
Before you continue... :
DID YOU SIFT YOUR STORY THROUGH THE THREE SIEVES?
Huh? The three what?
THE FIRST SIEVE IS THE SIEVE OF TRUTH! DID YOU VERIFY THE TRUTHFULNESS OF WHAT YOU WANT TO TELL ME...?
No, should I have...?
THE SECOND SIEVE IS THE SIEVE OF GOOD! IS IT SOMETHING GOOD YOU'LL SAY ABOUT MY FRIEND?
No, but it's funny!
THE THIRD SIEVE IS THE SIEVE OF NECESSITY! IS IT REALLY NECESSARY YOU SHOULD TELL ME THIS?
Hmm, strictly speaking NO I guess
WELL, THEN I DON'T NEED TO HEAR IT...!
Saves us all a lot of time, doesn't it?

THE SOCRATIC DISCOURSE

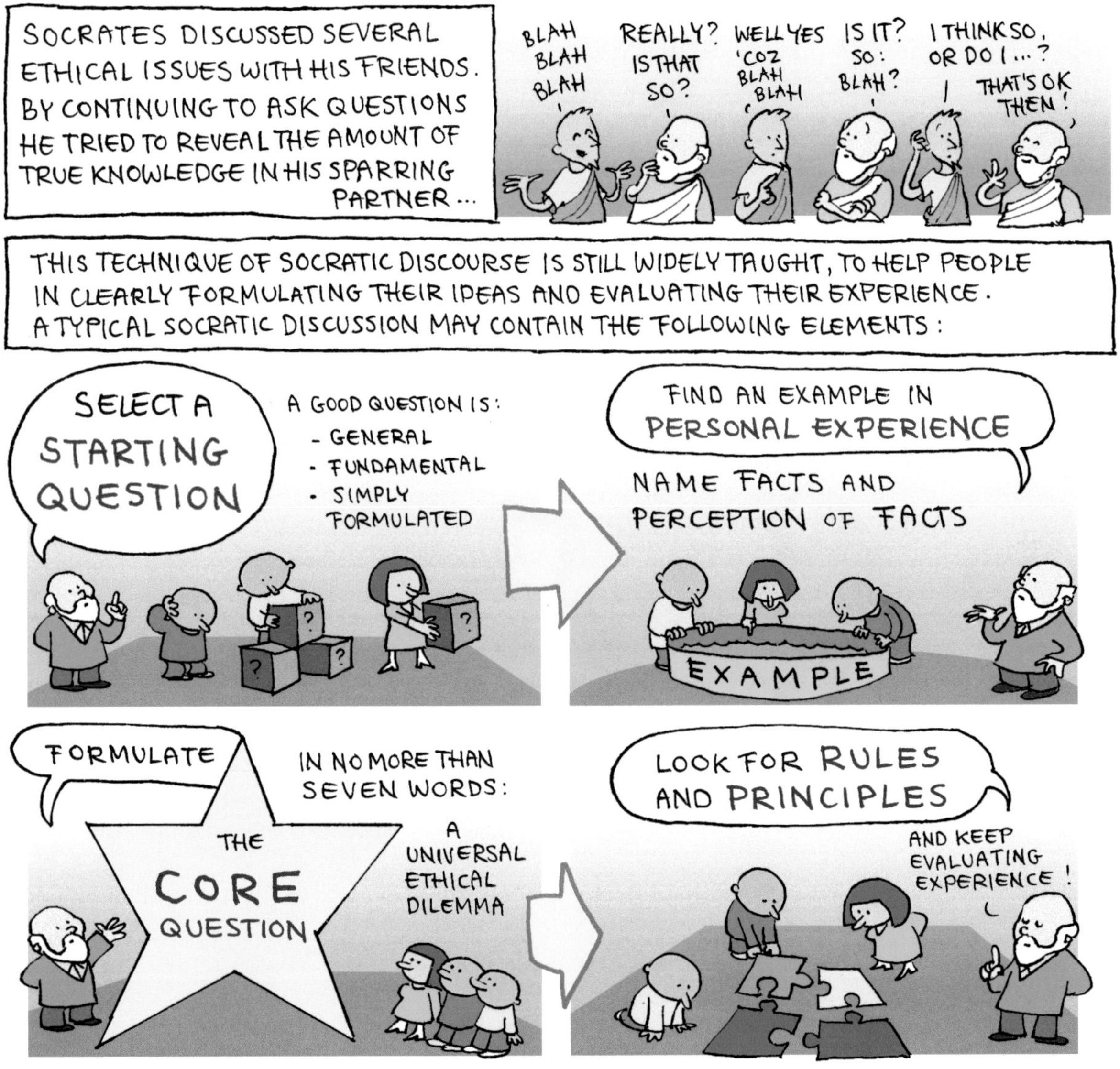
SOCRATES DISCUSSED SEVERAL ETHICAL ISSUES WITH HIS FRIENDS. BY CONTINUING TO ASK QUESTIONS HE TRIED TO REVEAL THE AMOUNT OF TRUE KNOWLEDGE IN HIS SPARRING PARTNER...
BLAH BLAH BLAH
REALLY? IS THAT SO?
WELL YES 'COZ BLAH BLAH
IS IT? SO: BLAH?
I THINK SO, OR DO I...?
THAT'S OK THEN!
THIS TECHNIQUE OF SOCRATIC DISCOURSE IS STILL WIDELY TAUGHT, TO HELP PEOPLE IN CLEARLY FORMULATING THEIR IDEAS AND EVALUATING THEIR EXPERIENCE. A TYPICAL SOCRATIC DISCUSSION MAY CONTAIN THE FOLLOWING ELEMENTS:
SELECT A STARTING QUESTION
A GOOD QUESTION IS:
- GENERAL
- FUNDAMENTAL
- SIMPLY FORMULATED
?
FIND AN EXAMPLE IN PERSONAL EXPERIENCE
NAME FACTS AND PERCEPTION OF FACTS
EXAMPLE
FORMULATE
THE CORE QUESTION
IN NO MORE THAN SEVEN WORDS:
A UNIVERSAL ETHICAL DILEMMA
LOOK FOR RULES AND PRINCIPLES
AND KEEP EVALUATING EXPERIENCE!

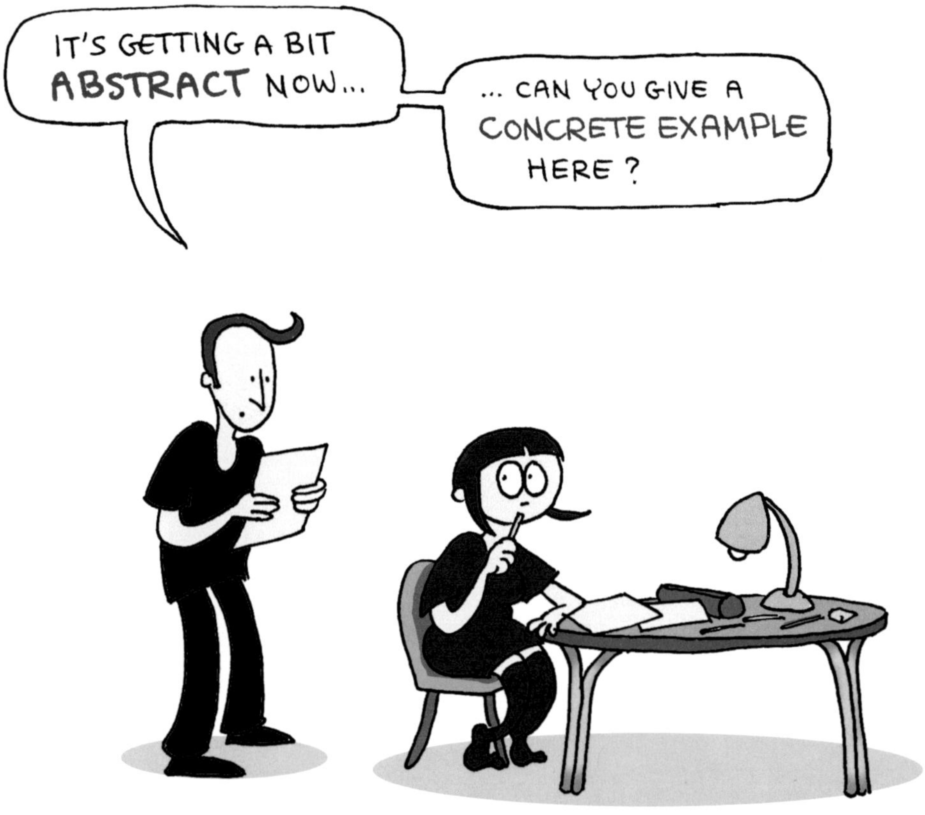
IT'S GETTING A BIT ABSTRACT NOW...
... CAN YOU GIVE A CONCRETE EXAMPLE HERE?

EXAMPLE OF A SOCRATIC DISCUSSION
STARTING QUESTION:
WHY IS EVERYONE AND EVERYTHING ALWAYS AGAINST ME?!
NAME FACTS & PERCEPTION OF FACTS:
WHY DO YOU THINK THAT...?
ARGH! I WAS IN THE STORE AND EVERYONE WAS IN MY WAY AND THE LINE WAS TOO LONG AND PEOPLE CUT IN FRONT OF ME AND THEN IT STARTED TO RAIN!
EVERYTHING HATES ME!!!
KEEP QUESTIONING... & QUESTIONING... & QUESTIONING...
WHY WAS IT SO CROWDED?
IT ALWAYS IS AROUND 5 'O CLOCK
... when everyone leaves work and they pop in the store for a few quick errands...
SO WHY DID YOU GO SHOPPING AT THAT TIME?
I had to finish a comic before 5 so I couldn't go out earlier...
WHY WERE YOU LATE FINISHING YOUR COMIC?
I only started at one, because I slept until twelve...
WHY DID YOU SLEEP SO LATE?
Er, because I was playing a game on the Wii until 3 AM...
... UNTIL THE CORE QUESTION IS REVEALED AND FORMULATED...
SO?! I work hard! Can't I relax once in a while?
SO THE CORE QUESTION IS:
HOW CAN I STRUCTURE WORK AND RELAXATION IN SUCH A WAY THAT IT DOESN'T DRIVE ME MAD?
OR PUT SIMPLY IN SIX WORDS:
HOW DO I BALANCE MY LIFE?

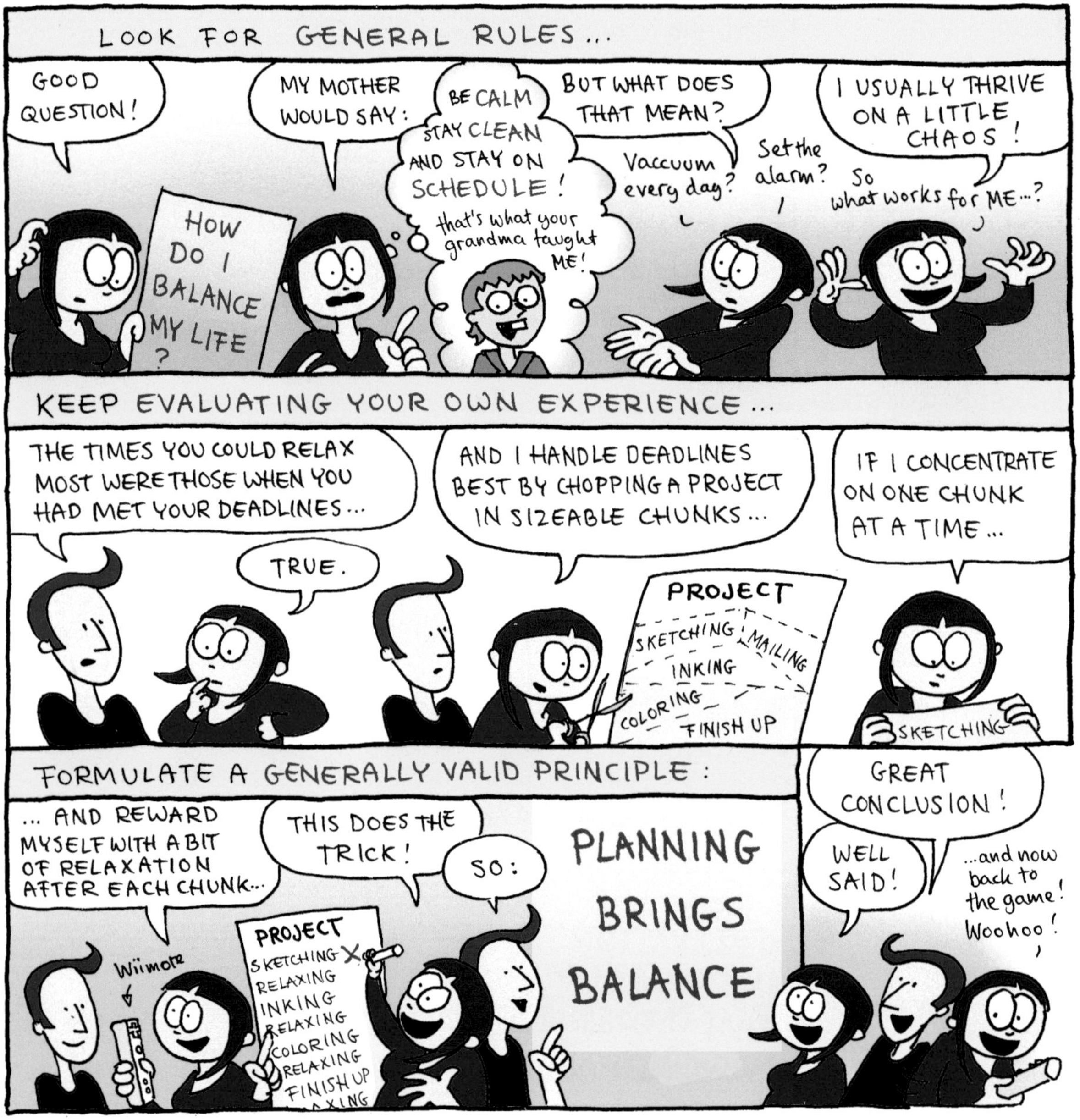
LOOK FOR GENERAL RULES...
GOOD QUESTION!
HOW DO I BALANCE MY LIFE?
MY MOTHER WOULD SAY:
BE CALM STAY CLEAN AND STAY ON SCHEDULE!
that's what your grandma taught ME!
BUT WHAT DOES THAT MEAN?
Vaccuum every day?
Set the alarm?
I USUALLY THRIVE ON A LITTLE CHAOS!
So what works for ME...?
KEEP EVALUATING YOUR OWN EXPERIENCE...
THE TIMES YOU COULD RELAX MOST WERE THOSE WHEN YOU HAD MET YOUR DEADLINES...
TRUE.
AND I HANDLE DEADLINES BEST BY CHOPPING A PROJECT IN SIZEABLE CHUNKS...
PROJECT
SKETCHING
MAILING
INKING
COLORING
FINISH UP
IF I CONCENTRATE ON ONE CHUNK AT A TIME...
SKETCHING
FORMULATE A GENERALLY VALID PRINCIPLE:
... AND REWARD MYSELF WITH A BIT OF RELAXATION AFTER EACH CHUNK...
Wiimote
THIS DOES THE TRICK!
PROJECT
SKETCHING
RELAXING
INKING
RELAXING
COLORING
RELAXING
FINISH UP
SO:
PLANNING BRINGS BALANCE
GREAT CONCLUSION!
WELL SAID!
...and now back to the game! Woohoo!

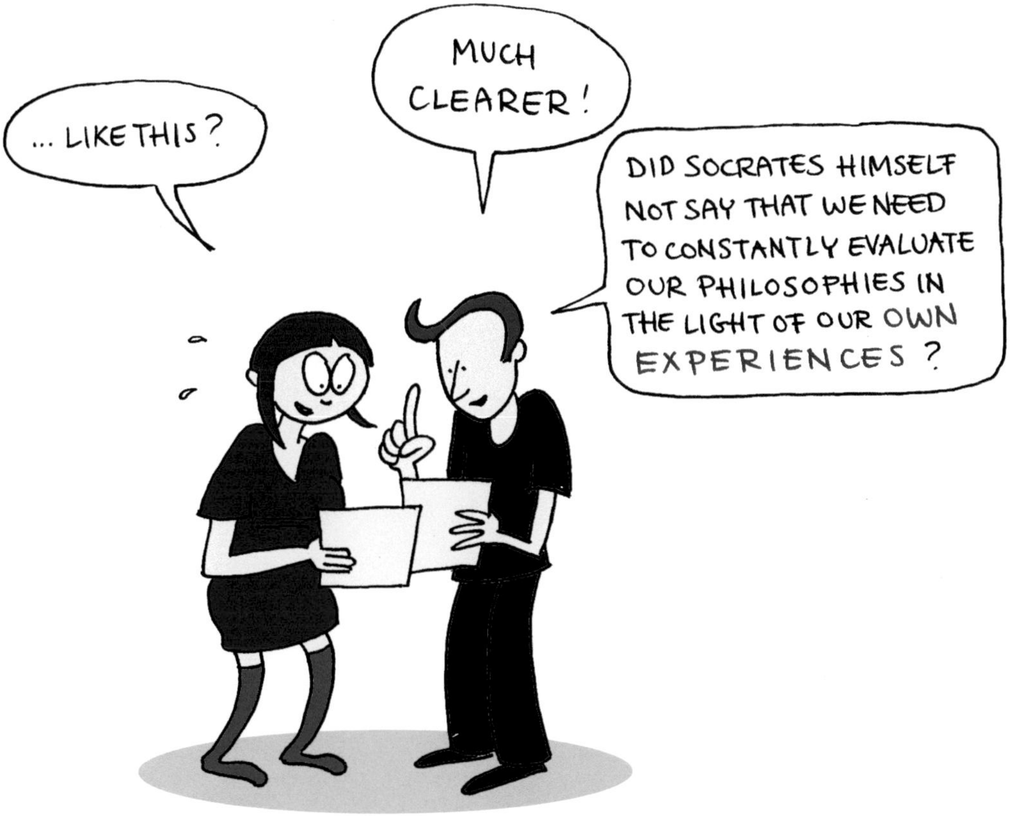
... LIKE THIS?
MUCH CLEARER!
DID SOCRATES HIMSELF NOT SAY THAT WE NEED TO CONSTANTLY EVALUATE OUR PHILOSOPHIES IN THE LIGHT OF OUR OWN EXPERIENCES?

SOCRATES DIDN'T LEAVE US ANY OF HIS OWN WRITINGS...

WE MAINLY KNOW ABOUT HIM THROUGH PLATO, WHO WROTE DOWN MANY OF HIS DIALOGUES AFTER SOCRATES' DEATH.

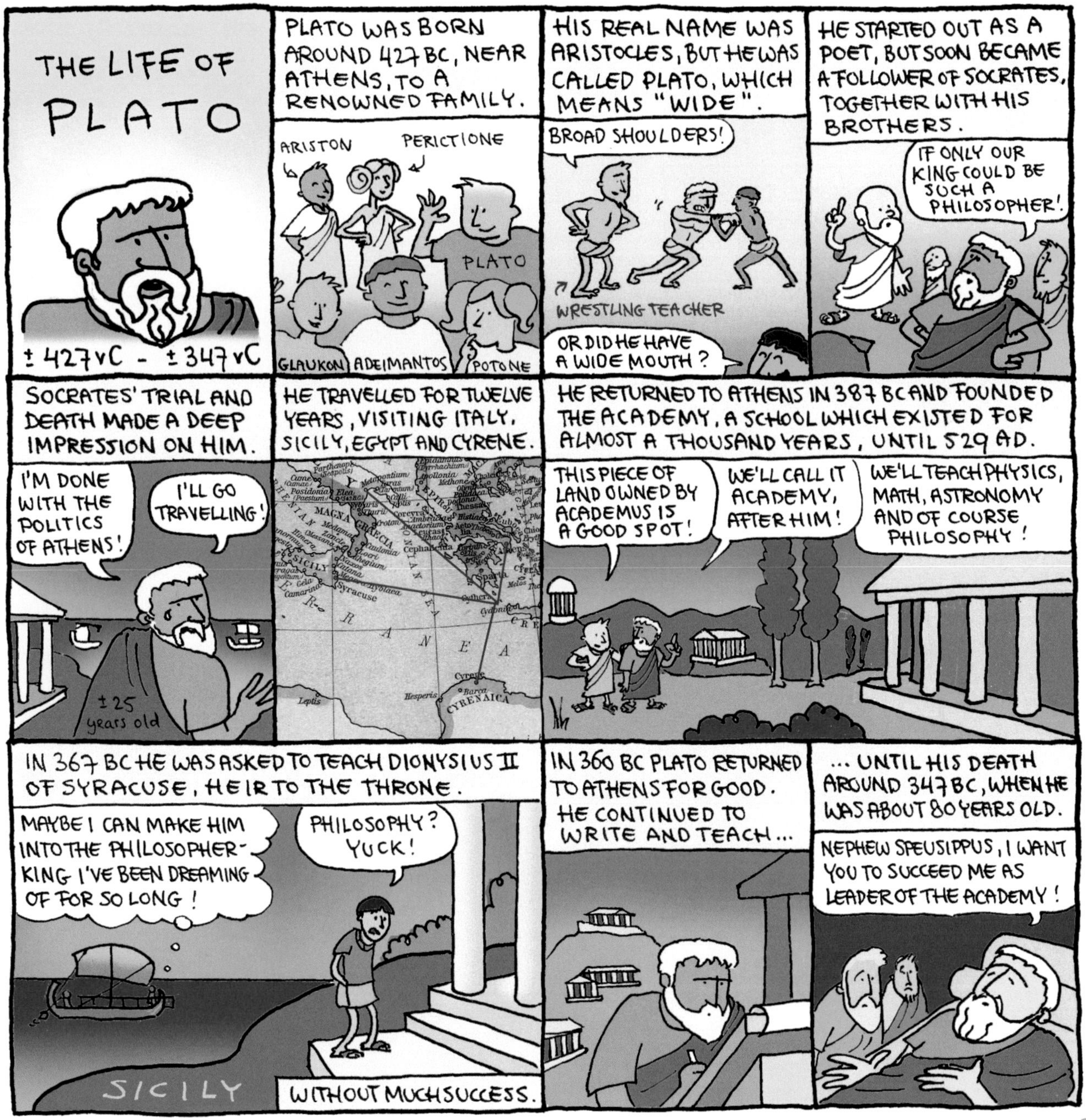

THE LIFE OF PLATO
± 427 vC - ± 347 vC
PLATO WAS BORN AROUND 427 BC, NEAR ATHENS, TO A RENOWNED FAMILY.
ARISTON
PERICTIONE
PLATO
GLAUKON
ADEIMANTOS
POTONE
HIS REAL NAME WAS ARISTOCLES, BUT HE WAS CALLED PLATO, WHICH MEANS "WIDE".
BROAD SHOULDERS!
WRESTLING TEACHER
OR DID HE HAVE A WIDE MOUTH?
HE STARTED OUT AS A POET, BUT SOON BECAME A FOLLOWER OF SOCRATES, TOGETHER WITH HIS BROTHERS.
IF ONLY OUR KING COULD BE SUCH A PHILOSOPHER!
SOCRATES' TRIAL AND DEATH MADE A DEEP IMPRESSION ON HIM.
I'M DONE WITH THE POLITICS OF ATHENS!
I'LL GO TRAVELLING!
± 25 years old
HE TRAVELLED FOR TWELVE YEARS, VISITING ITALY, SICILY, EGYPT AND CYRENE.
HE RETURNED TO ATHENS IN 387 BC AND FOUNDED THE ACADEMY, A SCHOOL WHICH EXISTED FOR ALMOST A THOUSAND YEARS, UNTIL 529 AD.
THIS PIECE OF LAND OWNED BY ACADEMUS IS A GOOD SPOT!
WE'LL CALL IT ACADEMY, AFTER HIM!
WE'LL TEACH PHYSICS, MATH, ASTRONOMY AND OF COURSE PHILOSOPHY!
IN 367 BC HE WAS ASKED TO TEACH DIONYSIUS II OF SYRACUSE, HEIR TO THE THRONE.
MAYBE I CAN MAKE HIM INTO THE PHILOSOPHER-KING I'VE BEEN DREAMING OF FOR SO LONG!
PHILOSOPHY? YUCK!
SICILY
WITHOUT MUCH SUCCESS.
IN 360 BC PLATO RETURNED TO ATHENS FOR GOOD. HE CONTINUED TO WRITE AND TEACH...
... UNTIL HIS DEATH AROUND 347 BC, WHEN HE WAS ABOUT 80 YEARS OLD.
NEPHEW SPEUSIPPUS, I WANT YOU TO SUCCEED ME AS LEADER OF THE ACADEMY!

THE BEST KNOWN WORK OF PLATO IS THE FAMOUS

ALLEGORY OF THE CAVE

THE ALLEGORY OF THE CAVE IS A DIALOGUE BETWEEN SOCRATES AND GLAUKON, PLATO'S BROTHER. IT IS WRITTEN DOWN IN THE BOOK CALLED 'THE STATE'.

LVX VENIT IN MVNDVN ET DILEXERVNT HOMINES MAGIS TENEBRAS QVAM LVCEM IO.3.19
ANTRVM PLATONICVM

EVEN THOUGH IT'S ABOUT SOCRATES, IT IS CLEAR THAT PLATO IS EXPLAINING HIS OWN PHILOSOPHY ABOUT THE WORLD OF TRUE FORMS, THE ETERNAL IDEAS OF WHICH THE PHYSICAL REALITY IS JUST A SHADOW.

I READ THE ALLEGORY OF THE CAVE IN COLLEGE
I SAW PARALLELS WITH BUDDHISM!
I KNOW THE ALLEGORY MAINLY AS INSPIRATION FOR MOVIES LIKE 'THE MATRIX' AND 'THE TRUMAN SHOW'!

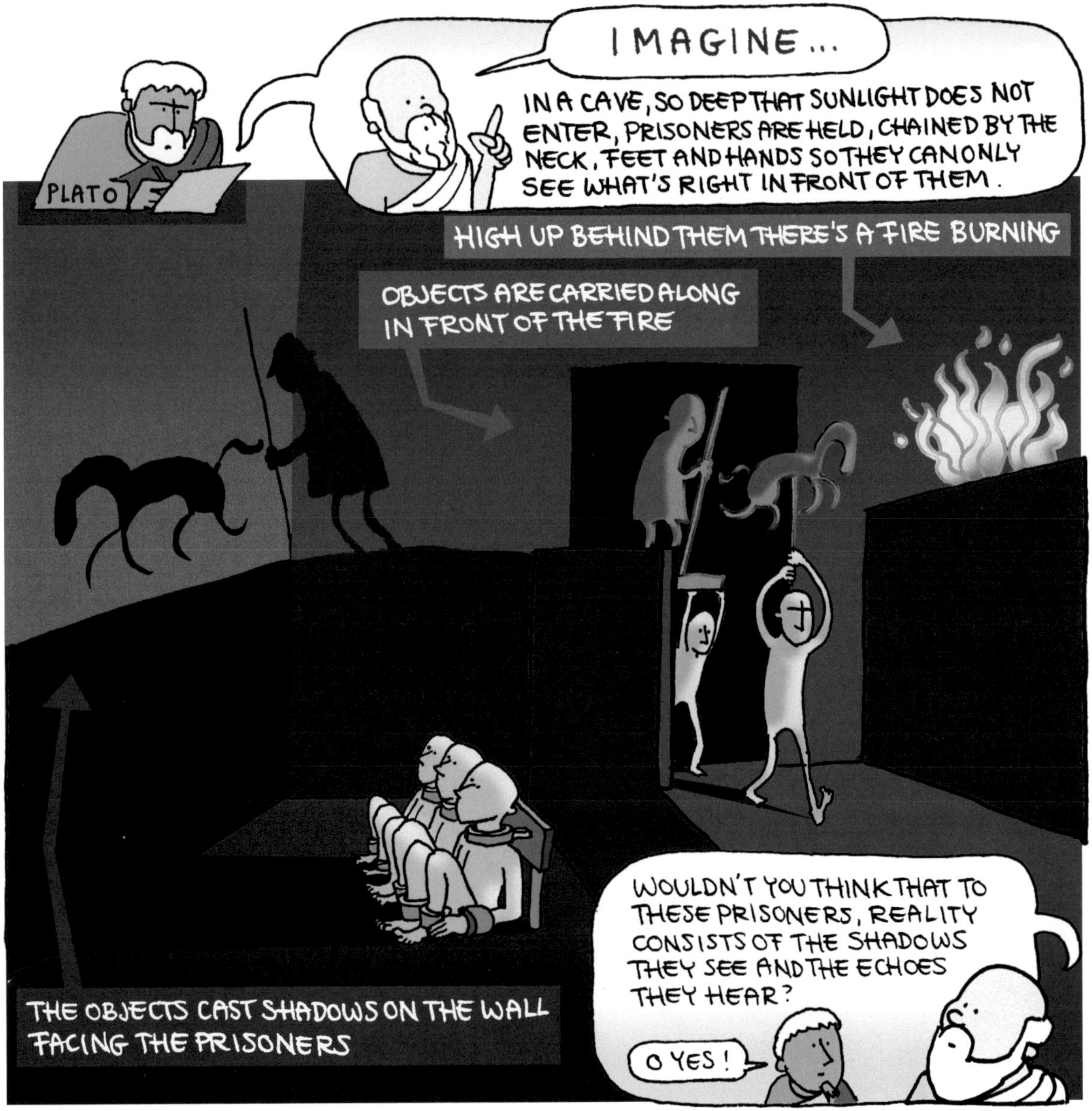
PLATO
IMAGINE...
IN A CAVE, SO DEEP THAT SUNLIGHT DOES NOT ENTER, PRISONERS ARE HELD, CHAINED BY THE NECK, FEET AND HANDS SO THEY CAN ONLY SEE WHAT'S RIGHT IN FRONT OF THEM.
HIGH UP BEHIND THEM THERE'S A FIRE BURNING
OBJECTS ARE CARRIED ALONG IN FRONT OF THE FIRE
THE OBJECTS CAST SHADOWS ON THE WALL FACING THE PRISONERS
WOULDN'T YOU THINK THAT TO THESE PRISONERS, REALITY CONSISTS OF THE SHADOWS THEY SEE AND THE ECHOES THEY HEAR?
O YES!

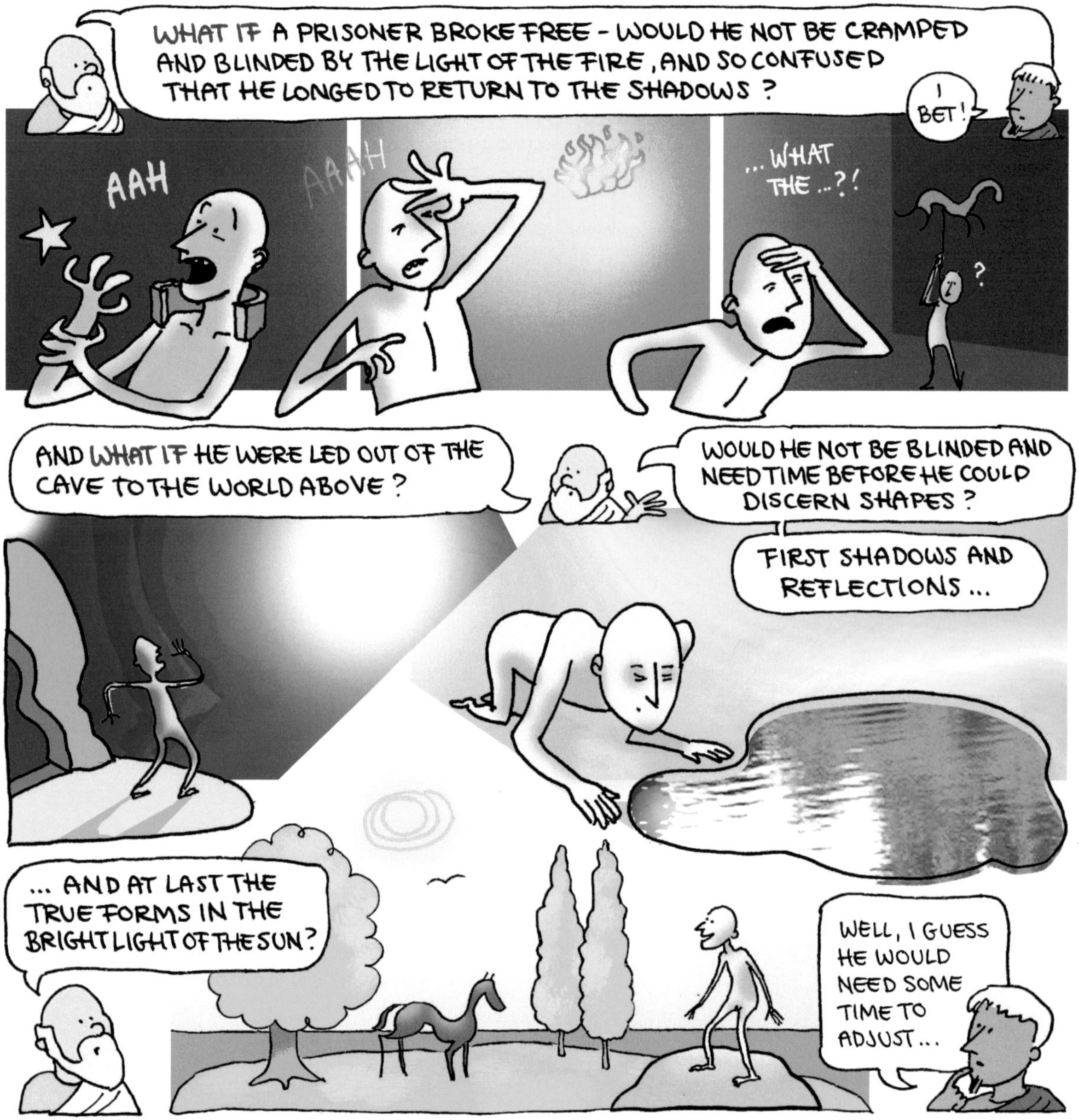
WHAT IF A PRISONER BROKE FREE - WOULD HE NOT BE CRAMPED AND BLINDED BY THE LIGHT OF THE FIRE, AND SO CONFUSED THAT HE LONGED TO RETURN TO THE SHADOWS ?
I BET!
AAH
AAAH
... WHAT THE ...?!
?
AND WHAT IF HE WERE LED OUT OF THE CAVE TO THE WORLD ABOVE ?
WOULD HE NOT BE BLINDED AND NEED TIME BEFORE HE COULD DISCERN SHAPES ?
FIRST SHADOWS AND REFLECTIONS ...
... AND AT LAST THE TRUE FORMS IN THE BRIGHT LIGHT OF THE SUN ?
WELL, I GUESS HE WOULD NEED SOME TIME TO ADJUST...

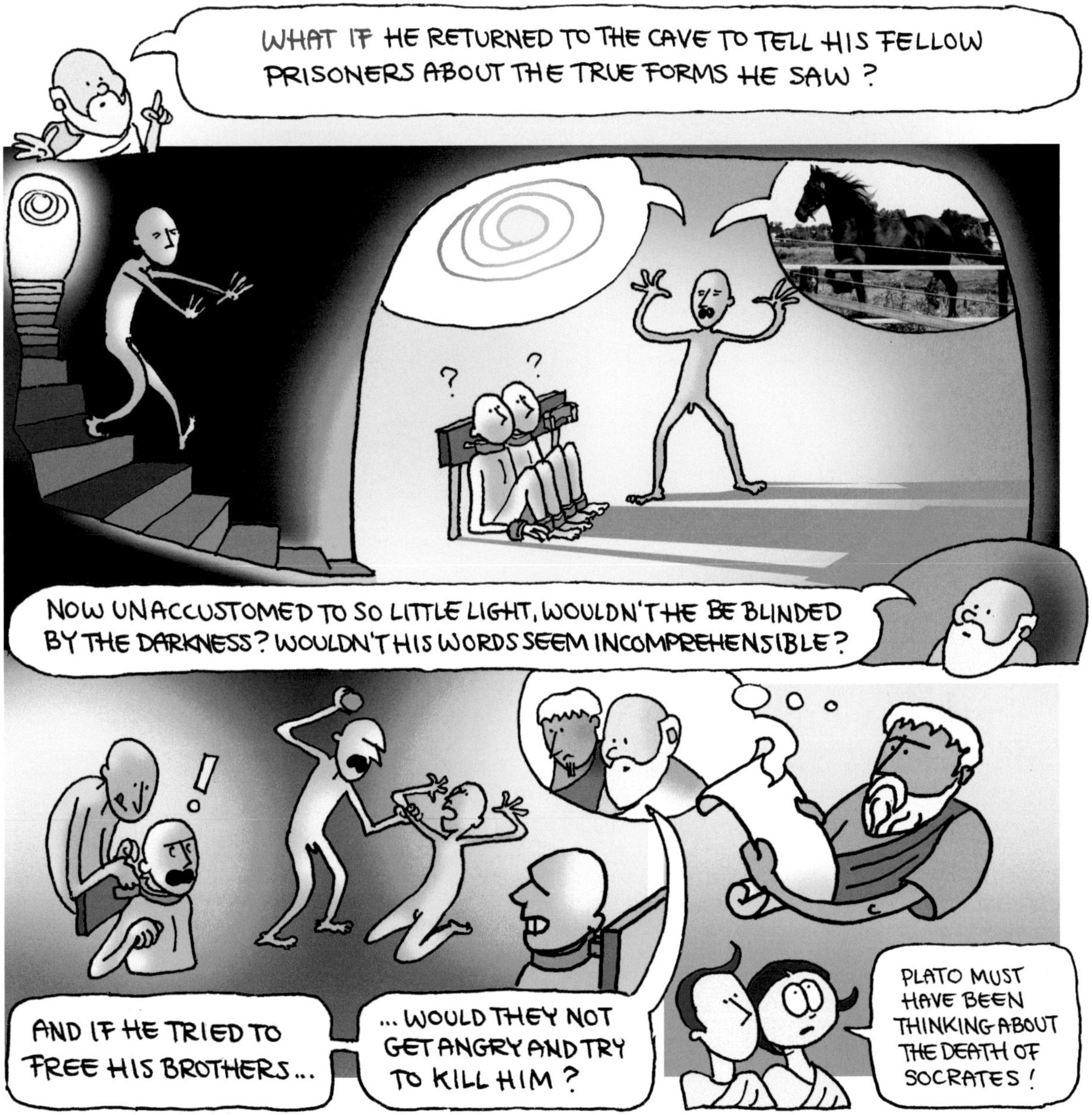
WHAT IF HE RETURNED TO THE CAVE TO TELL HIS FELLOW PRISONERS ABOUT THE TRUE FORMS HE SAW ?
NOW UNACCUSTOMED TO SO LITTLE LIGHT, WOULDN'T HE BE BLINDED BY THE DARKNESS? WOULDN'T HIS WORDS SEEM INCOMPREHENSIBLE?
AND IF HE TRIED TO FREE HIS BROTHERS...
... WOULD THEY NOT GET ANGRY AND TRY TO KILL HIM ?
PLATO MUST HAVE BEEN THINKING ABOUT THE DEATH OF SOCRATES !

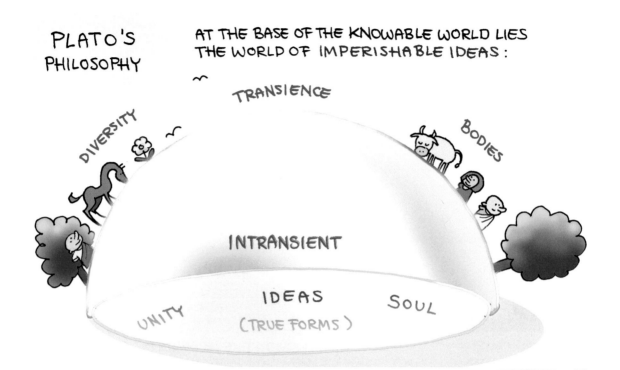

PLATO'S PHILOSOPHY

AT THE BASE OF THE KNOWABLE WORLD LIES THE WORLD OF IMPERISHABLE IDEAS:

TRANSIENCE

DIVERSITY

BODIES

INTRANSIENT

IDEAS
(TRUE FORMS)

UNITY

SOUL

THE MOST IMPORTANT GOAL IN LIFE FOR AN INTELLIGENT HUMAN IS TO SEE THROUGH THE SURFACE, SO WE CAN BEHOLD ACTUAL REALITY!

THOSE WHO HAVE ATTAINED THIS ENLIGHTENMENT...

...HAVE A DUTY TO PASS ON THIS WISDOM, FOR THE GOOD OF MANKIND AND THE STATE!

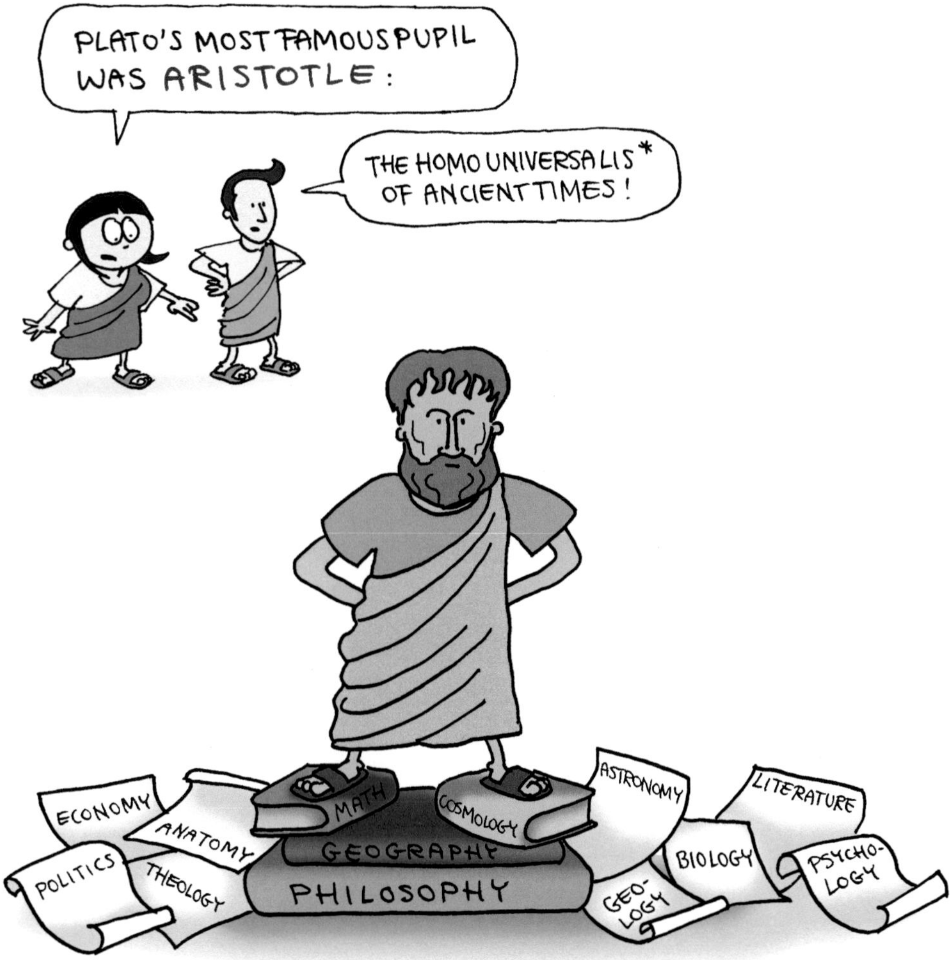
PLATO'S MOST FAMOUS PUPIL WAS ARISTOTLE:
THE HOMO UNIVERSALIS* OF ANCIENT TIMES!
ECONOMY
ANATOMY
POLITICS
THEOLOGY
MATH
COSMOLOGY
GEOGRAPHY
PHILOSOPHY
ASTRONOMY
LITERATURE
BIOLOGY
PSYCHO-LOGY
GEO-LOGY

* HOMO UNIVERSALIS = UNIVERSAL MAN : A PERSON WHOSE EXPERTISE SPANS A SIGNIFICANT NUMBER OF DIFFERENT SUBJECT AREAS.

THE LIFE OF ARISTOTLE

384 B.C. – 322 B.C.

ARISTOTLE WAS BORN IN STAGEIRA, NEAR MODERN THESSALONIKI.

Nicomachus (royal physician)

uncle Proxenus raised him after his parents' deaths

WHEN HE WAS 17, HE WENT TO ATHENS TO STUDY AT PLATO'S ACADEMY.

AH! KNOWLEDGE!

HE STAYED THERE FOR ALMOST 20 YEARS, UNTIL PLATO'S DEATH IN 347 B.C.

WILL YOU BE SUCCEEDING PLATO?

NAH— I HAVE VERY DIFFERENT VIEWS!

HE TRAVELLED TO THE COURT OF HIS FRIEND HERMIAS OF ATARNEUS, IN ASIA MINOR.

SHALL WE VISIT LESBOS ON OUR WAY?

YEAH! WE CAN STUDY ITS FLORA AND FAUNA!

ARISTOTLE MARRIED PYTHIAS, HERMIAS' NIECE. THEY HAD A DAUGHTER: PYTHIAS.

AFTER HERMIAS' DEATH IN 343 BC, ARISTOTLE TAUGHT YOUNG ALEXANDER THE GREAT.

I'D EXPAND THE EMPIRE TO THE EAST, IF I WERE YOU...

NOTHING BUT BARBARIANS THERE!

age 13

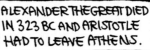

HE BECAME HEAD OF THE ROYAL ACADEMY OF MACEDONIA.

He taught Kassander (king of Macedonia) and Ptolemy (ruler of Egypt)

IN 335 BC ARISTOTLE RETURNED TO ATHENS WHERE HE FOUNDED THE LYCEUM.

I CALL IT THE SCHOOL OF PERI-PATHETICS – BECAUSE I LIKE TO TEACH WHILE I WALK!

AFTER THE DEATH OF HIS WIFE HE HAD A SON WITH HERPYLLIS.

THEY SAY HE'S ALSO INVOLVED WITH A YOUNG MAN!

Who isn't these days?

ALEXANDER THE GREAT DIED IN 323 BC AND ARISTOTLE HAD TO LEAVE ATHENS.

ALEXANDER WAS A JERK!

ARISTOTLE USED TO TEACH HIM! LET'S GET HIM!

I'D BETTER LEAVE BEFORE THEY HAVE ME END UP LIKE SOCRATES!

HE DIED LESS THAN A YEAR LATER IN CHALKIS, 61 YEARS OF AGE.

HE WAS A SWEET FATHER AND HE WAS KIND TO HIS SLAVES!

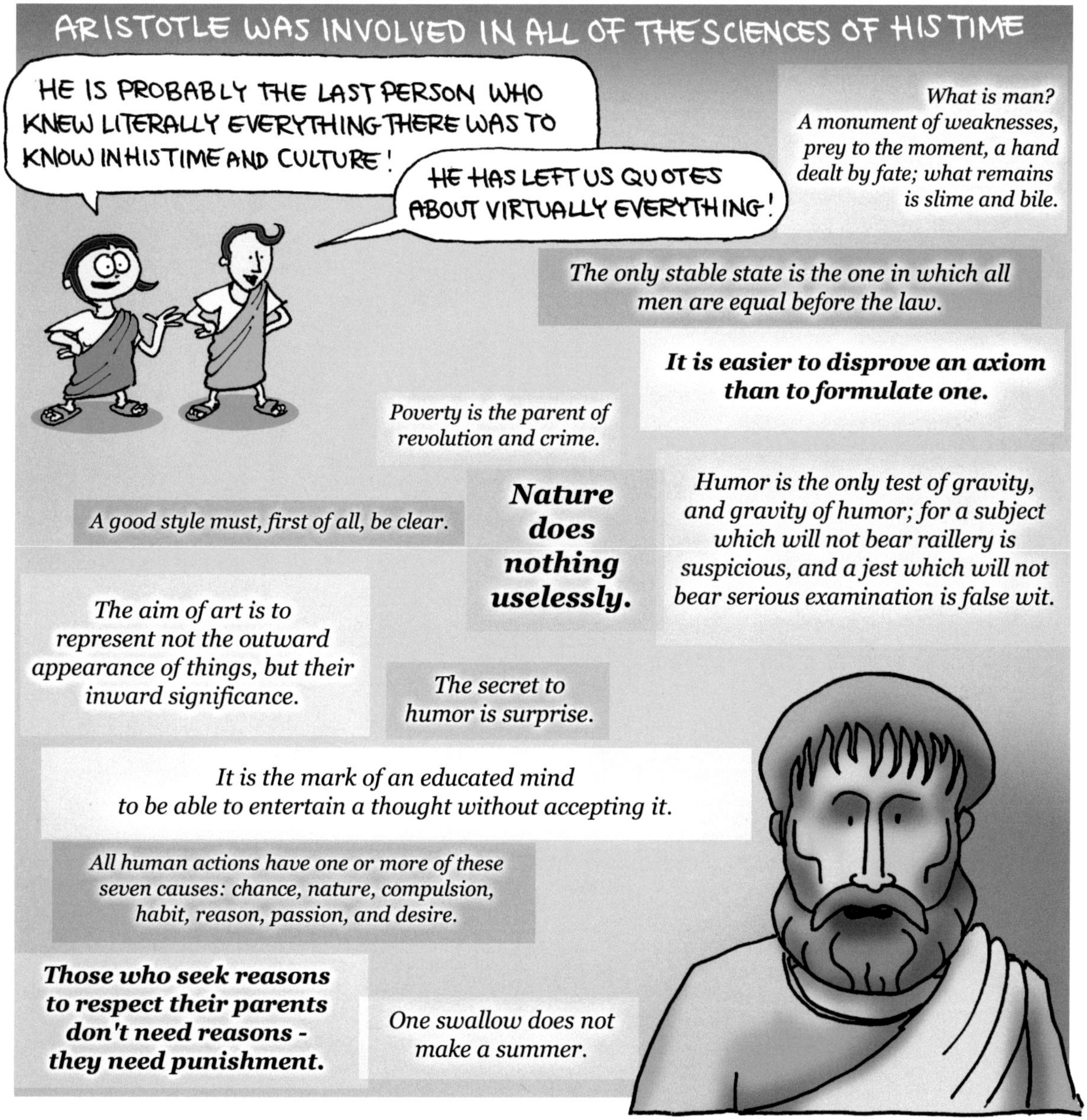
ARISTOTLE WAS INVOLVED IN ALL OF THE SCIENCES OF HIS TIME
HE IS PROBABLY THE LAST PERSON WHO KNEW LITERALLY EVERYTHING THERE WAS TO KNOW IN HIS TIME AND CULTURE!
HE HAS LEFT US QUOTES ABOUT VIRTUALLY EVERYTHING!
What is man? A monument of weaknesses, prey to the moment, a hand dealt by fate; what remains is slime and bile.
The only stable state is the one in which all men are equal before the law.
It is easier to disprove an axiom than to formulate one.
Poverty is the parent of revolution and crime.
A good style must, first of all, be clear.
Nature does nothing uselessly.
Humor is the only test of gravity, and gravity of humor; for a subject which will not bear raillery is suspicious, and a jest which will not bear serious examination is false wit.
The aim of art is to represent not the outward appearance of things, but their inward significance.
The secret to humor is surprise.
It is the mark of an educated mind to be able to entertain a thought without accepting it.
All human actions have one or more of these seven causes: chance, nature, compulsion, habit, reason, passion, and desire.
Those who seek reasons to respect their parents don't need reasons - they need punishment.
One swallow does not make a summer.

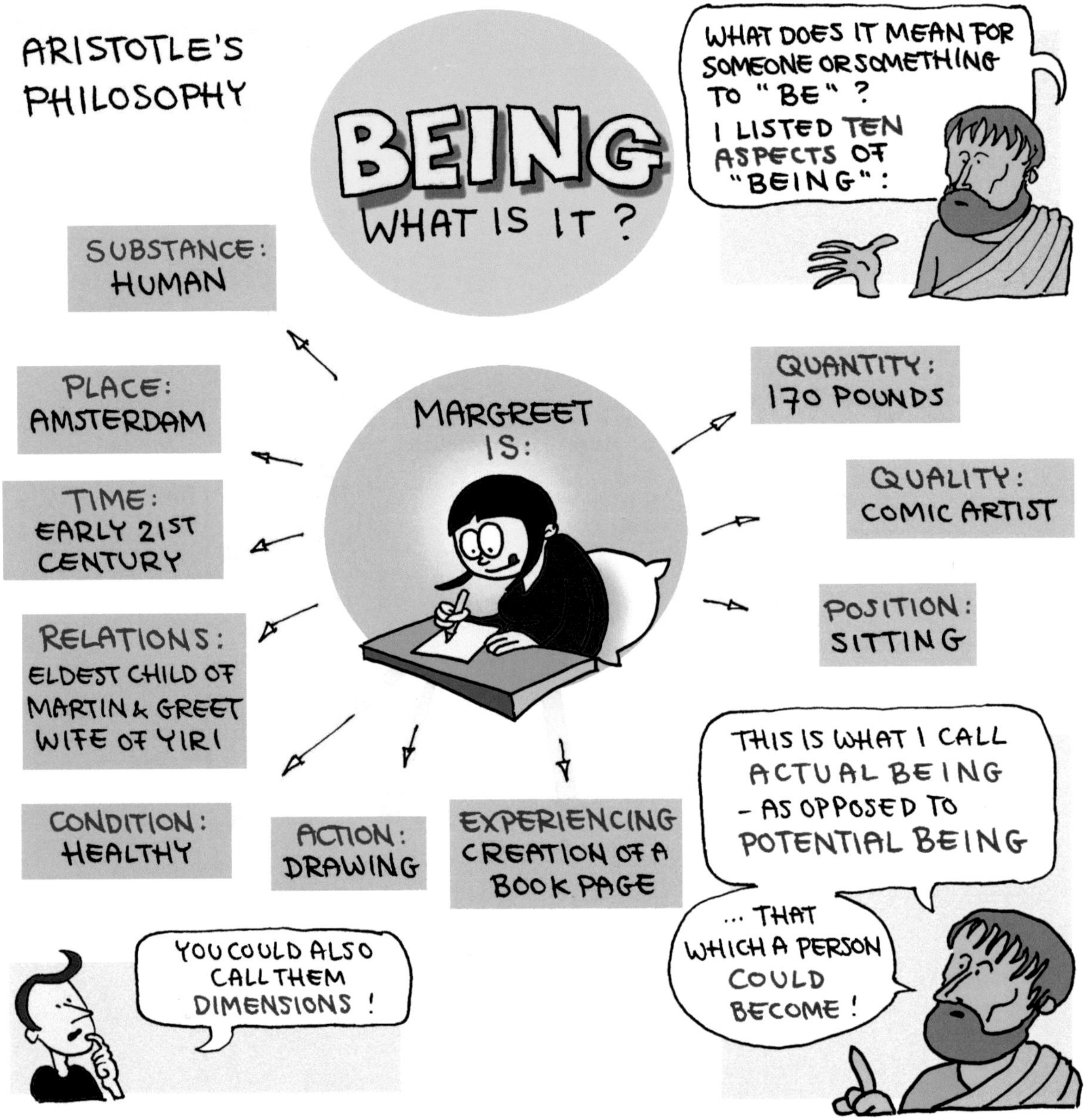
ARISTOTLE'S PHILOSOPHY
BEING
WHAT IS IT?
WHAT DOES IT MEAN FOR SOMEONE OR SOMETHING TO "BE"? I LISTED TEN ASPECTS OF "BEING":
SUBSTANCE: HUMAN
MARGREET IS:
PLACE: AMSTERDAM
TIME: EARLY 21ST CENTURY
RELATIONS: ELDEST CHILD OF MARTIN & GREET WIFE OF YIRI
CONDITION: HEALTHY
ACTION: DRAWING
EXPERIENCING CREATION OF A BOOK PAGE
QUANTITY: 170 POUNDS
QUALITY: COMIC ARTIST
POSITION: SITTING
THIS IS WHAT I CALL ACTUAL BEING - AS OPPOSED TO POTENTIAL BEING
... THAT WHICH A PERSON COULD BECOME!
YOU COULD ALSO CALL THEM DIMENSIONS!

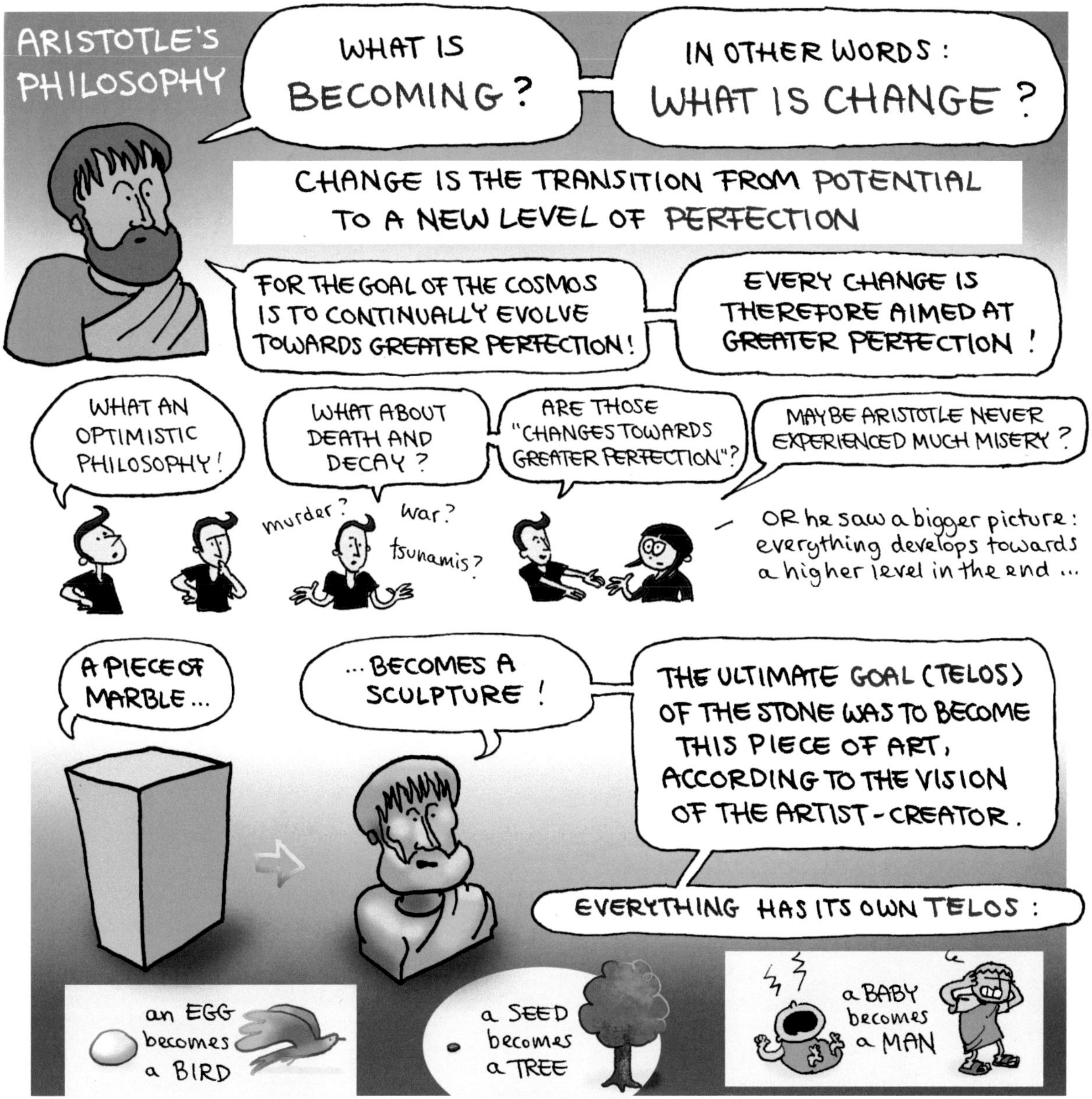

ARISTOTLE'S PHILOSOPHY
WHAT IS BECOMING?
IN OTHER WORDS: WHAT IS CHANGE?
CHANGE IS THE TRANSITION FROM POTENTIAL TO A NEW LEVEL OF PERFECTION
FOR THE GOAL OF THE COSMOS IS TO CONTINUALLY EVOLVE TOWARDS GREATER PERFECTION!
EVERY CHANGE IS THEREFORE AIMED AT GREATER PERFECTION!
WHAT AN OPTIMISTIC PHILOSOPHY!
WHAT ABOUT DEATH AND DECAY?
murder?
war?
tsunamis?
ARE THOSE "CHANGES TOWARDS GREATER PERFECTION"?
MAYBE ARISTOTLE NEVER EXPERIENCED MUCH MISERY?
– OR he saw a bigger picture: everything develops towards a higher level in the end ...
A PIECE OF MARBLE ...
... BECOMES A SCULPTURE!
THE ULTIMATE GOAL (TELOS) OF THE STONE WAS TO BECOME THIS PIECE OF ART, ACCORDING TO THE VISION OF THE ARTIST-CREATOR.
EVERYTHING HAS ITS OWN TELOS:
an EGG becomes a BIRD
a SEED becomes a TREE
a BABY becomes a MAN

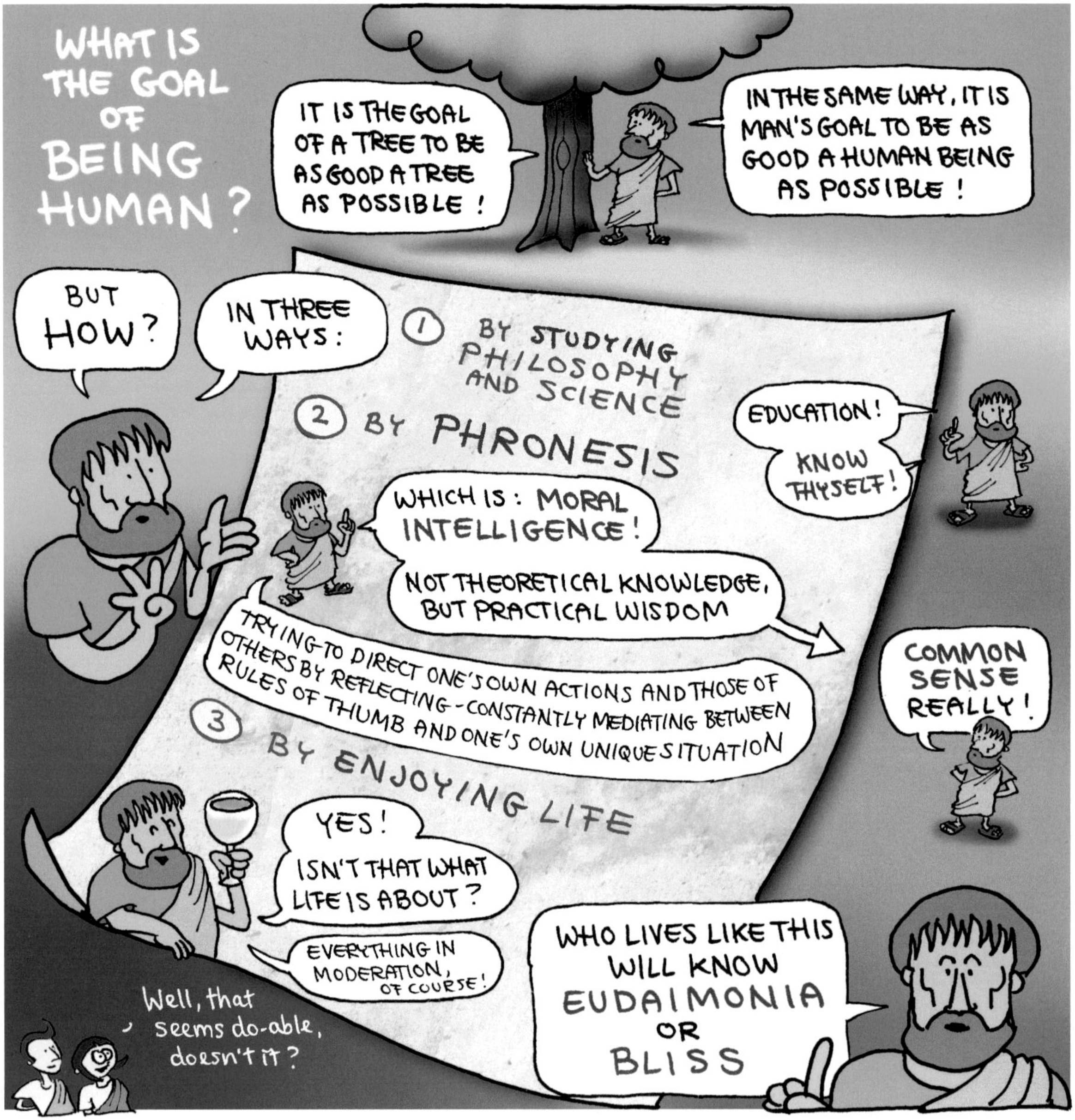
WHAT IS THE GOAL OF BEING HUMAN?
IT IS THE GOAL OF A TREE TO BE AS GOOD A TREE AS POSSIBLE!
IN THE SAME WAY, IT IS MAN'S GOAL TO BE AS GOOD A HUMAN BEING AS POSSIBLE!
BUT HOW?
IN THREE WAYS:
1 BY STUDYING PHILOSOPHY AND SCIENCE
EDUCATION!
KNOW THYSELF!
2 BY PHRONESIS
WHICH IS: MORAL INTELLIGENCE!
NOT THEORETICAL KNOWLEDGE, BUT PRACTICAL WISDOM
TRYING TO DIRECT ONE'S OWN ACTIONS AND THOSE OF OTHERS BY REFLECTING - CONSTANTLY MEDIATING BETWEEN RULES OF THUMB AND ONE'S OWN UNIQUE SITUATION
COMMON SENSE REALLY!
3 BY ENJOYING LIFE
YES!
ISN'T THAT WHAT LIFE IS ABOUT?
EVERYTHING IN MODERATION, OF COURSE!
WHO LIVES LIKE THIS WILL KNOW EUDAIMONIA OR BLISS
Well, that seems do-able, doesn't it?

AND THAT IS MERELY A FRACTION OF EVERYTHING THAT ARISTOTLE HAS WRITTEN AND THOUGHT ABOUT!

HE IS ALSO KNOWN FOR THE SYSTEMATIC WAY HE STUDIED NATURAL PHENOMENA – THE SCIENTIFIC METHOD, BASED ON OBSERVATION AND LOGIC, AS WE STILL KNOW IT TODAY!

THE MIND CAN GRASP ANYTHING!

EMPIRICISM
ANALYSIS
INDUCTION + DEDUCTION

MOST OF HIS WORK HAS BEEN LOST – WHAT REMAINS ARE MAINLY TUTORIALS AND NOTES MADE FOR HIS OWN REFERENCE!

CENTURIES LATER, ARISTOTLE'S WORK WAS "REDISCOVERED" IN THE WEST, AND IT BECAME THE FOUNDATION OF WESTERN THINKING!

What an output!

I ALSO PUBLISHED A LOT OF BOOKS, LIKE THIS ONE, WHICH YOU WILL NEVER KNOW!

DIALOGUES

I translated it from Greek into Arabic!

We translated it from Arabic into Latin!

So that I could base my work on it!

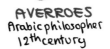

AVERROES
Arabic philosopher
12th century

DOMINICANS
12th/13th century

THOMAS AQUINAS
13th century

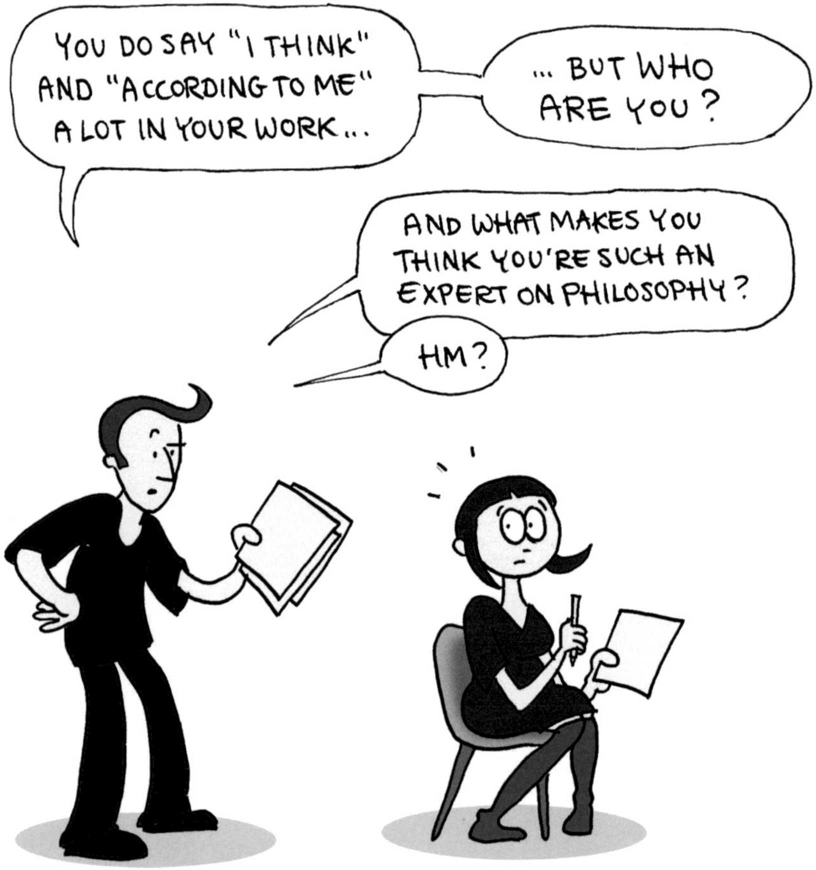
YOU DO SAY "I THINK" AND "ACCORDING TO ME" A LOT IN YOUR WORK...
... BUT WHO ARE YOU ?
AND WHAT MAKES YOU THINK YOU'RE SUCH AN EXPERT ON PHILOSOPHY ?
HM ?

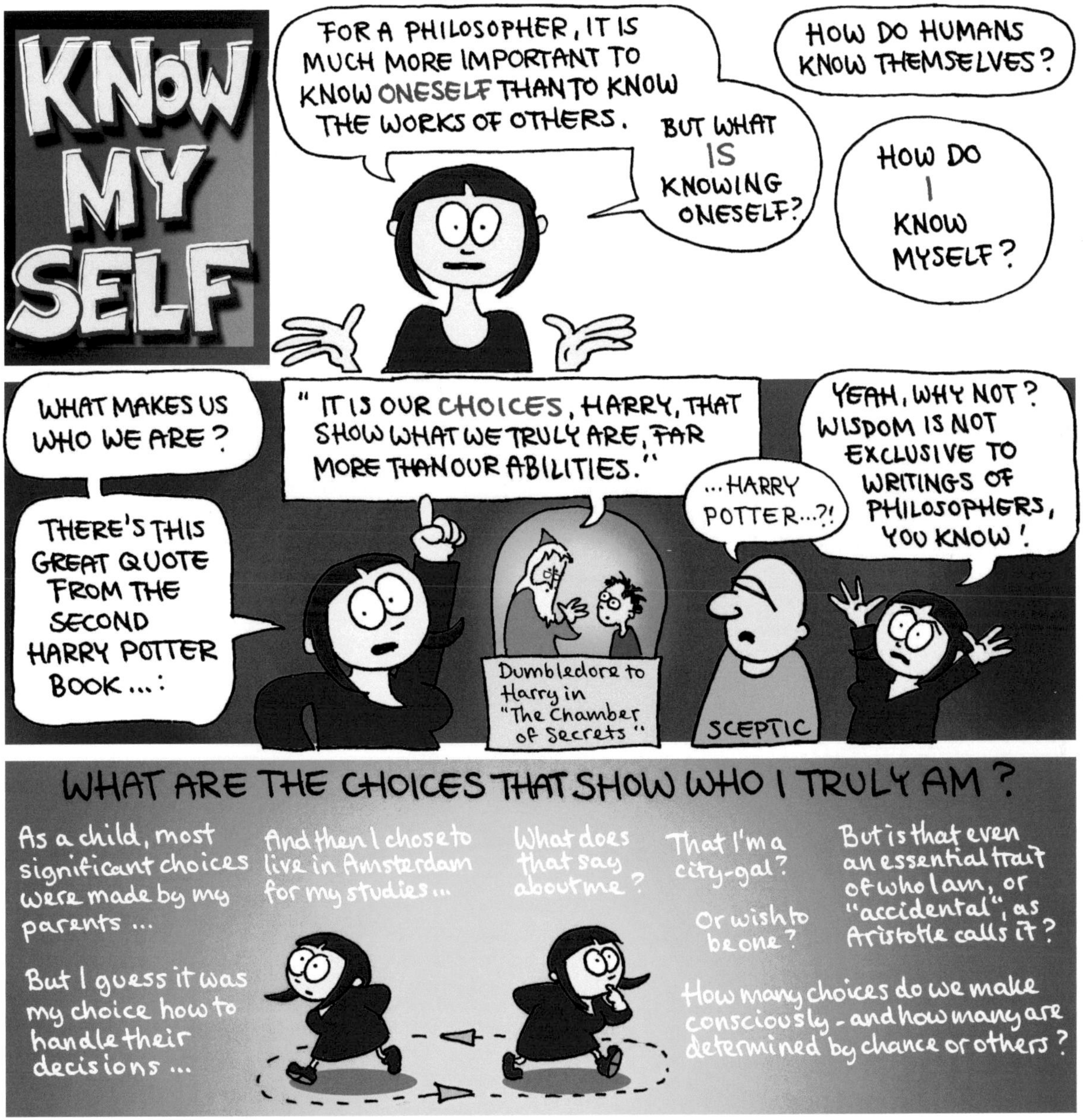
KNOW MY SELF
FOR A PHILOSOPHER, IT IS MUCH MORE IMPORTANT TO KNOW ONESELF THAN TO KNOW THE WORKS OF OTHERS.
BUT WHAT IS KNOWING ONESELF?
HOW DO HUMANS KNOW THEMSELVES?
HOW DO I KNOW MYSELF?
WHAT MAKES US WHO WE ARE?
THERE'S THIS GREAT QUOTE FROM THE SECOND HARRY POTTER BOOK...:
" IT IS OUR CHOICES, HARRY, THAT SHOW WHAT WE TRULY ARE, FAR MORE THAN OUR ABILITIES."
Dumbledore to Harry in "The Chamber of Secrets"
...HARRY POTTER...?!
SCEPTIC
YEAH, WHY NOT? WISDOM IS NOT EXCLUSIVE TO WRITINGS OF PHILOSOPHERS, YOU KNOW!
WHAT ARE THE CHOICES THAT SHOW WHO I TRULY AM?
As a child, most significant choices were made by my parents...
But I guess it was my choice how to handle their decisions...
And then I chose to live in Amsterdam for my studies...
What does that say about me?
That I'm a city-gal?
Or wish to be one?
But is that even an essential trait of who I am, or "accidental", as Aristotle calls it?
How many choices do we make consciously - and how many are determined by chance or others?

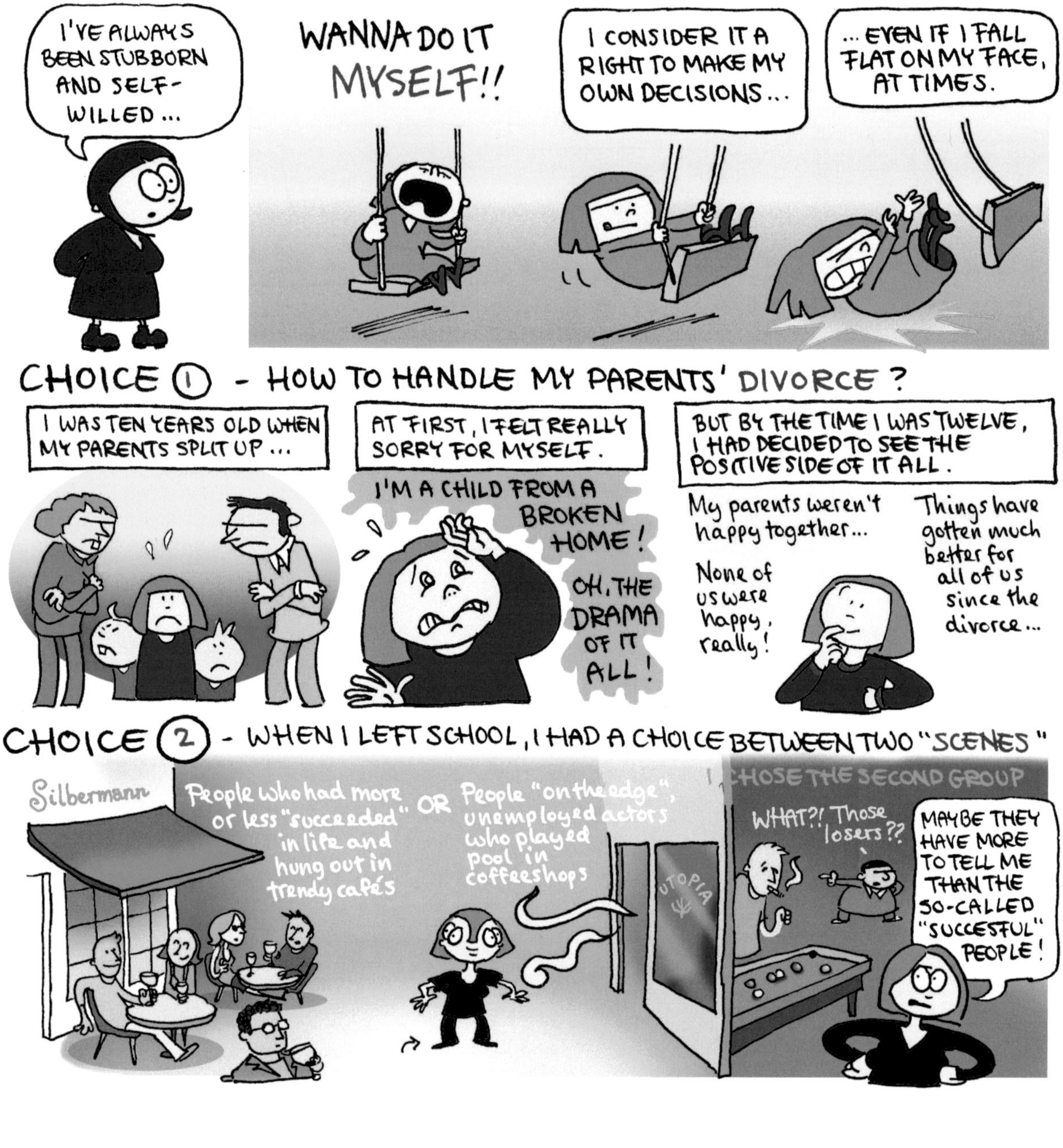
I'VE ALWAYS BEEN STUBBORN AND SELF-WILLED...
WANNA DO IT MYSELF!!
I CONSIDER IT A RIGHT TO MAKE MY OWN DECISIONS...
...EVEN IF I FALL FLAT ON MY FACE, AT TIMES.
CHOICE 1 - HOW TO HANDLE MY PARENTS' DIVORCE?
I WAS TEN YEARS OLD WHEN MY PARENTS SPLIT UP...
AT FIRST, I FELT REALLY SORRY FOR MYSELF.
I'M A CHILD FROM A BROKEN HOME!
OH, THE DRAMA OF IT ALL!
BUT BY THE TIME I WAS TWELVE, I HAD DECIDED TO SEE THE POSITIVE SIDE OF IT ALL.
My parents weren't happy together...
None of us were happy, really!
Things have gotten much better for all of us since the divorce...
CHOICE 2 - WHEN I LEFT SCHOOL, I HAD A CHOICE BETWEEN TWO "SCENES"
Silbermann
People who had more or less "succeeded" in life and hung out in trendy cafés
OR
People "on the edge", unemployed actors who played pool in coffeeshops
UTOPIA
I CHOSE THE SECOND GROUP
WHAT?! Those losers??
MAYBE THEY HAVE MORE TO TELL ME THAN THE SO-CALLED "SUCCESFUL" PEOPLE!

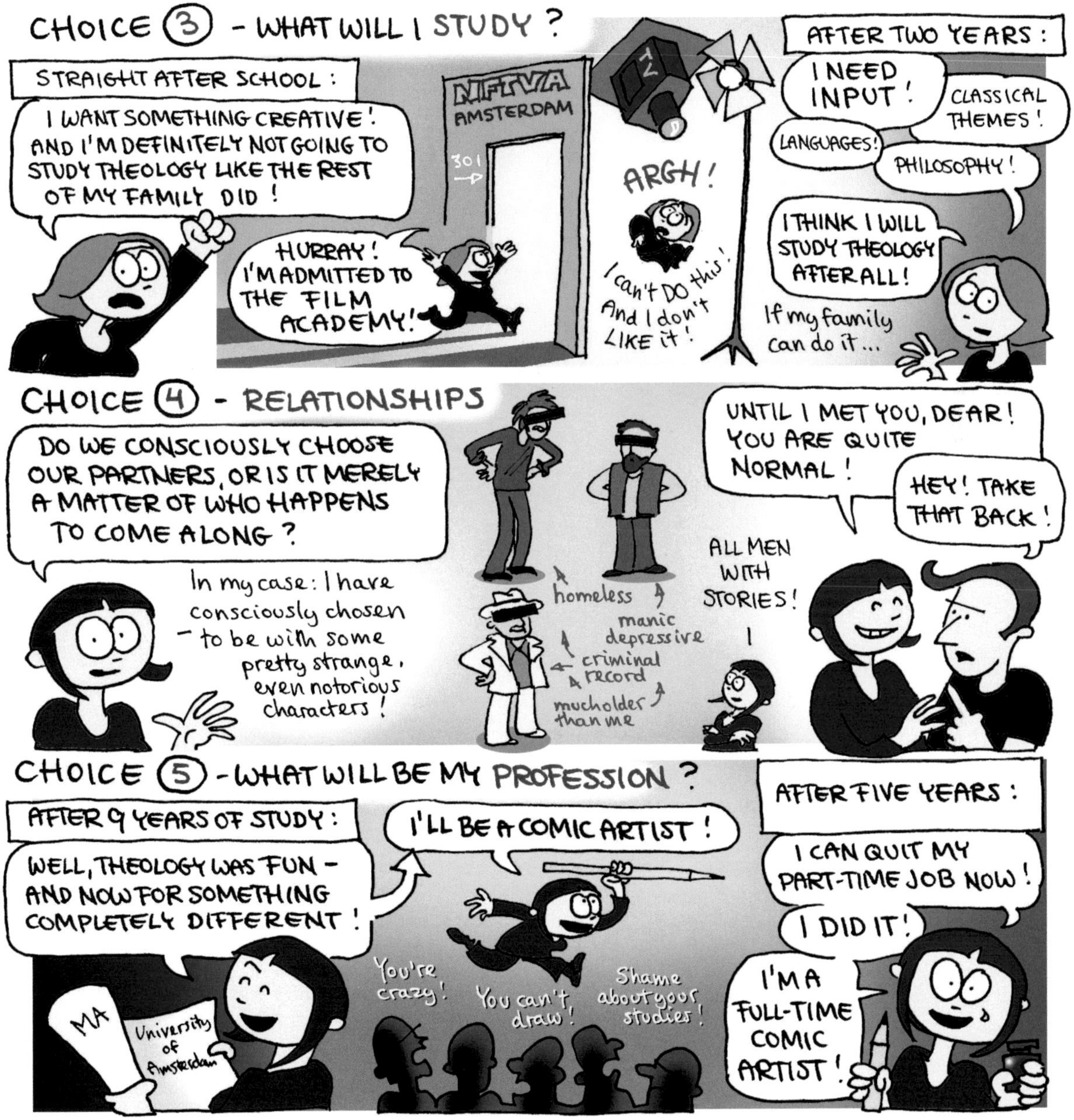
CHOICE 3 - WHAT WILL I STUDY?
STRAIGHT AFTER SCHOOL:
I WANT SOMETHING CREATIVE! AND I'M DEFINITELY NOT GOING TO STUDY THEOLOGY LIKE THE REST OF MY FAMILY DID!
NFTVA AMSTERDAM
301
HURRAY! I'M ADMITTED TO THE FILM ACADEMY!
TV
ARGH!
I can't DO this! And I don't LIKE it!
AFTER TWO YEARS:
I NEED INPUT!
CLASSICAL THEMES!
LANGUAGES!
PHILOSOPHY!
I THINK I WILL STUDY THEOLOGY AFTER ALL!
If my family can do it...
CHOICE 4 - RELATIONSHIPS
DO WE CONSCIOUSLY CHOOSE OUR PARTNERS, OR IS IT MERELY A MATTER OF WHO HAPPENS TO COME ALONG?
In my case: I have consciously chosen to be with some pretty strange, even notorious characters!
homeless
manic depressive
criminal record
much older than me
ALL MEN WITH STORIES!
UNTIL I MET YOU, DEAR! YOU ARE QUITE NORMAL!
HEY! TAKE THAT BACK!
CHOICE 5 - WHAT WILL BE MY PROFESSION?
AFTER 9 YEARS OF STUDY:
WELL, THEOLOGY WAS FUN - AND NOW FOR SOMETHING COMPLETELY DIFFERENT!
MA
University of Amsterdam
I'LL BE A COMIC ARTIST!
You're crazy!
You can't draw!
Shame about your studies!
AFTER FIVE YEARS:
I CAN QUIT MY PART-TIME JOB NOW!
I DID IT!
I'M A FULL-TIME COMIC ARTIST!

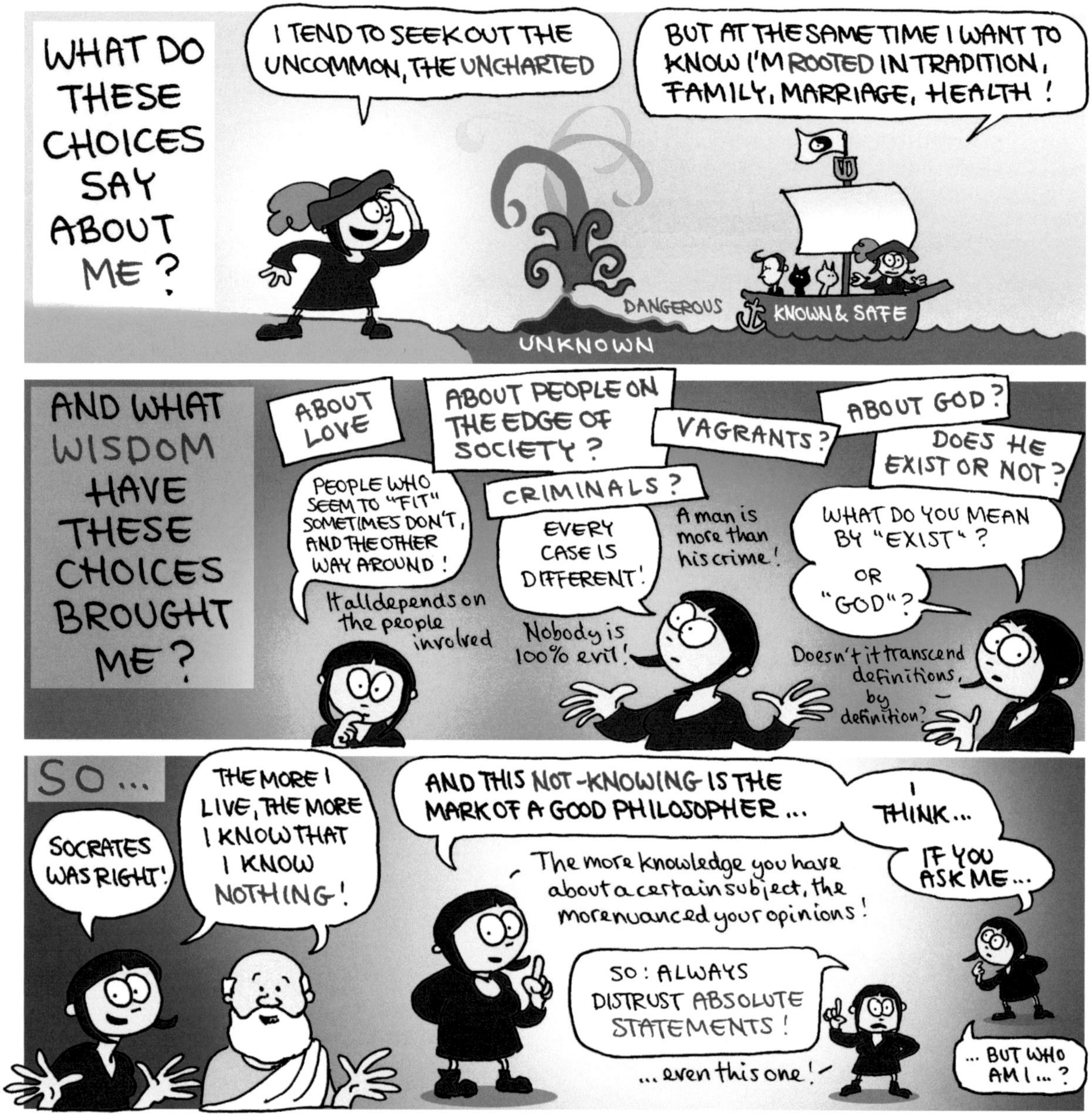
WHAT DO THESE CHOICES SAY ABOUT ME?
I TEND TO SEEK OUT THE UNCOMMON, THE UNCHARTED
BUT AT THE SAME TIME I WANT TO KNOW I'M ROOTED IN TRADITION, FAMILY, MARRIAGE, HEALTH!
DANGEROUS
UNKNOWN
KNOWN & SAFE
AND WHAT WISDOM HAVE THESE CHOICES BROUGHT ME?
ABOUT LOVE
PEOPLE WHO SEEM TO "FIT" SOMETIMES DON'T, AND THE OTHER WAY AROUND!
It all depends on the people involved
ABOUT PEOPLE ON THE EDGE OF SOCIETY?
VAGRANTS?
CRIMINALS?
EVERY CASE IS DIFFERENT!
A man is more than his crime!
Nobody is 100% evil!
ABOUT GOD?
DOES HE EXIST OR NOT?
WHAT DO YOU MEAN BY "EXIST"?
OR "GOD"?
Doesn't it transcend definitions, by definition?
SO...
SOCRATES WAS RIGHT!
THE MORE I LIVE, THE MORE I KNOW THAT I KNOW NOTHING!
AND THIS NOT-KNOWING IS THE MARK OF A GOOD PHILOSOPHER...
The more knowledge you have about a certain subject, the more nuanced your opinions!
SO: ALWAYS DISTRUST ABSOLUTE STATEMENTS!
... even this one!
I THINK...
IF YOU ASK ME...
... BUT WHO AM I...?

MEDIEVAL PHILOSOPHY

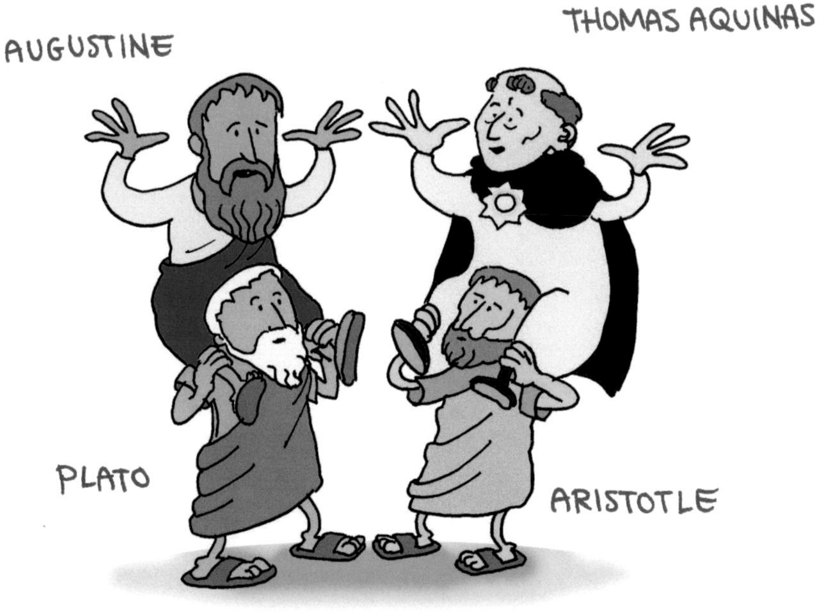
AUGUSTINE
THOMAS AQUINAS
PLATO
ARISTOTLE

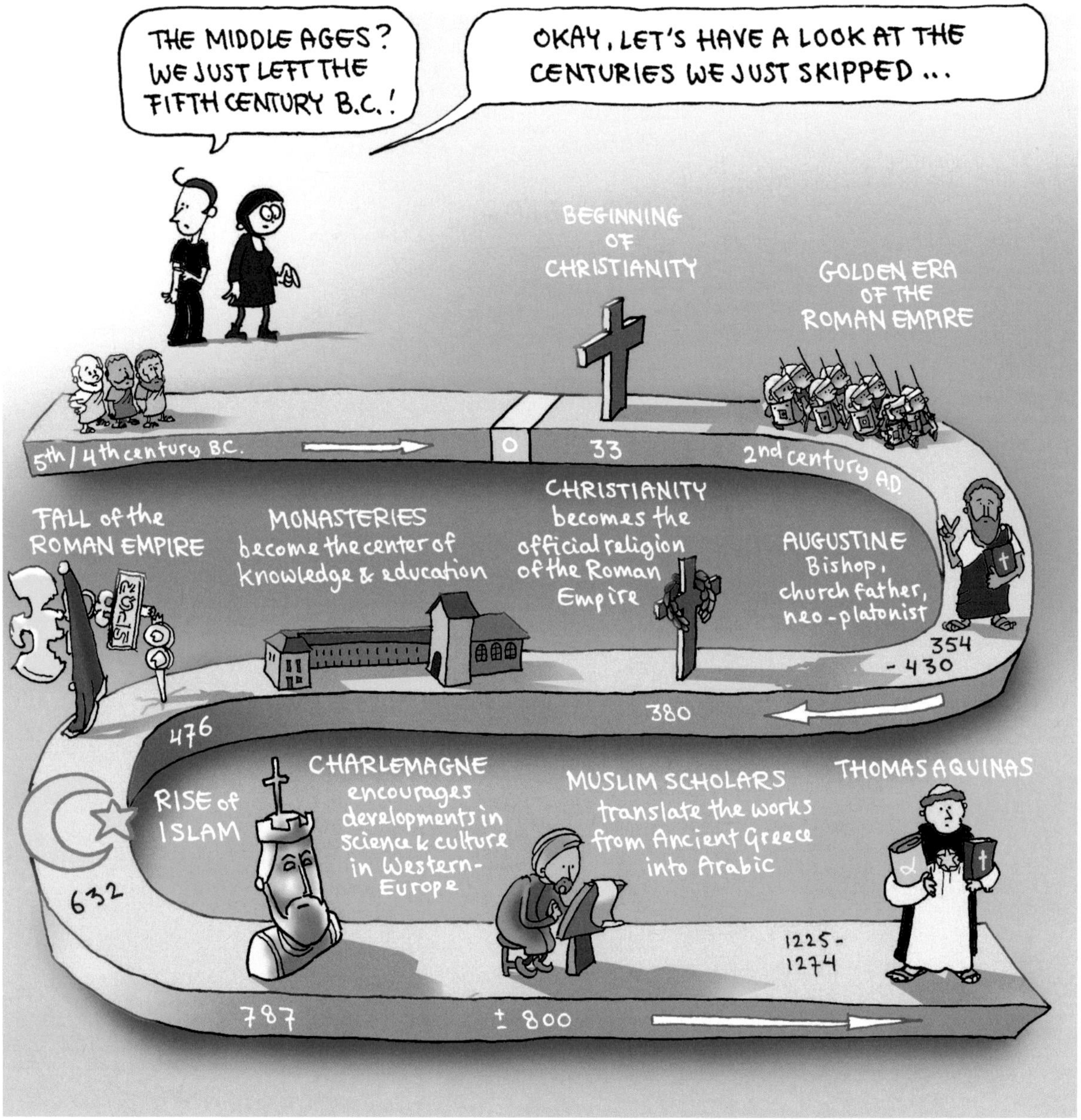
THE MIDDLE AGES? WE JUST LEFT THE FIFTH CENTURY B.C.!
OKAY, LET'S HAVE A LOOK AT THE CENTURIES WE JUST SKIPPED ...
5th / 4th century B.C.
0
BEGINNING OF CHRISTIANITY
33
GOLDEN ERA OF THE ROMAN EMPIRE
2nd century A.D.
AUGUSTINE Bishop, church father, neo-platonist
354 - 430
CHRISTIANITY becomes the official religion of the Roman Empire
380
MONASTERIES become the center of knowledge & education
FALL of the ROMAN EMPIRE
476
RISE of ISLAM
632
CHARLEMAGNE encourages developments in science & culture in Western-Europe
787
MUSLIM SCHOLARS translate the works from Ancient Greece into Arabic
± 800
THOMAS AQUINAS
1225-1274

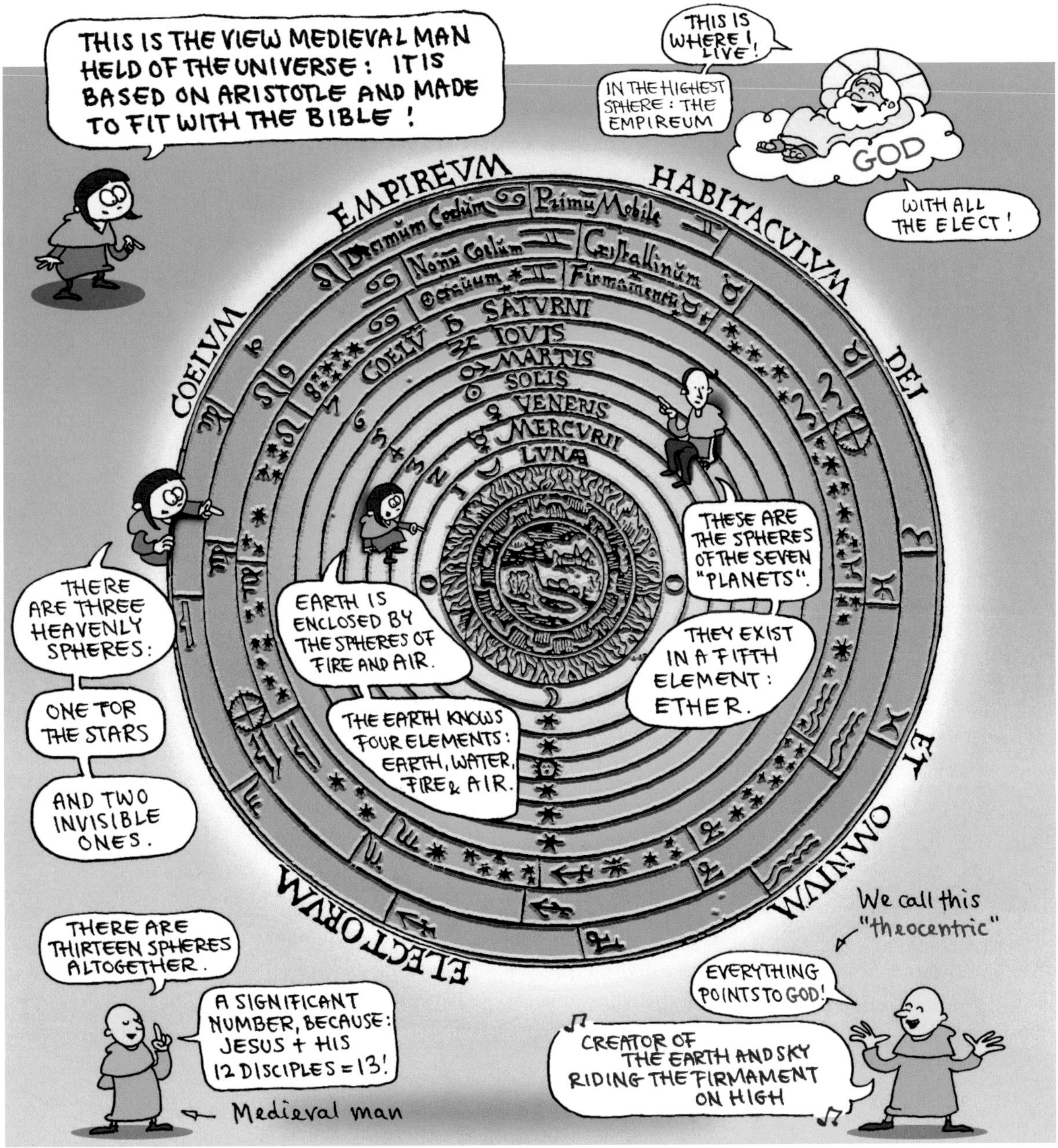
THIS IS THE VIEW MEDIEVAL MAN HELD OF THE UNIVERSE: IT IS BASED ON ARISTOTLE AND MADE TO FIT WITH THE BIBLE!
THIS IS WHERE I LIVE!
IN THE HIGHEST SPHERE: THE EMPIREUM
GOD
WITH ALL THE ELECT!
EMPIREVM HABITACVLVM DEI ET OMNIVM ELECTORVM
COELVM
Primu Mobile
Cristallinum
Firmamentum
SATVRNI
IOVIS
MARTIS
SOLIS
VENERIS
MERCVRII
LVNA
THESE ARE THE SPHERES OF THE SEVEN "PLANETS".
THEY EXIST IN A FIFTH ELEMENT: ETHER.
THERE ARE THREE HEAVENLY SPHERES:
ONE FOR THE STARS
AND TWO INVISIBLE ONES.
EARTH IS ENCLOSED BY THE SPHERES OF FIRE AND AIR.
THE EARTH KNOWS FOUR ELEMENTS: EARTH, WATER, FIRE & AIR.
THERE ARE THIRTEEN SPHERES ALTOGETHER.
A SIGNIFICANT NUMBER, BECAUSE: JESUS + HIS 12 DISCIPLES = 13!
Medieval man
We call this "theocentric"
EVERYTHING POINTS TO GOD!
CREATOR OF THE EARTH AND SKY RIDING THE FIRMAMENT ON HIGH

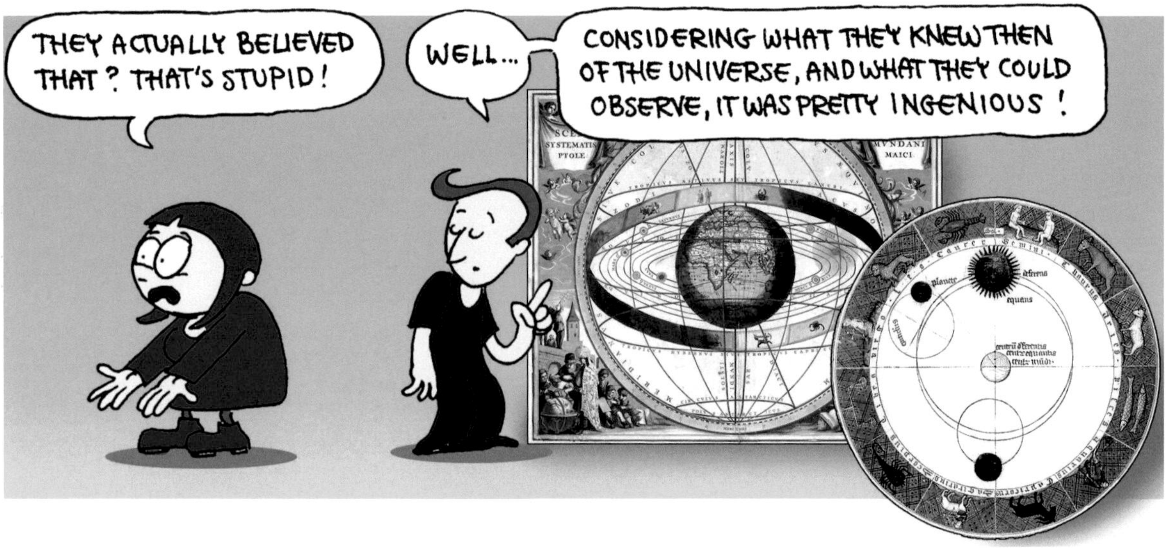
THEY ACTUALLY BELIEVED THAT? THAT'S STUPID!
WELL...
CONSIDERING WHAT THEY KNEW THEN OF THE UNIVERSE, AND WHAT THEY COULD OBSERVE, IT WAS PRETTY INGENIOUS!

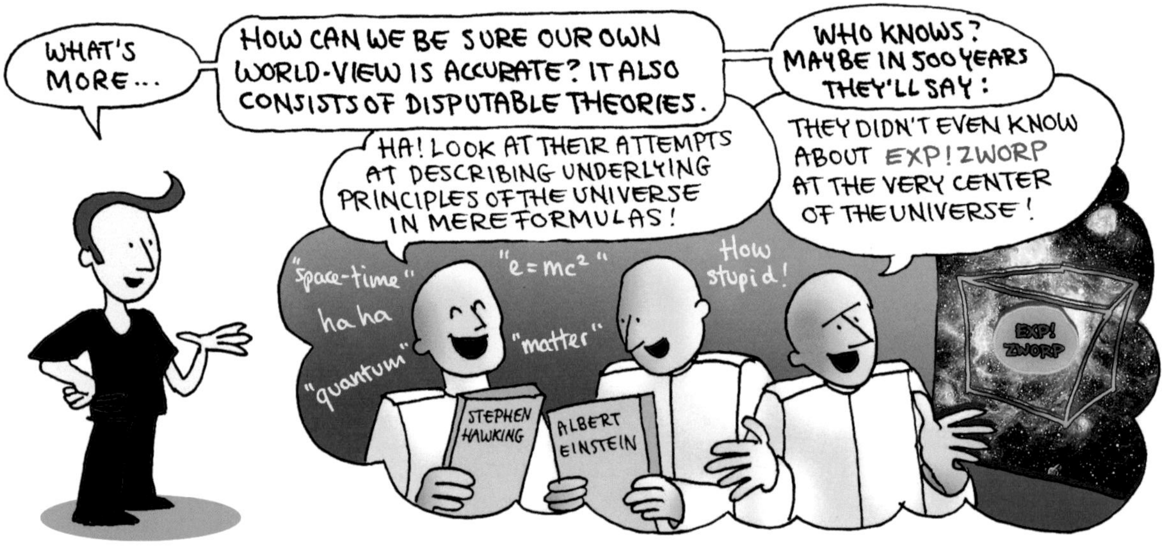
WHAT'S MORE...
HOW CAN WE BE SURE OUR OWN WORLD-VIEW IS ACCURATE? IT ALSO CONSISTS OF DISPUTABLE THEORIES.
WHO KNOWS? MAYBE IN 500 YEARS THEY'LL SAY:
HA! LOOK AT THEIR ATTEMPTS AT DESCRIBING UNDERLYING PRINCIPLES OF THE UNIVERSE IN MERE FORMULAS!
THEY DIDN'T EVEN KNOW ABOUT EXP!ZWORP AT THE VERY CENTER OF THE UNIVERSE!
"space-time"
"e = mc²"
How stupid!
ha ha
"matter"
"quantum"
STEPHEN HAWKING
ALBERT EINSTEIN
EXP! ZWORP

MEDIEVAL PHILOSOPHY =

ANCIENT GREEK + CHRISTIAN DOCTRINE

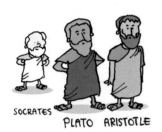

SOCRATES
PLATO ARISTOTLE

+ SUBJECTS AGREED UPON IN SO-CALLED "COUNCILS"

- Which books belong in the Bible and which don't?
- was Jesus man or God?
- what is God's "trinity"?
- how to deal with non-Christians?

Great meeting!

Glad we agree!

NICEA 325 + 787
CONSTANTINOPLE 381, 553 + 680
EPHESOS 431
CHALCEDON 451

MEDIEVAL PHILOSOPHY IS CHARACTERIZED BY:

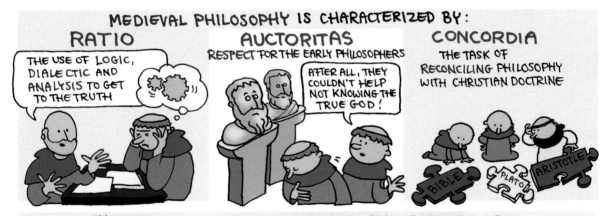

RATIO
THE USE OF LOGIC, DIALECTIC AND ANALYSIS TO GET TO THE TRUTH

AUCTORITAS
RESPECT FOR THE EARLY PHILOSOPHERS

AFTER ALL, THEY COULDN'T HELP NOT KNOWING THE TRUE GOD!

CONCORDIA
THE TASK OF RECONCILING PHILOSOPHY WITH CHRISTIAN DOCTRINE

BIBLE   PLATO   ARISTOTLE

THE TWO MOST IMPORTANT MEDIEVAL PHILOSOPHERS ARE:

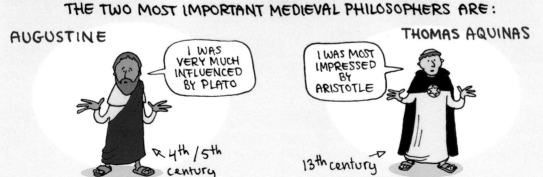

AUGUSTINE
I WAS VERY MUCH INFLUENCED BY PLATO

4th/5th century

THOMAS AQUINAS
I WAS MOST IMPRESSED BY ARISTOTLE

13th century

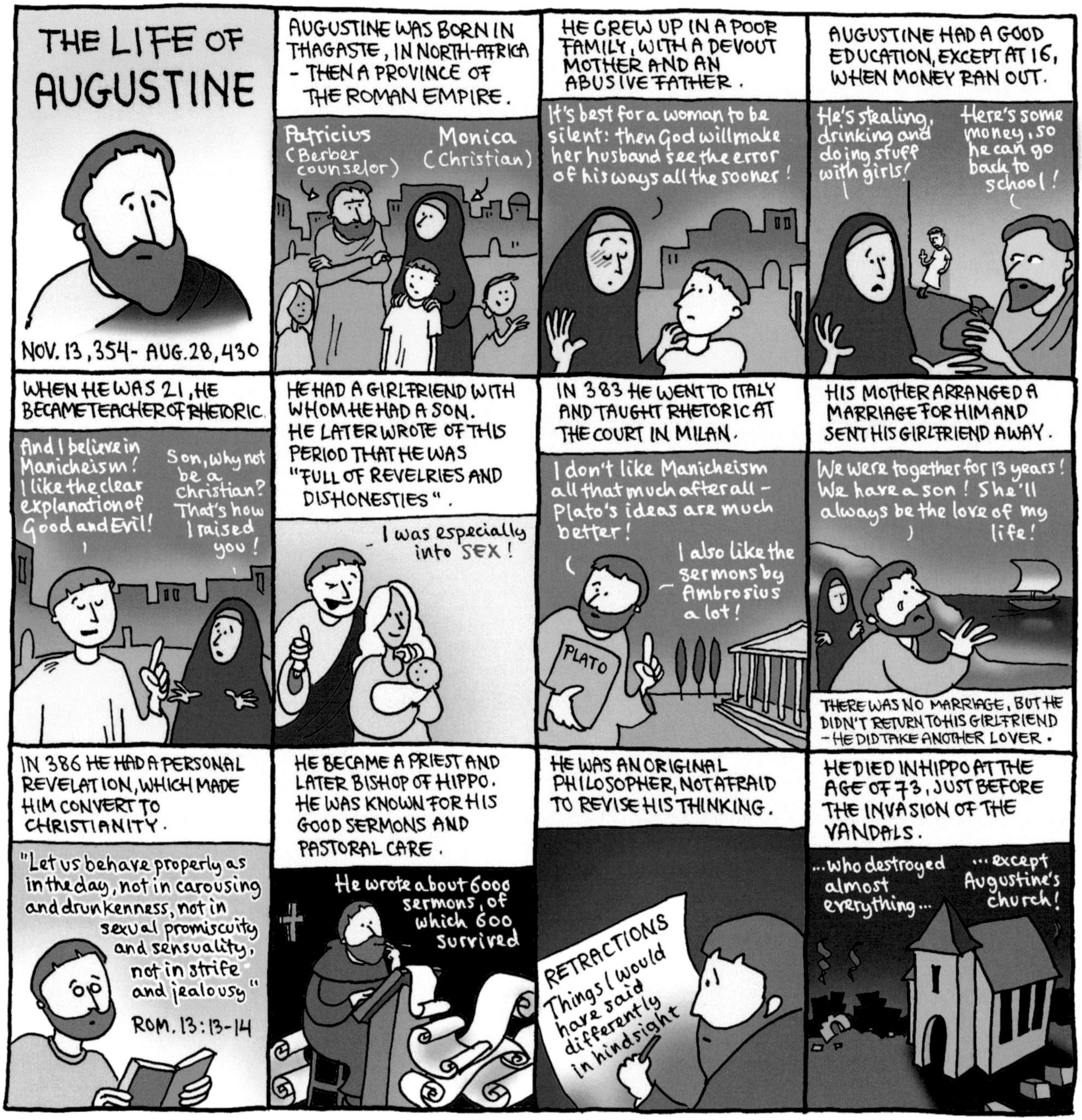
THE LIFE OF AUGUSTINE
NOV. 13, 354- AUG. 28, 430
AUGUSTINE WAS BORN IN THAGASTE, IN NORTH-AFRICA - THEN A PROVINCE OF THE ROMAN EMPIRE.
Patricius (Berber counselor)
Monica (Christian)
HE GREW UP IN A POOR FAMILY, WITH A DEVOUT MOTHER AND AN ABUSIVE FATHER.
It's best for a woman to be silent: then God will make her husband see the error of his ways all the sooner!
AUGUSTINE HAD A GOOD EDUCATION, EXCEPT AT 16, WHEN MONEY RAN OUT.
He's stealing, drinking and doing stuff with girls!
Here's some money, so he can go back to school!
WHEN HE WAS 21, HE BECAME TEACHER OF RHETORIC.
And I believe in Manicheism! I like the clear explanation of Good and Evil!
Son, why not be a christian? That's how I raised you!
HE HAD A GIRLFRIEND WITH WHOM HE HAD A SON. HE LATER WROTE OF THIS PERIOD THAT HE WAS "FULL OF REVELRIES AND DISHONESTIES".
- I was especially into SEX!
IN 383 HE WENT TO ITALY AND TAUGHT RHETORIC AT THE COURT IN MILAN.
I don't like Manicheism all that much after all - Plato's ideas are much better!
I also like the sermons by Ambrosius a lot!
PLATO
HIS MOTHER ARRANGED A MARRIAGE FOR HIM AND SENT HIS GIRLFRIEND AWAY.
We were together for 13 years! We have a son! She'll always be the love of my life!
THERE WAS NO MARRIAGE, BUT HE DIDN'T RETURN TO HIS GIRLFRIEND - HE DID TAKE ANOTHER LOVER.
IN 386 HE HAD A PERSONAL REVELATION, WHICH MADE HIM CONVERT TO CHRISTIANITY.
"Let us behave properly as in the day, not in carousing and drunkenness, not in sexual promiscuity and sensuality, not in strife and jealousy" ROM. 13:13-14
HE BECAME A PRIEST AND LATER BISHOP OF HIPPO. HE WAS KNOWN FOR HIS GOOD SERMONS AND PASTORAL CARE.
He wrote about 6000 sermons, of which 600 survived
HE WAS AN ORIGINAL PHILOSOPHER, NOT AFRAID TO REVISE HIS THINKING.
RETRACTIONS
Things I would have said differently in hindsight
HE DIED IN HIPPO AT THE AGE OF 73, JUST BEFORE THE INVASION OF THE VANDALS.
...who destroyed almost everything...
...except Augustine's church!

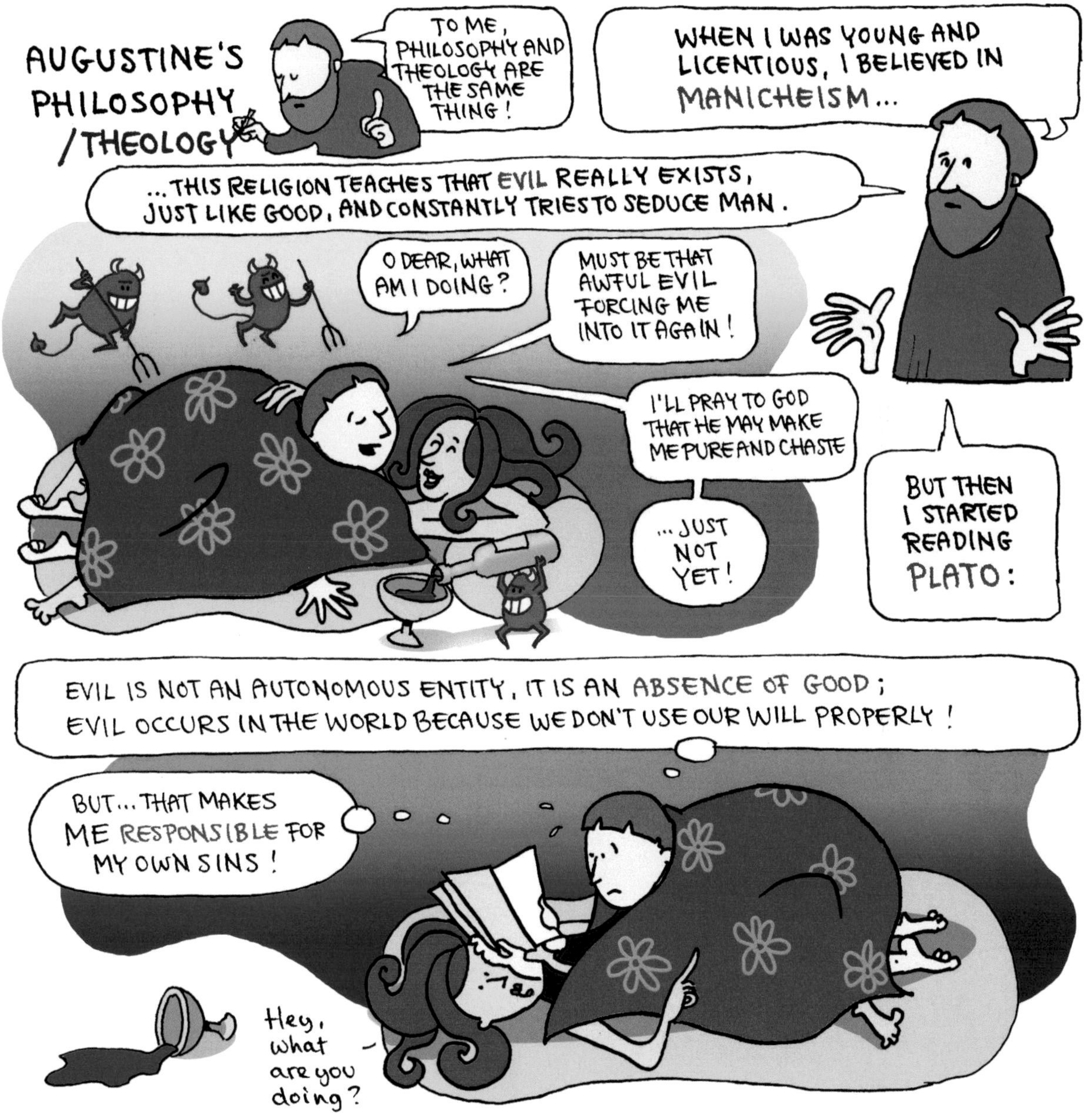
AUGUSTINE'S PHILOSOPHY /THEOLOGY
TO ME, PHILOSOPHY AND THEOLOGY ARE THE SAME THING!
WHEN I WAS YOUNG AND LICENTIOUS, I BELIEVED IN MANICHEISM...
...THIS RELIGION TEACHES THAT EVIL REALLY EXISTS, JUST LIKE GOOD, AND CONSTANTLY TRIES TO SEDUCE MAN.
O DEAR, WHAT AM I DOING?
MUST BE THAT AWFUL EVIL FORCING ME INTO IT AGAIN!
I'LL PRAY TO GOD THAT HE MAY MAKE ME PURE AND CHASTE
...JUST NOT YET!
BUT THEN I STARTED READING PLATO:
EVIL IS NOT AN AUTONOMOUS ENTITY, IT IS AN ABSENCE OF GOOD; EVIL OCCURS IN THE WORLD BECAUSE WE DON'T USE OUR WILL PROPERLY!
BUT... THAT MAKES ME RESPONSIBLE FOR MY OWN SINS!
Hey, what are you doing?

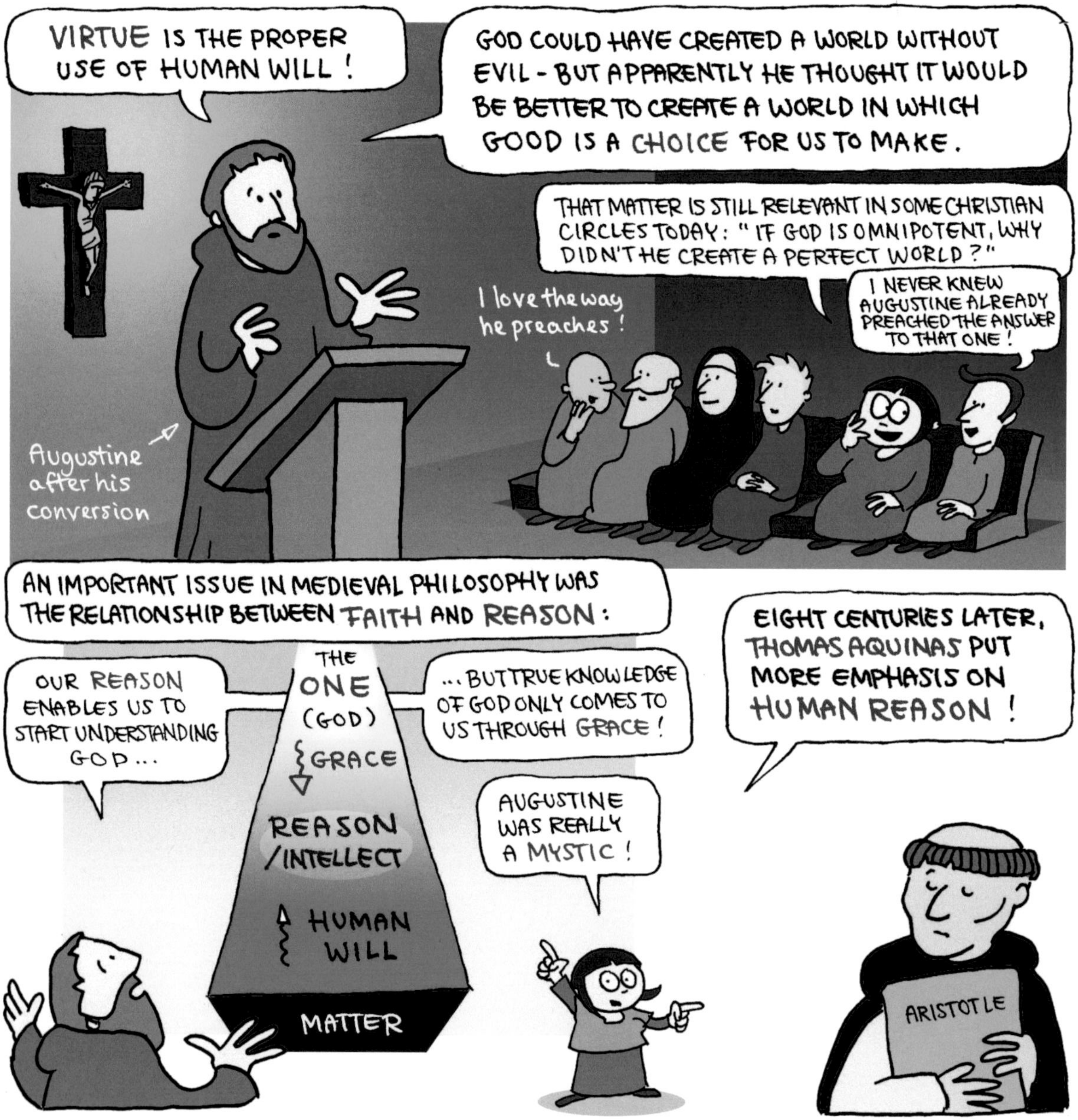
VIRTUE IS THE PROPER USE OF HUMAN WILL!
GOD COULD HAVE CREATED A WORLD WITHOUT EVIL - BUT APPARENTLY HE THOUGHT IT WOULD BE BETTER TO CREATE A WORLD IN WHICH GOOD IS A CHOICE FOR US TO MAKE.
THAT MATTER IS STILL RELEVANT IN SOME CHRISTIAN CIRCLES TODAY: "IF GOD IS OMNIPOTENT, WHY DIDN'T HE CREATE A PERFECT WORLD?"
I NEVER KNEW AUGUSTINE ALREADY PREACHED THE ANSWER TO THAT ONE!
I love the way he preaches!
Augustine after his conversion
AN IMPORTANT ISSUE IN MEDIEVAL PHILOSOPHY WAS THE RELATIONSHIP BETWEEN FAITH AND REASON:
OUR REASON ENABLES US TO START UNDERSTANDING GOD...
...BUT TRUE KNOWLEDGE OF GOD ONLY COMES TO US THROUGH GRACE!
THE ONE (GOD)
GRACE
REASON /INTELLECT
HUMAN WILL
MATTER
AUGUSTINE WAS REALLY A MYSTIC!
EIGHT CENTURIES LATER, THOMAS AQUINAS PUT MORE EMPHASIS ON HUMAN REASON!
ARISTOTLE

THE LIFE OF THOMAS AQUINAS

JAN. 28, 1225 – MARCH 7, 1274

THOMAS WAS BORN IN CASTLE ROCCASECCA, NEAR NAPLES, ITALY.

Another son!

This one will become a Benedictine!

AT AGE NINETEEN, HE JOINED THE ORDER OF DOMINICANS.

WHAT?! Why not the Benedictines?

Dominicans are much cooler! They study Aristotle!

IN 1246, HE WENT TO PARIS TO STUDY WITH PHILOSOPHER ALBERTUS MAGNUS.

He knows everything about Aristotle! I even followed him to Cologne!

AT AGE 27, HE STARTED TEACHING IN PARIS.

PARIS IS NOW THE CENTER OF KNOWLEDGE IN EUROPE!

Under construction: the Notre Dame

BETWEEN 1259 AND 1265, HE WORKED AT THE PAPAL COURT IN ANAGNI, ITALY.

He's always going on about Aristotle! Isn't that a heathen doctrine?

BETWEEN 1269 AND 1273 HE TAUGHT IN PARIS AND WROTE HIS BEST KNOWN WORKS.

SUMMA THEOLOGIAE

SUMMA CONTRA GENTILES

AT THE END OF 1273, HE WAS PROBABLY HIT BY A STROKE.

...what sense does it all make...?

ON MARCH 7, 1274, THOMAS AQUINAS DIED AT THE ABBEY OF FOSSANOVA.

THREE YEARS LATER, SOME OF HIS THESES WERE CONDEMNED BY ROME.

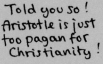

Told you so! Aristotle is just too pagan for Christianity!

BUT IN 1323 THE VERDICT WAS RETRACTED AND THOMAS AQUINAS WAS CANONIZED.

PLING!

RECOGNITION!

ARISTOTLE

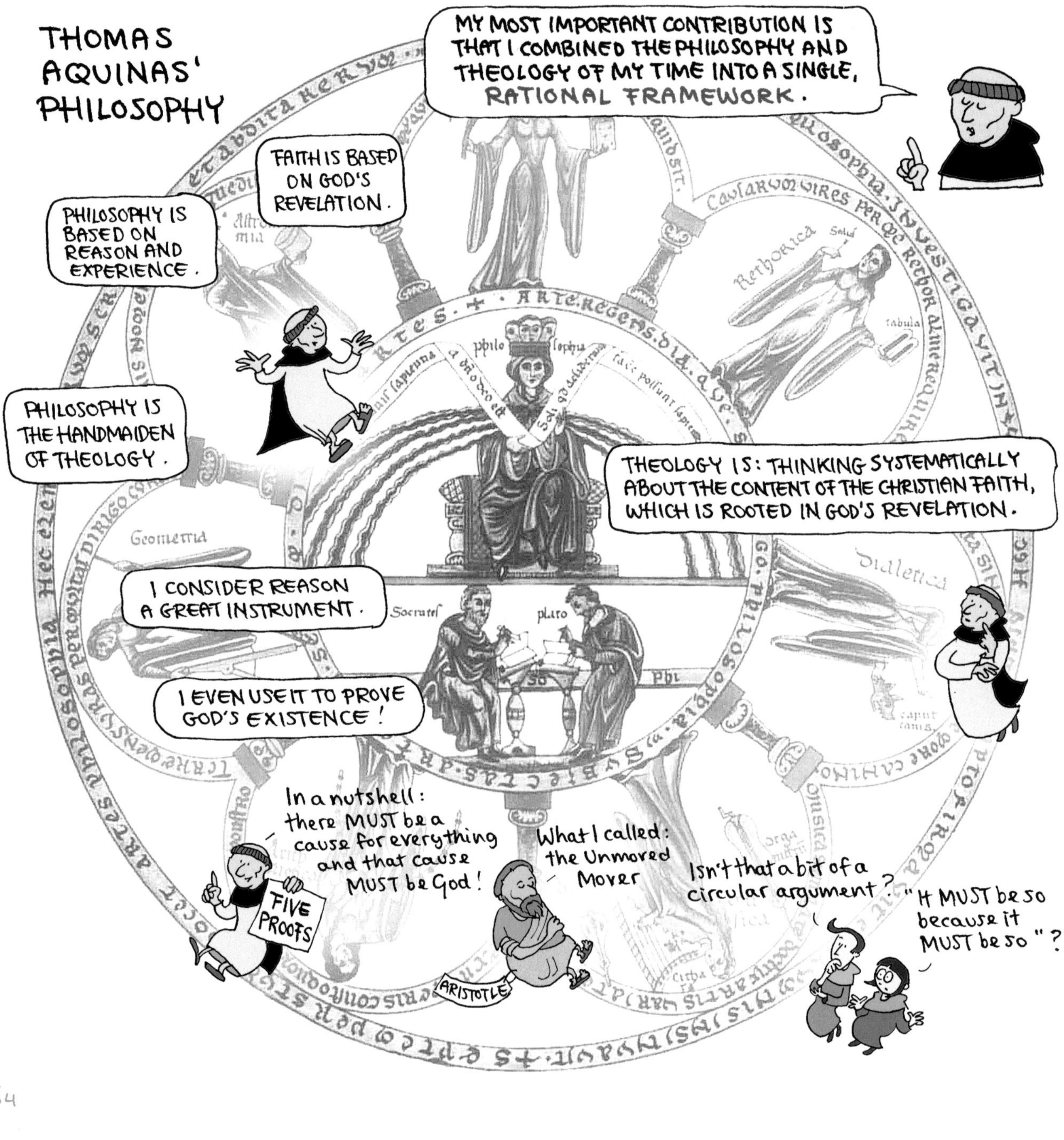
THOMAS AQUINAS' PHILOSOPHY
MY MOST IMPORTANT CONTRIBUTION IS THAT I COMBINED THE PHILOSOPHY AND THEOLOGY OF MY TIME INTO A SINGLE, RATIONAL FRAMEWORK.
FAITH IS BASED ON GOD'S REVELATION.
PHILOSOPHY IS BASED ON REASON AND EXPERIENCE.
PHILOSOPHY IS THE HANDMAIDEN OF THEOLOGY.
THEOLOGY IS: THINKING SYSTEMATICALLY ABOUT THE CONTENT OF THE CHRISTIAN FAITH, WHICH IS ROOTED IN GOD'S REVELATION.
I CONSIDER REASON A GREAT INSTRUMENT.
I EVEN USE IT TO PROVE GOD'S EXISTENCE!
In a nutshell: there MUST be a cause for everything and that cause MUST be God!
FIVE PROOFS
What I called: the Unmoved Mover
ARISTOTLE
Isn't that a bit of a circular argument?
"It MUST be so because it MUST be so"?
Socrates
plato
philo
sophia
Geometria
Rethorica
Dialectica

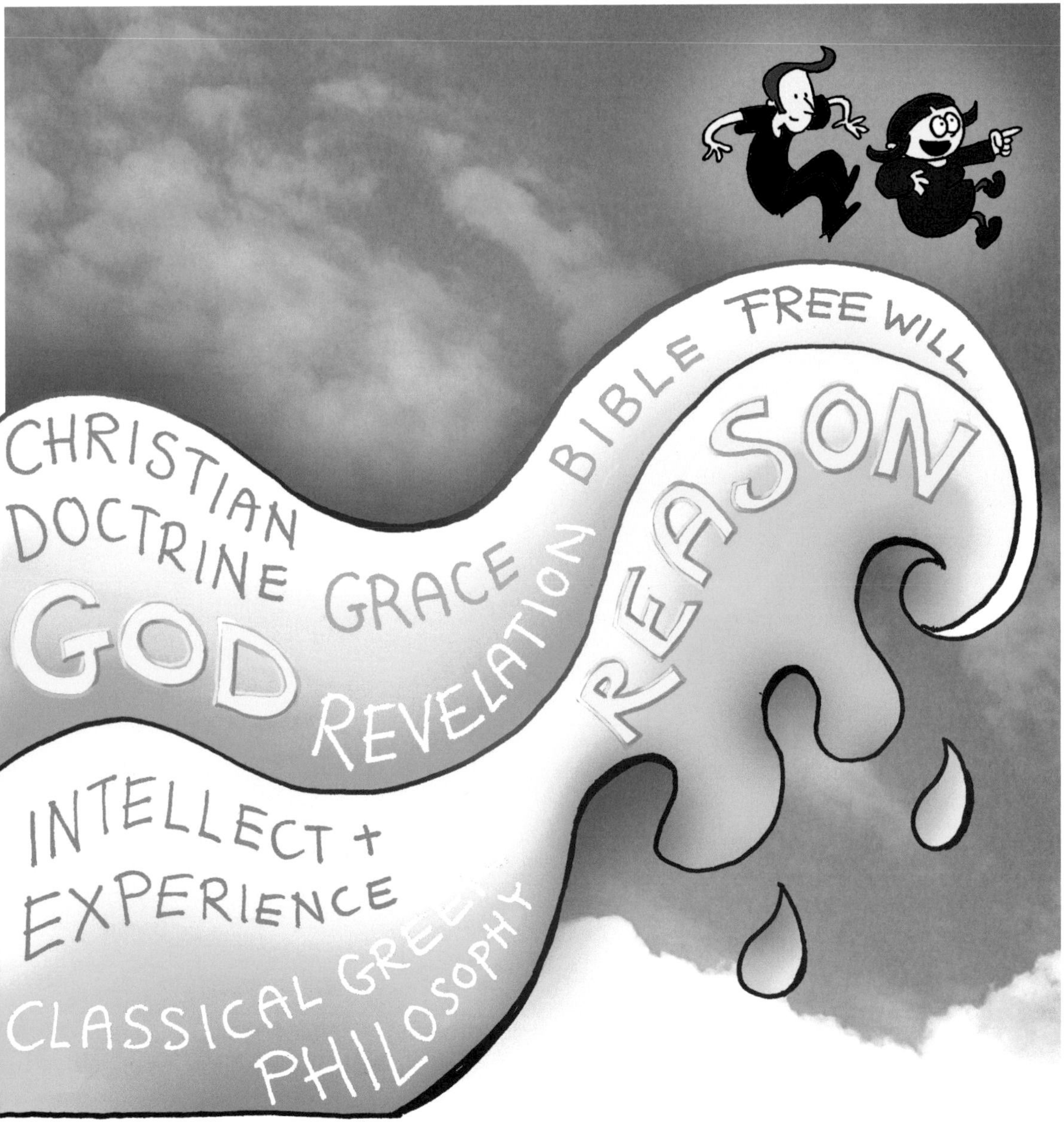
CHRISTIAN
DOCTRINE
GRACE
BIBLE
FREE WILL
GOD
REVELATION
REASON
INTELLECT +
EXPERIENCE
CLASSICAL GREEK
PHILOSOPHY

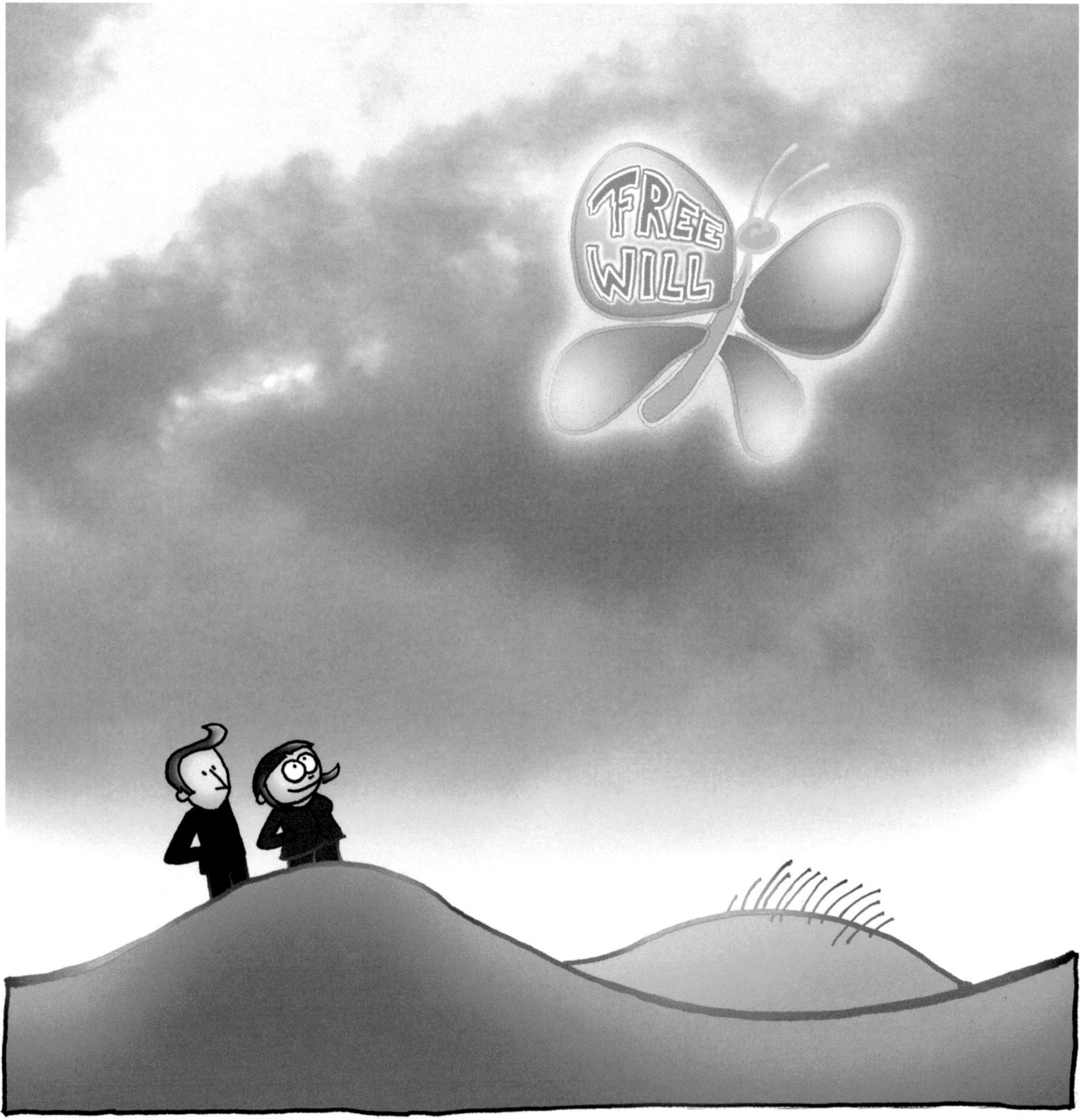
FREE
WILL

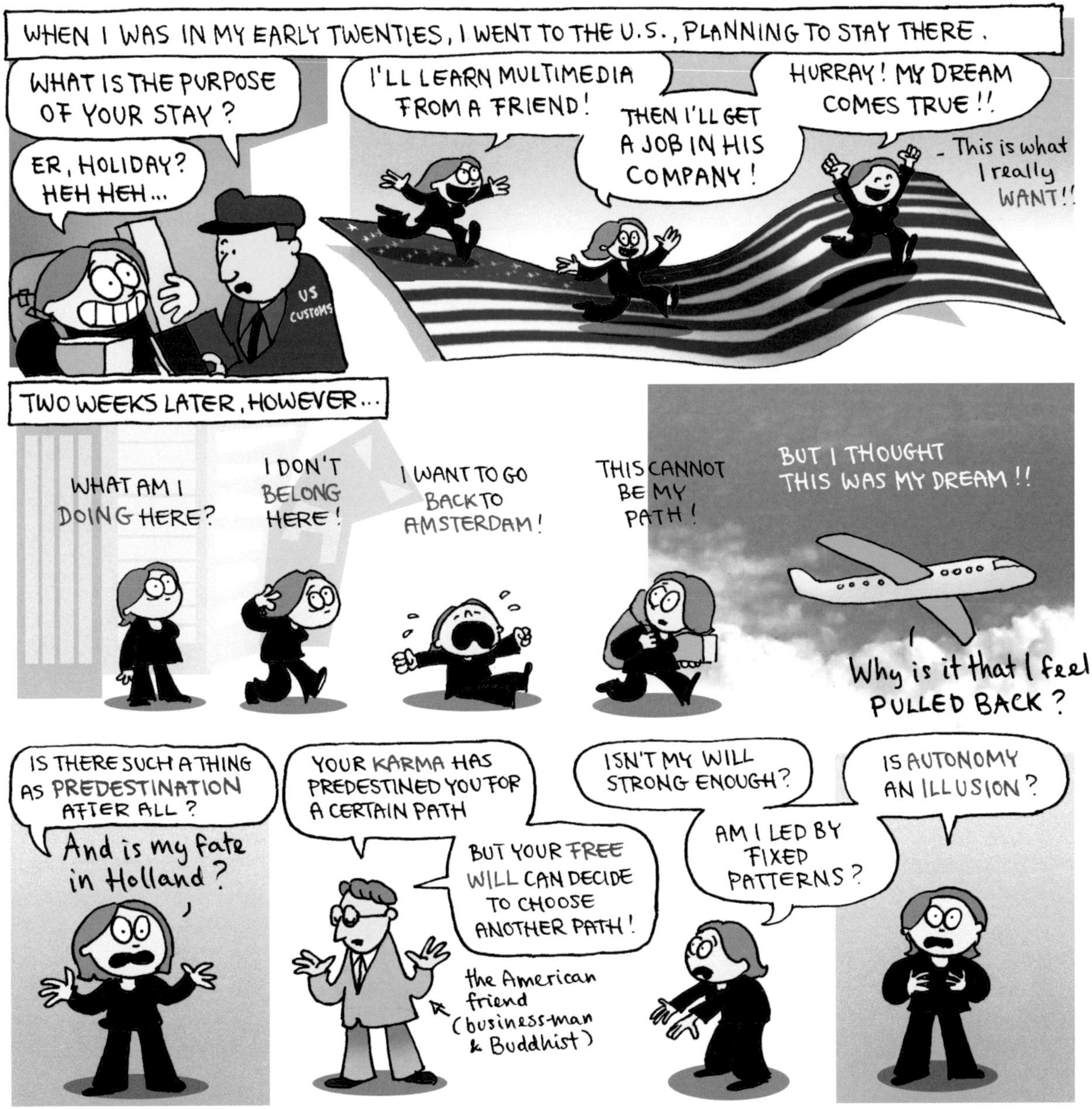
WHEN I WAS IN MY EARLY TWENTIES, I WENT TO THE U.S., PLANNING TO STAY THERE.
WHAT IS THE PURPOSE OF YOUR STAY?
ER, HOLIDAY? HEH HEH...
US CUSTOMS
I'LL LEARN MULTIMEDIA FROM A FRIEND!
THEN I'LL GET A JOB IN HIS COMPANY!
HURRAY! MY DREAM COMES TRUE!!
- This is what I really WANT!!
TWO WEEKS LATER, HOWEVER...
WHAT AM I DOING HERE?
I DON'T BELONG HERE!
I WANT TO GO BACK TO AMSTERDAM!
THIS CANNOT BE MY PATH!
BUT I THOUGHT THIS WAS MY DREAM!!
Why is it that I feel PULLED BACK?
IS THERE SUCH A THING AS PREDESTINATION AFTER ALL?
And is my fate in Holland?
YOUR KARMA HAS PREDESTINED YOU FOR A CERTAIN PATH
BUT YOUR FREE WILL CAN DECIDE TO CHOOSE ANOTHER PATH!
the American friend (business-man & Buddhist)
ISN'T MY WILL STRONG ENOUGH?
AM I LED BY FIXED PATTERNS?
IS AUTONOMY AN ILLUSION?

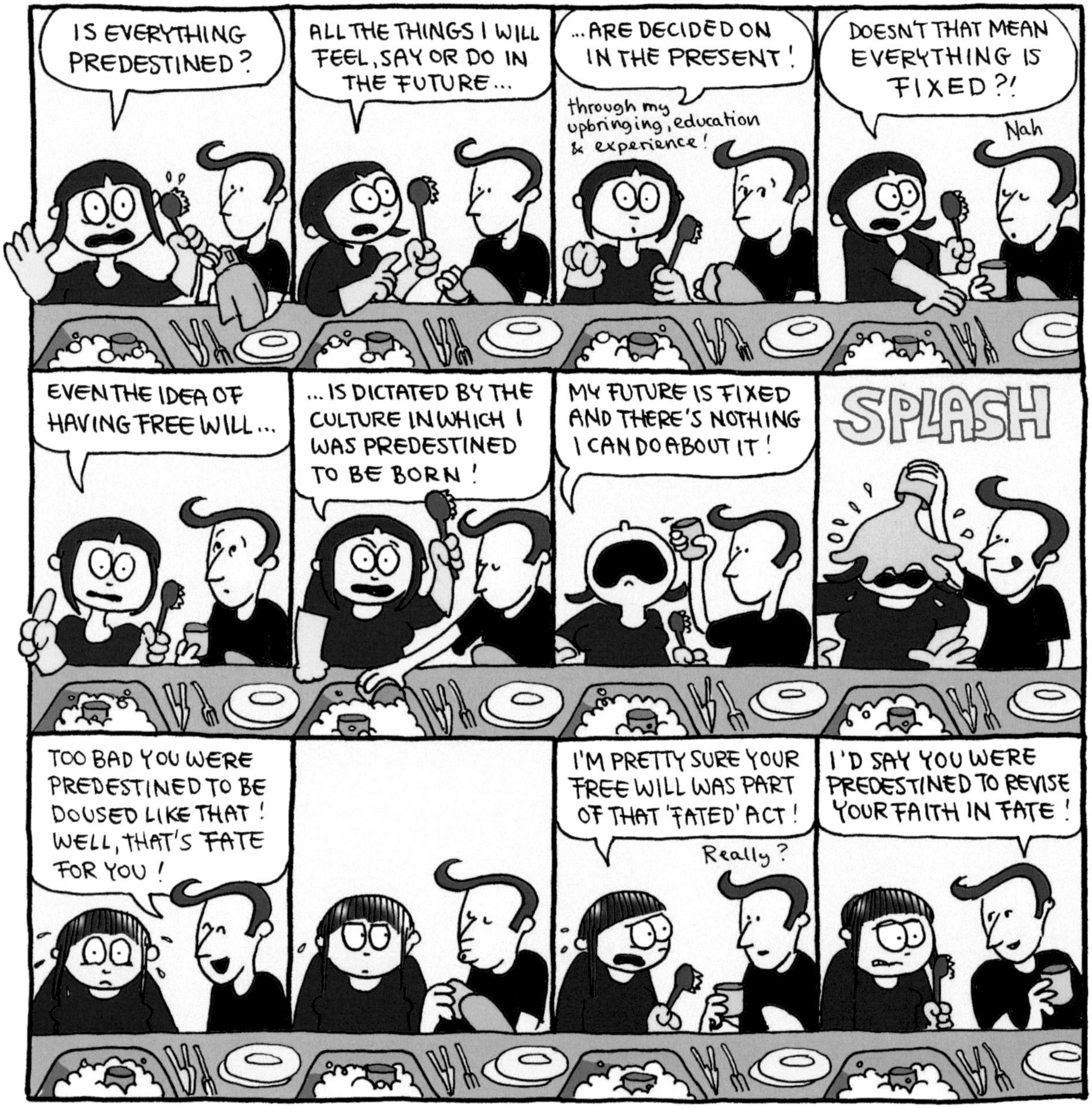
IS EVERYTHING PREDESTINED?
ALL THE THINGS I WILL FEEL, SAY OR DO IN THE FUTURE...
...ARE DECIDED ON IN THE PRESENT!
through my upbringing, education & experience!
DOESN'T THAT MEAN EVERYTHING IS FIXED?!
Nah
EVEN THE IDEA OF HAVING FREE WILL...
...IS DICTATED BY THE CULTURE IN WHICH I WAS PREDESTINED TO BE BORN!
MY FUTURE IS FIXED AND THERE'S NOTHING I CAN DO ABOUT IT!
SPLASH
TOO BAD YOU WERE PREDESTINED TO BE DOUSED LIKE THAT! WELL, THAT'S FATE FOR YOU!
I'M PRETTY SURE YOUR FREE WILL WAS PART OF THAT 'FATED' ACT!
Really?
I'D SAY YOU WERE PREDESTINED TO REVISE YOUR FAITH IN FATE!

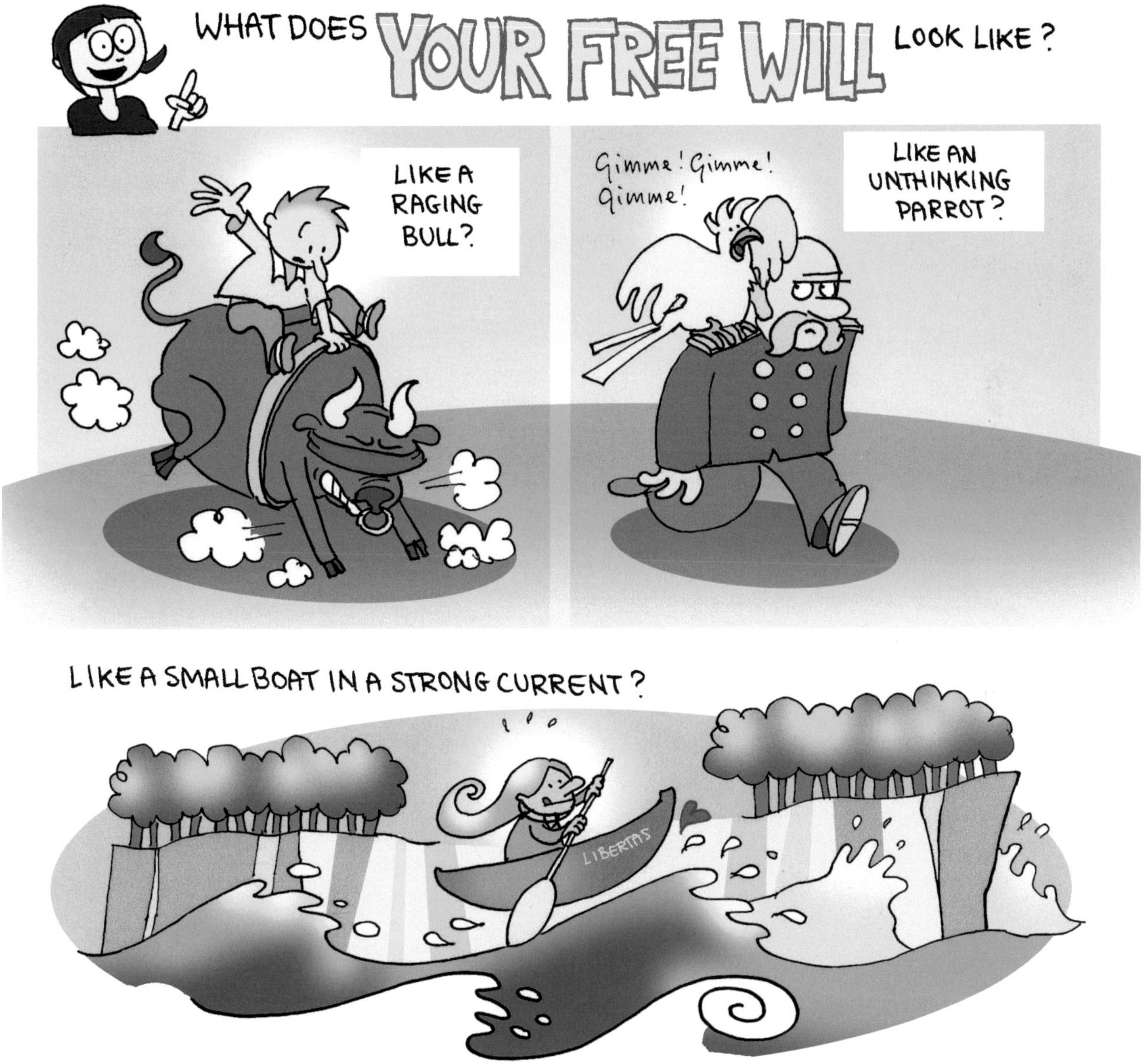
WHAT DOES YOUR FREE WILL LOOK LIKE?
LIKE A RAGING BULL?
Gimme! Gimme! Gimme!
LIKE AN UNTHINKING PARROT?
LIKE A SMALL BOAT IN A STRONG CURRENT?
LIBERTAS

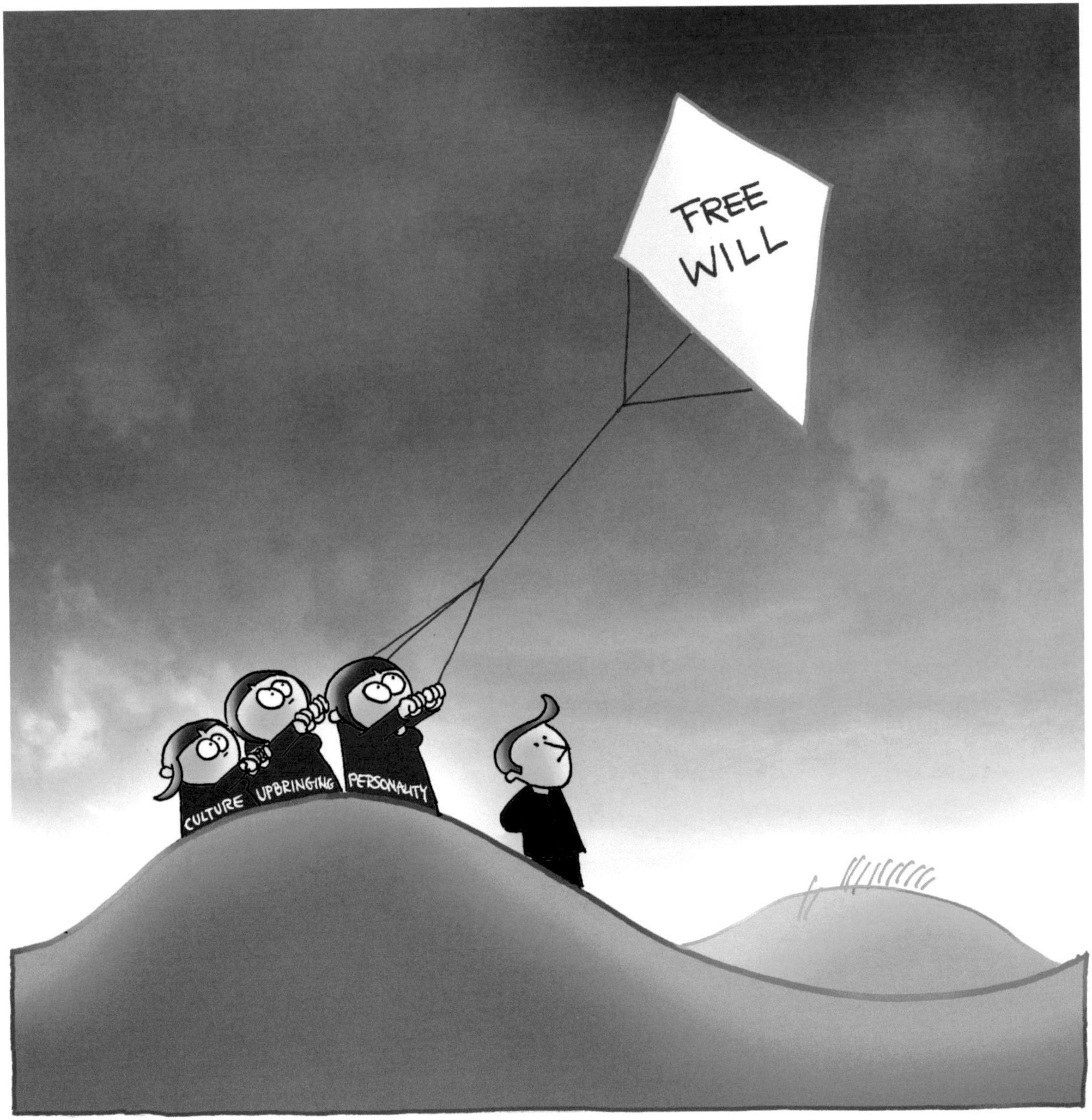
FREE WILL
CULTURE
UPBRINGING
PERSONALITY

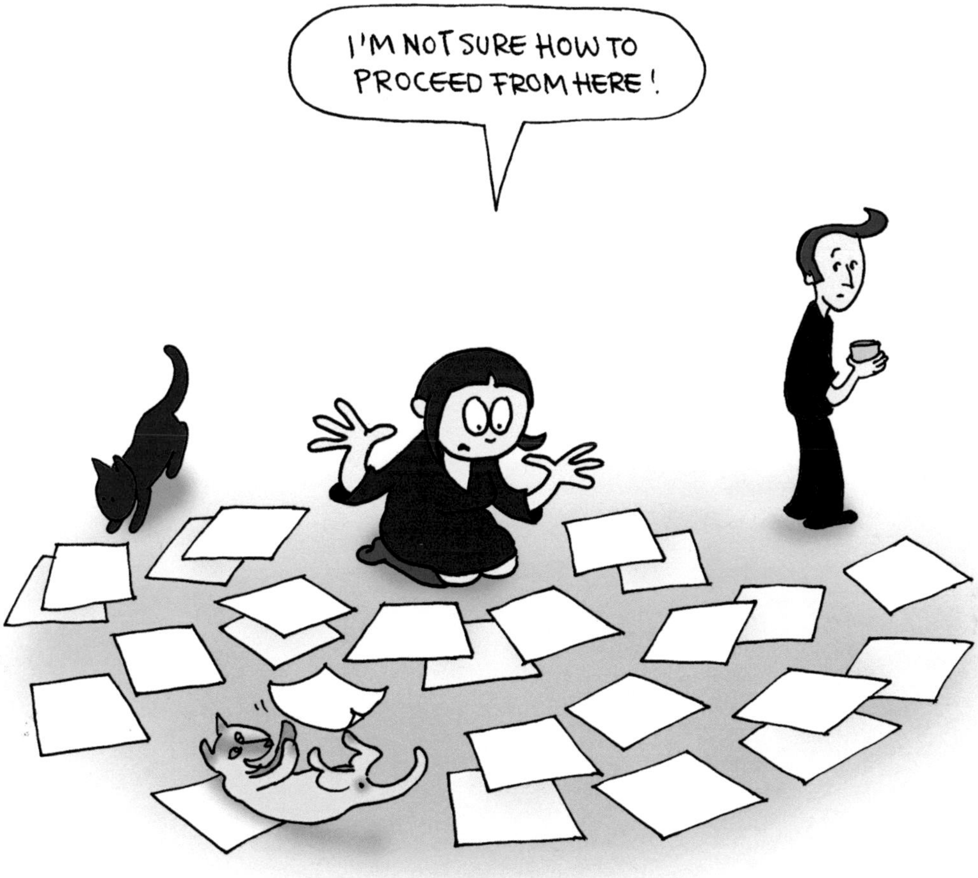
I'M NOT SURE HOW TO PROCEED FROM HERE!

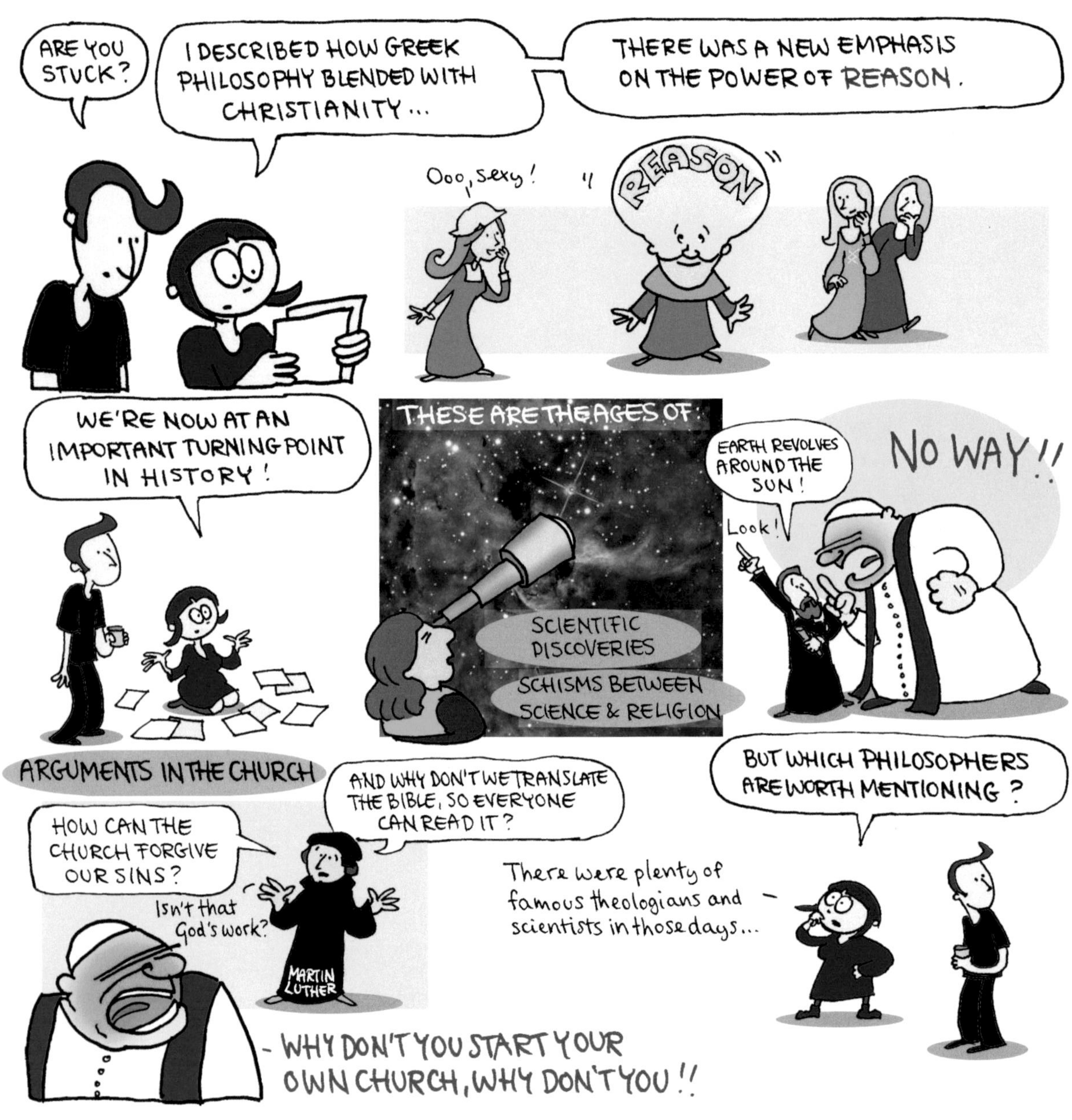
ARE YOU STUCK?
I DESCRIBED HOW GREEK PHILOSOPHY BLENDED WITH CHRISTIANITY...
THERE WAS A NEW EMPHASIS ON THE POWER OF REASON.
Ooo, sexy!
"REASON"
WE'RE NOW AT AN IMPORTANT TURNING POINT IN HISTORY!
THESE ARE THE AGES OF:
SCIENTIFIC DISCOVERIES
SCHISMS BETWEEN SCIENCE & RELIGION
EARTH REVOLVES AROUND THE SUN!
Look!
NO WAY!!
ARGUMENTS IN THE CHURCH
HOW CAN THE CHURCH FORGIVE OUR SINS?
Isn't that God's work?
AND WHY DON'T WE TRANSLATE THE BIBLE, SO EVERYONE CAN READ IT?
MARTIN LUTHER
- WHY DON'T YOU START YOUR OWN CHURCH, WHY DON'T YOU!!
BUT WHICH PHILOSOPHERS ARE WORTH MENTIONING?
There were plenty of famous theologians and scientists in those days... -

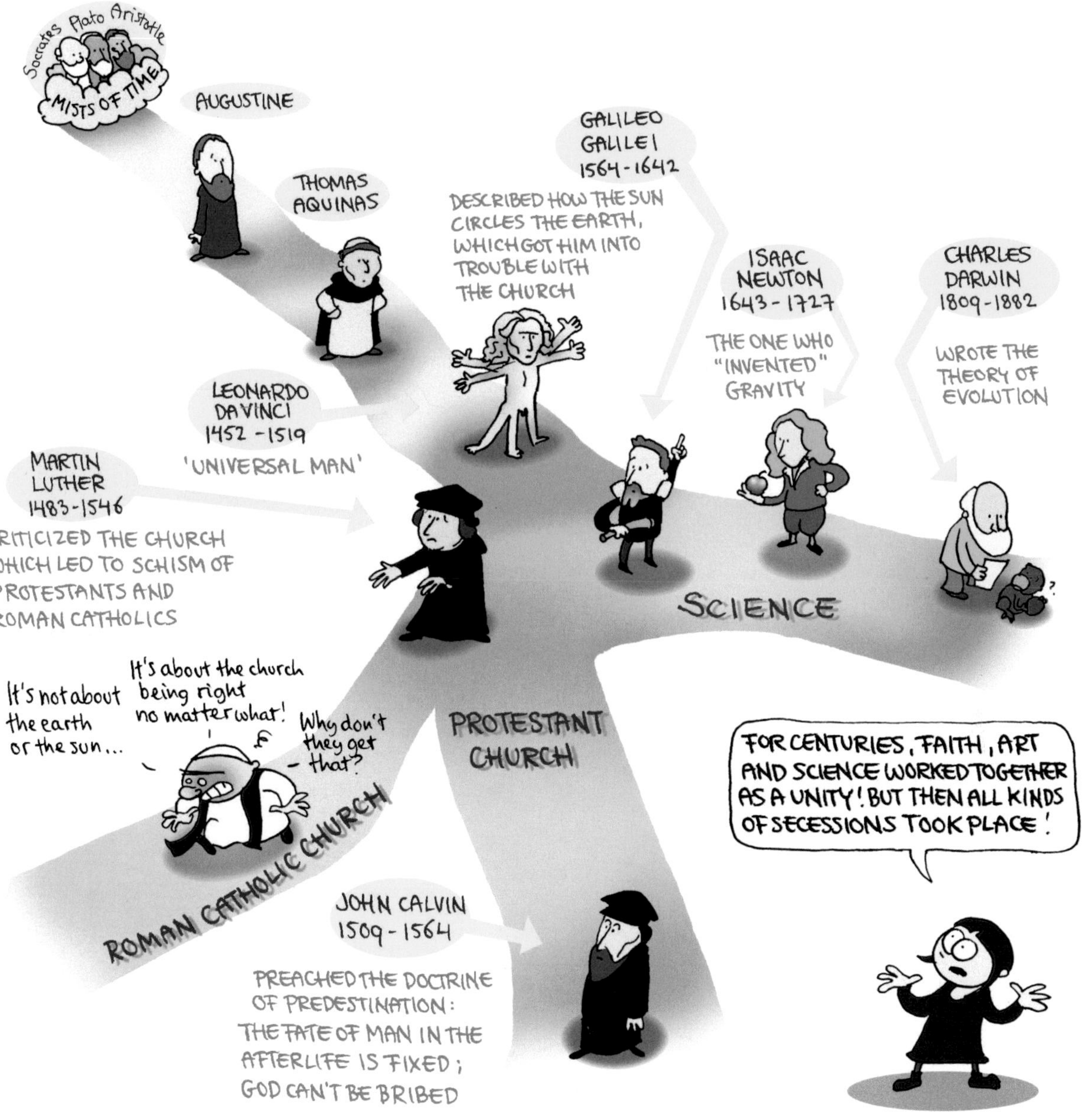
Socrates Plato Aristotle
MISTS OF TIME
AUGUSTINE
THOMAS AQUINAS
GALILEO GALILEI 1564-1642
DESCRIBED HOW THE SUN CIRCLES THE EARTH, WHICH GOT HIM INTO TROUBLE WITH THE CHURCH
ISAAC NEWTON 1643-1727
THE ONE WHO "INVENTED" GRAVITY
CHARLES DARWIN 1809-1882
WROTE THE THEORY OF EVOLUTION
LEONARDO DA VINCI 1452-1519
'UNIVERSAL MAN'
MARTIN LUTHER 1483-1546
CRITICIZED THE CHURCH WHICH LED TO SCHISM OF PROTESTANTS AND ROMAN CATHOLICS
SCIENCE
It's not about the earth or the sun...
It's about the church being right no matter what!
Why don't they get that?
PROTESTANT CHURCH
ROMAN CATHOLIC CHURCH
FOR CENTURIES, FAITH, ART AND SCIENCE WORKED TOGETHER AS A UNITY! BUT THEN ALL KINDS OF SECESSIONS TOOK PLACE!
JOHN CALVIN 1509-1564
PREACHED THE DOCTRINE OF PREDESTINATION: THE FATE OF MAN IN THE AFTERLIFE IS FIXED; GOD CAN'T BE BRIBED

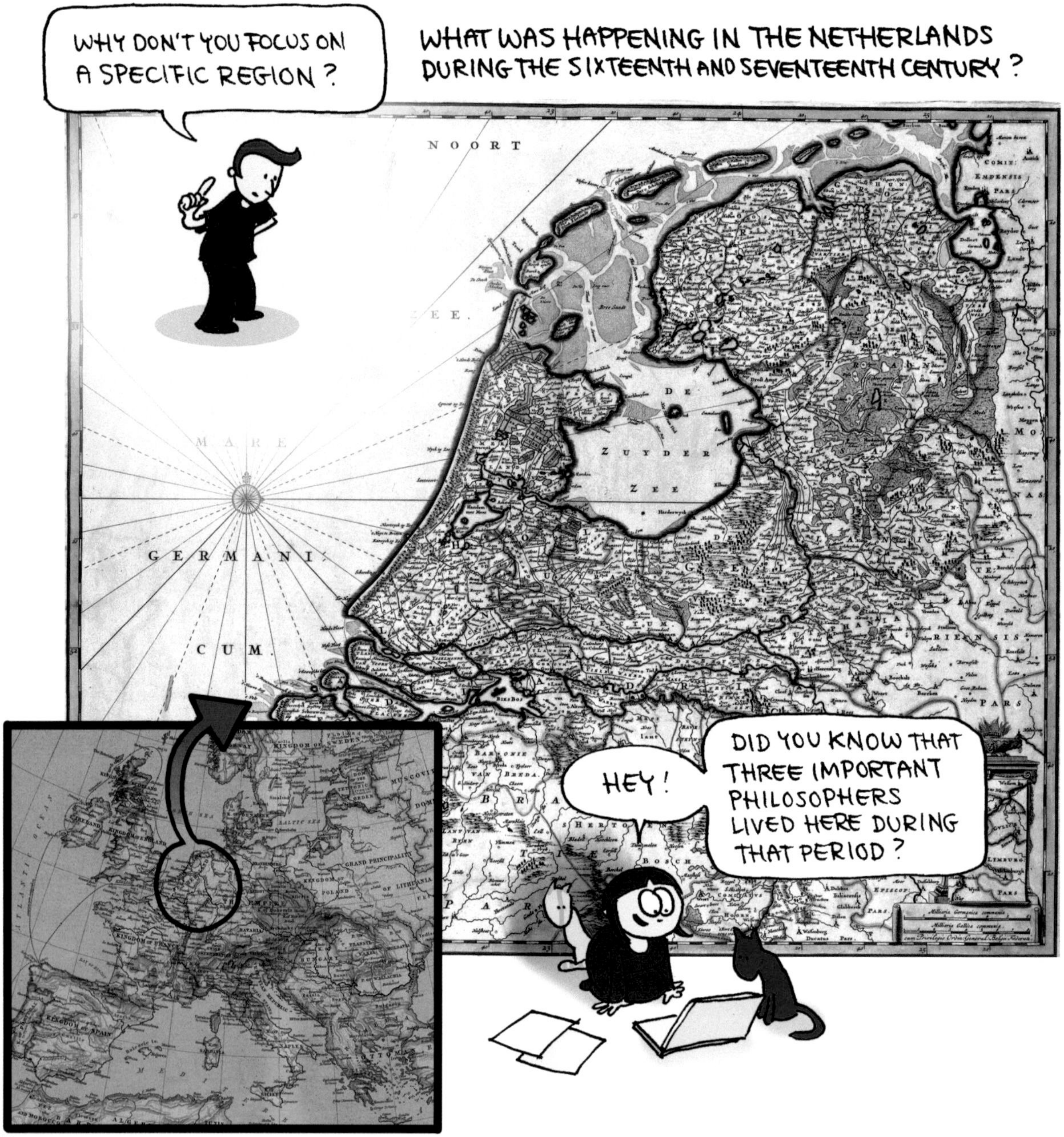
WHY DON'T YOU FOCUS ON A SPECIFIC REGION?
WHAT WAS HAPPENING IN THE NETHERLANDS DURING THE SIXTEENTH AND SEVENTEENTH CENTURY?
NOORT
MARE
GERMANI
CUM.
ZUYDER
ZEE
HEY!
DID YOU KNOW THAT THREE IMPORTANT PHILOSOPHERS LIVED HERE DURING THAT PERIOD?

ERASMUS, DESCARTES & SPINOZA

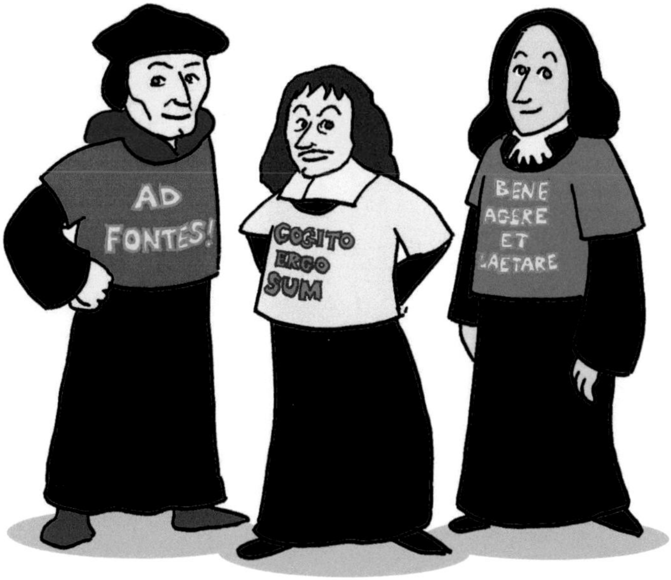

AD FONTES!
COGITO ERGO SUM
BENE AGERE ET LAETARE

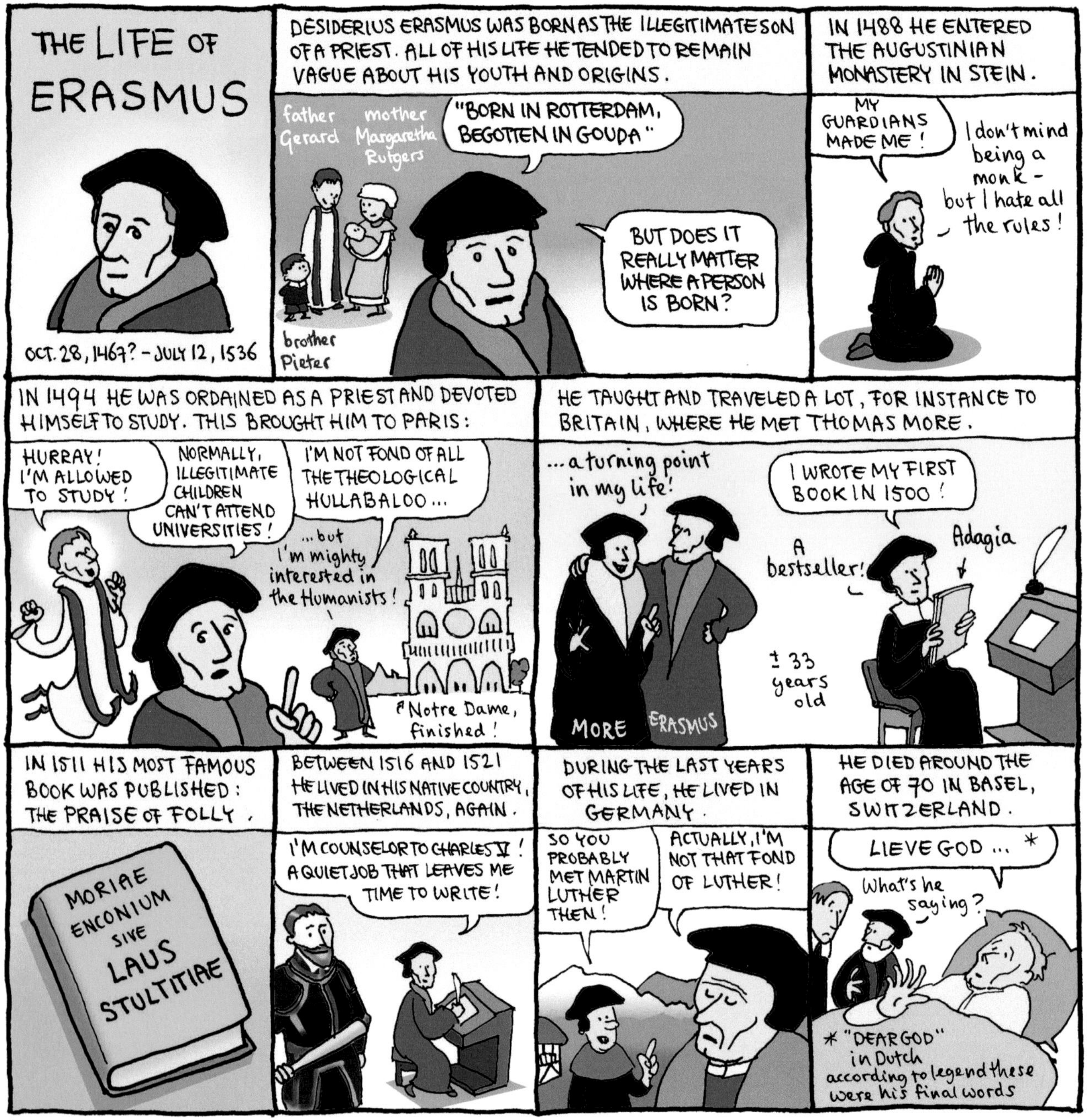
THE LIFE OF ERASMUS
OCT. 28, 1467? – JULY 12, 1536
DESIDERIUS ERASMUS WAS BORN AS THE ILLEGITIMATE SON OF A PRIEST. ALL OF HIS LIFE HE TENDED TO REMAIN VAGUE ABOUT HIS YOUTH AND ORIGINS.
father Gerard
mother Margaretha Rutgers
brother Pieter
"BORN IN ROTTERDAM, BEGOTTEN IN GOUDA"
BUT DOES IT REALLY MATTER WHERE A PERSON IS BORN?
IN 1488 HE ENTERED THE AUGUSTINIAN MONASTERY IN STEIN.
MY GUARDIANS MADE ME!
I don't mind being a monk - but I hate all the rules!
IN 1494 HE WAS ORDAINED AS A PRIEST AND DEVOTED HIMSELF TO STUDY. THIS BROUGHT HIM TO PARIS:
HURRAY! I'M ALLOWED TO STUDY!
NORMALLY, ILLEGITIMATE CHILDREN CAN'T ATTEND UNIVERSITIES!
I'M NOT FOND OF ALL THE THEOLOGICAL HULLABALOO...
...but I'm mighty interested in the Humanists!
Notre Dame, finished!
HE TAUGHT AND TRAVELED A LOT, FOR INSTANCE TO BRITAIN, WHERE HE MET THOMAS MORE.
...a turning point in my life!
MORE
ERASMUS
I WROTE MY FIRST BOOK IN 1500!
A bestseller!
Adagia
± 33 years old
IN 1511 HIS MOST FAMOUS BOOK WAS PUBLISHED: THE PRAISE OF FOLLY.
MORIAE ENCONIUM SIVE LAUS STULTITIAE
BETWEEN 1516 AND 1521 HE LIVED IN HIS NATIVE COUNTRY, THE NETHERLANDS, AGAIN.
I'M COUNSELOR TO CHARLES V! A QUIET JOB THAT LEAVES ME TIME TO WRITE!
DURING THE LAST YEARS OF HIS LIFE, HE LIVED IN GERMANY.
SO YOU PROBABLY MET MARTIN LUTHER THEN!
ACTUALLY, I'M NOT THAT FOND OF LUTHER!
HE DIED AROUND THE AGE OF 70 IN BASEL, SWITZERLAND.
LIEVE GOD... *
What's he saying?
* "DEAR GOD" in Dutch according to legend these were his final words

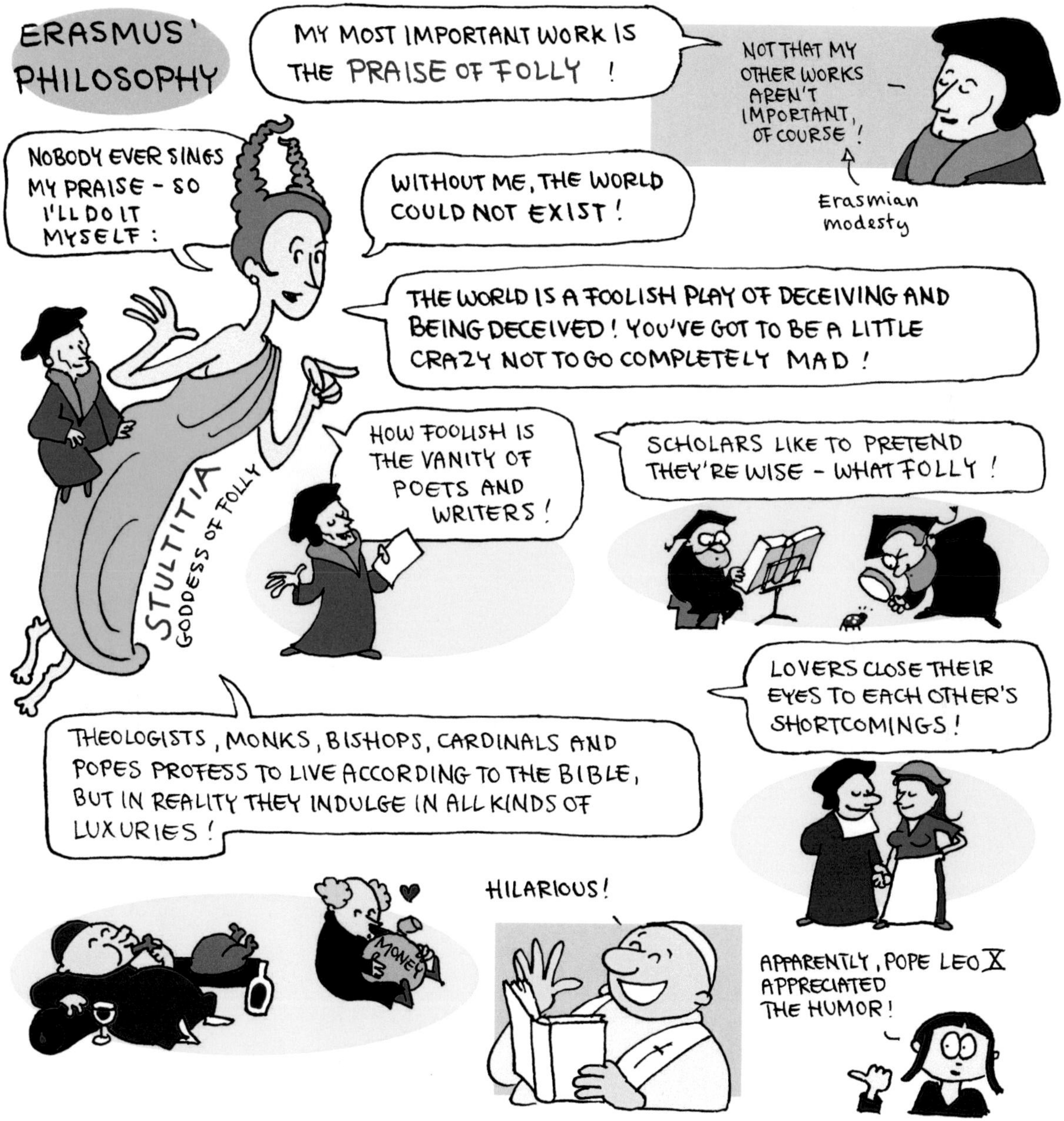

ERASMUS' PHILOSOPHY
MY MOST IMPORTANT WORK IS THE PRAISE OF FOLLY !
NOT THAT MY OTHER WORKS AREN'T IMPORTANT, OF COURSE !
Erasmian modesty
NOBODY EVER SINGS MY PRAISE - SO I'LL DO IT MYSELF :
WITHOUT ME, THE WORLD COULD NOT EXIST !
THE WORLD IS A FOOLISH PLAY OF DECEIVING AND BEING DECEIVED ! YOU'VE GOT TO BE A LITTLE CRAZY NOT TO GO COMPLETELY MAD !
STULTITIA
GODDESS OF FOLLY
HOW FOOLISH IS THE VANITY OF POETS AND WRITERS !
SCHOLARS LIKE TO PRETEND THEY'RE WISE - WHAT FOLLY !
LOVERS CLOSE THEIR EYES TO EACH OTHER'S SHORTCOMINGS !
THEOLOGISTS, MONKS, BISHOPS, CARDINALS AND POPES PROFESS TO LIVE ACCORDING TO THE BIBLE, BUT IN REALITY THEY INDULGE IN ALL KINDS OF LUXURIES !
MONEY
HILARIOUS !
APPARENTLY, POPE LEO X APPRECIATED THE HUMOR !

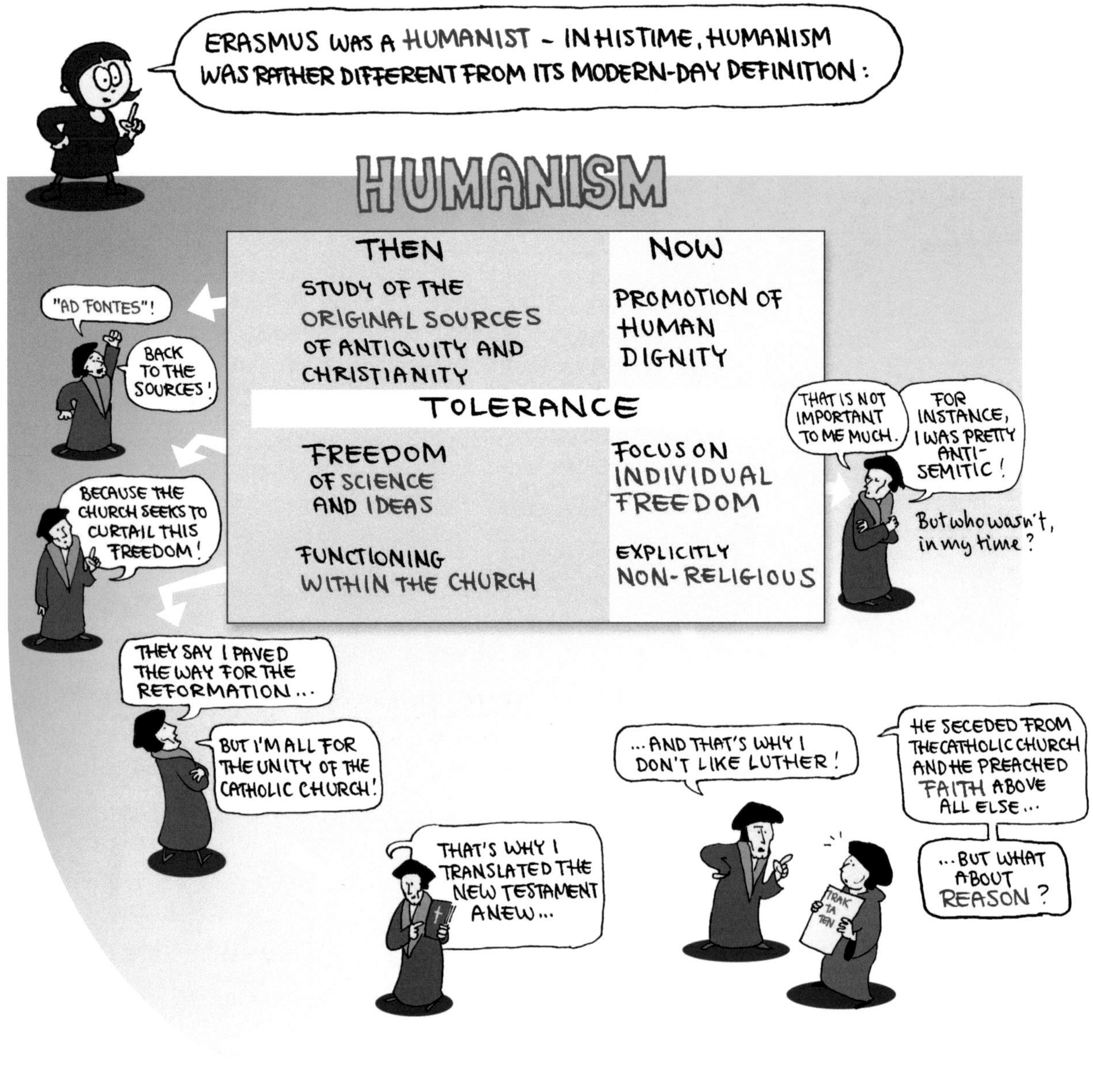
ERASMUS WAS A HUMANIST - IN HIS TIME, HUMANISM WAS RATHER DIFFERENT FROM ITS MODERN-DAY DEFINITION:
HUMANISM
THEN
NOW
STUDY OF THE ORIGINAL SOURCES OF ANTIQUITY AND CHRISTIANITY
PROMOTION OF HUMAN DIGNITY
TOLERANCE
FREEDOM OF SCIENCE AND IDEAS
FOCUS ON INDIVIDUAL FREEDOM
FUNCTIONING WITHIN THE CHURCH
EXPLICITLY NON-RELIGIOUS
"AD FONTES"!
BACK TO THE SOURCES!
BECAUSE THE CHURCH SEEKS TO CURTAIL THIS FREEDOM!
THEY SAY I PAVED THE WAY FOR THE REFORMATION...
BUT I'M ALL FOR THE UNITY OF THE CATHOLIC CHURCH!
THAT IS NOT IMPORTANT TO ME MUCH.
FOR INSTANCE, I WAS PRETTY ANTI-SEMITIC!
But who wasn't, in my time?
THAT'S WHY I TRANSLATED THE NEW TESTAMENT ANEW...
...AND THAT'S WHY I DON'T LIKE LUTHER!
HE SECEDED FROM THE CATHOLIC CHURCH AND HE PREACHED FAITH ABOVE ALL ELSE...
...BUT WHAT ABOUT REASON?
TRAK TA TEN

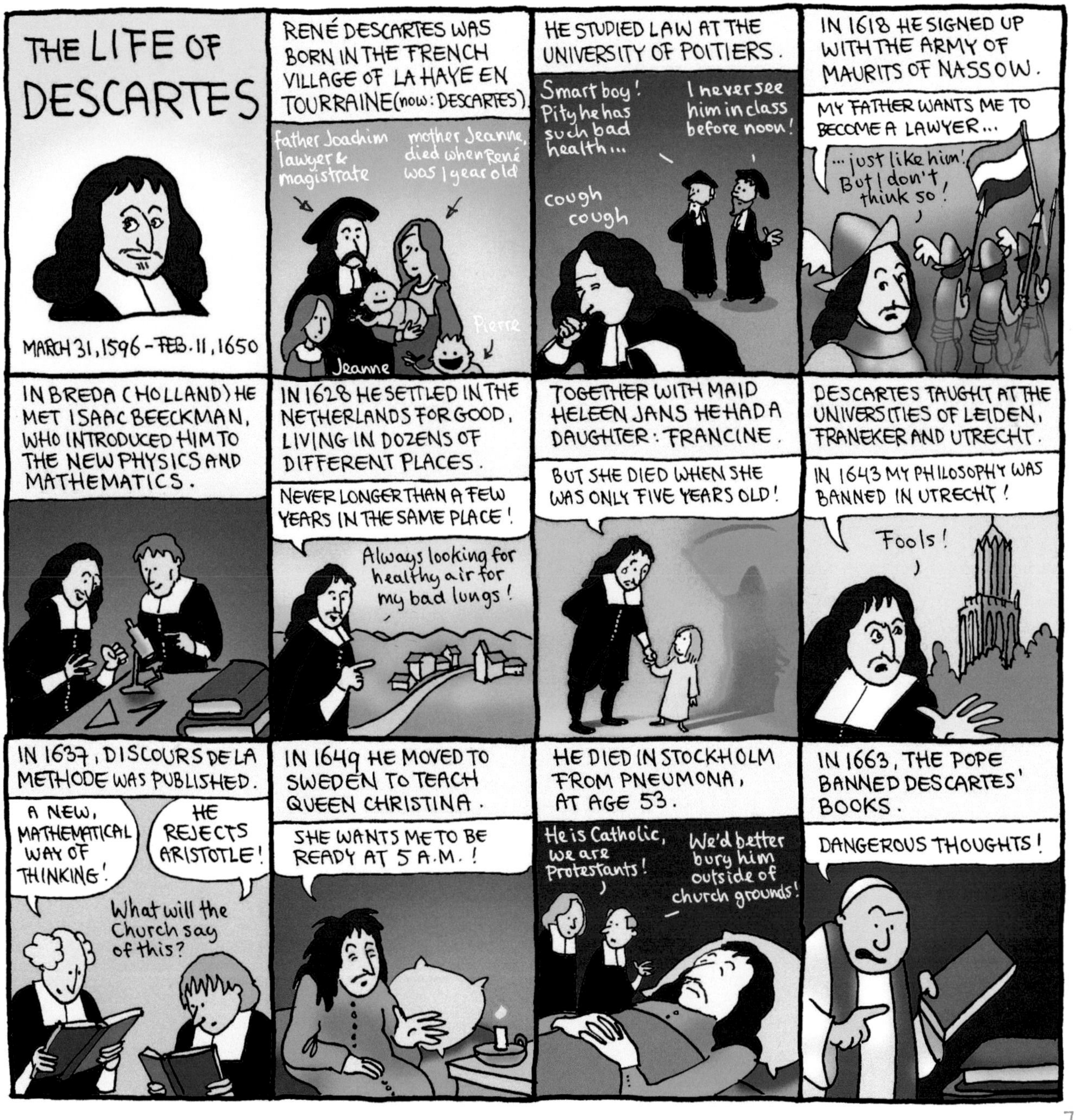
THE LIFE OF DESCARTES
MARCH 31, 1596 - FEB. 11, 1650
RENÉ DESCARTES WAS BORN IN THE FRENCH VILLAGE OF LA HAYE EN TOURRAINE (now: DESCARTES).
father Joachim lawyer & magistrate
mother Jeanne, died when René was 1 year old
Pierre
Jeanne
HE STUDIED LAW AT THE UNIVERSITY OF POITIERS.
Smart boy! Pity he has such bad health...
I never see him in class before noon!
cough cough
IN 1618 HE SIGNED UP WITH THE ARMY OF MAURITS OF NASSOW.
MY FATHER WANTS ME TO BECOME A LAWYER...
...just like him! But I don't think so!
IN BREDA (HOLLAND) HE MET ISAAC BEECKMAN, WHO INTRODUCED HIM TO THE NEW PHYSICS AND MATHEMATICS.
IN 1628 HE SETTLED IN THE NETHERLANDS FOR GOOD, LIVING IN DOZENS OF DIFFERENT PLACES.
NEVER LONGER THAN A FEW YEARS IN THE SAME PLACE!
Always looking for healthy air for my bad lungs!
TOGETHER WITH MAID HELEEN JANS HE HAD A DAUGHTER: FRANCINE.
BUT SHE DIED WHEN SHE WAS ONLY FIVE YEARS OLD!
DESCARTES TAUGHT AT THE UNIVERSITIES OF LEIDEN, FRANEKER AND UTRECHT.
IN 1643 MY PHILOSOPHY WAS BANNED IN UTRECHT!
Fools!
IN 1637, DISCOURS DE LA METHODE WAS PUBLISHED.
A NEW, MATHEMATICAL WAY OF THINKING!
HE REJECTS ARISTOTLE!
What will the Church say of this?
IN 1649 HE MOVED TO SWEDEN TO TEACH QUEEN CHRISTINA.
SHE WANTS ME TO BE READY AT 5 A.M.!
HE DIED IN STOCKHOLM FROM PNEUMONA, AT AGE 53.
He is Catholic, we are Protestants!
We'd better bury him outside of church grounds!
IN 1663, THE POPE BANNED DESCARTES' BOOKS.
DANGEROUS THOUGHTS!

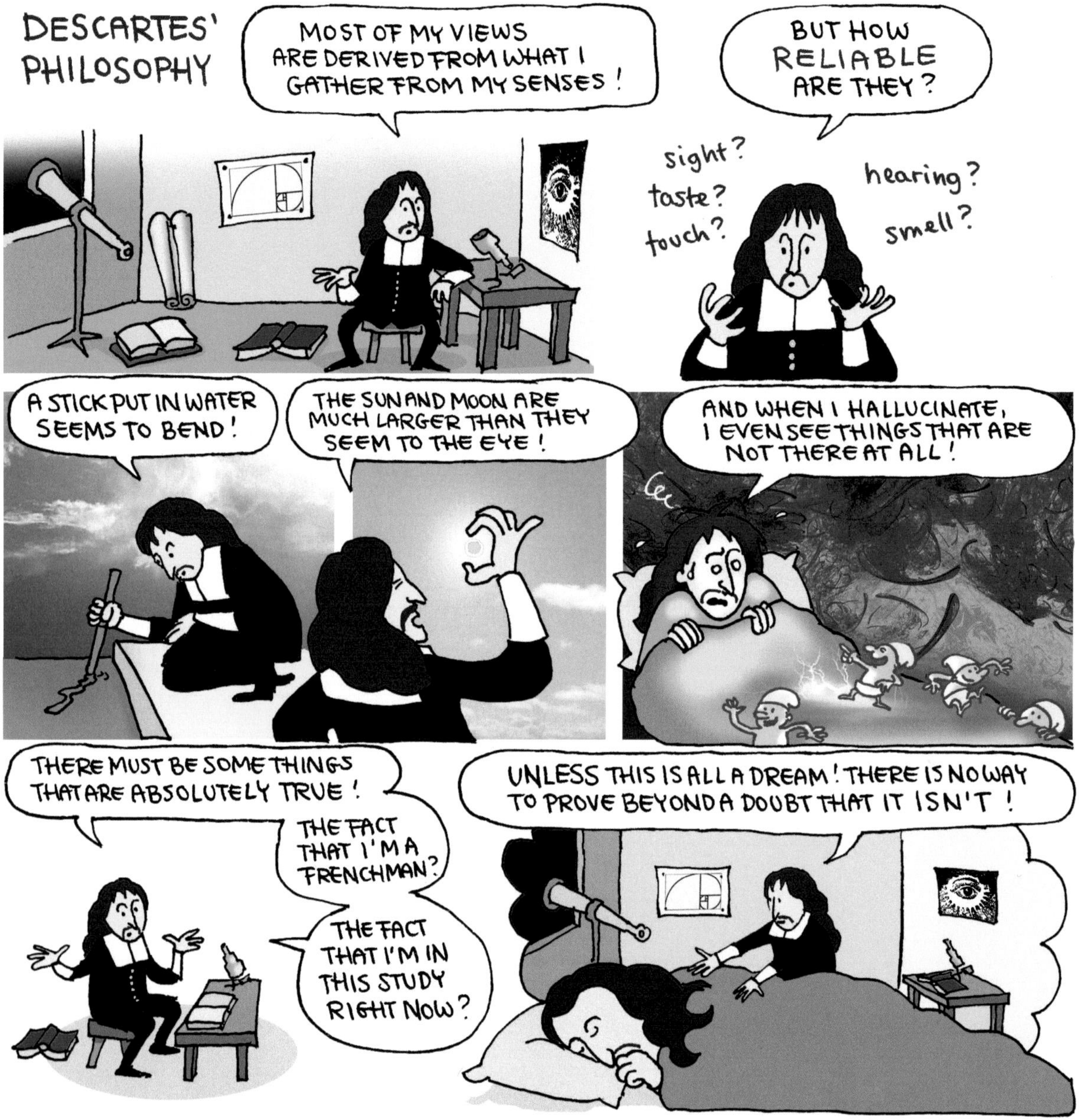
DESCARTES' PHILOSOPHY
MOST OF MY VIEWS ARE DERIVED FROM WHAT I GATHER FROM MY SENSES!
BUT HOW RELIABLE ARE THEY?
sight?
taste?
touch?
hearing?
smell?
A STICK PUT IN WATER SEEMS TO BEND!
THE SUN AND MOON ARE MUCH LARGER THAN THEY SEEM TO THE EYE!
AND WHEN I HALLUCINATE, I EVEN SEE THINGS THAT ARE NOT THERE AT ALL!
THERE MUST BE SOME THINGS THAT ARE ABSOLUTELY TRUE!
THE FACT THAT I'M A FRENCHMAN?
THE FACT THAT I'M IN THIS STUDY RIGHT NOW?
UNLESS THIS IS ALL A DREAM! THERE IS NO WAY TO PROVE BEYOND A DOUBT THAT IT ISN'T!

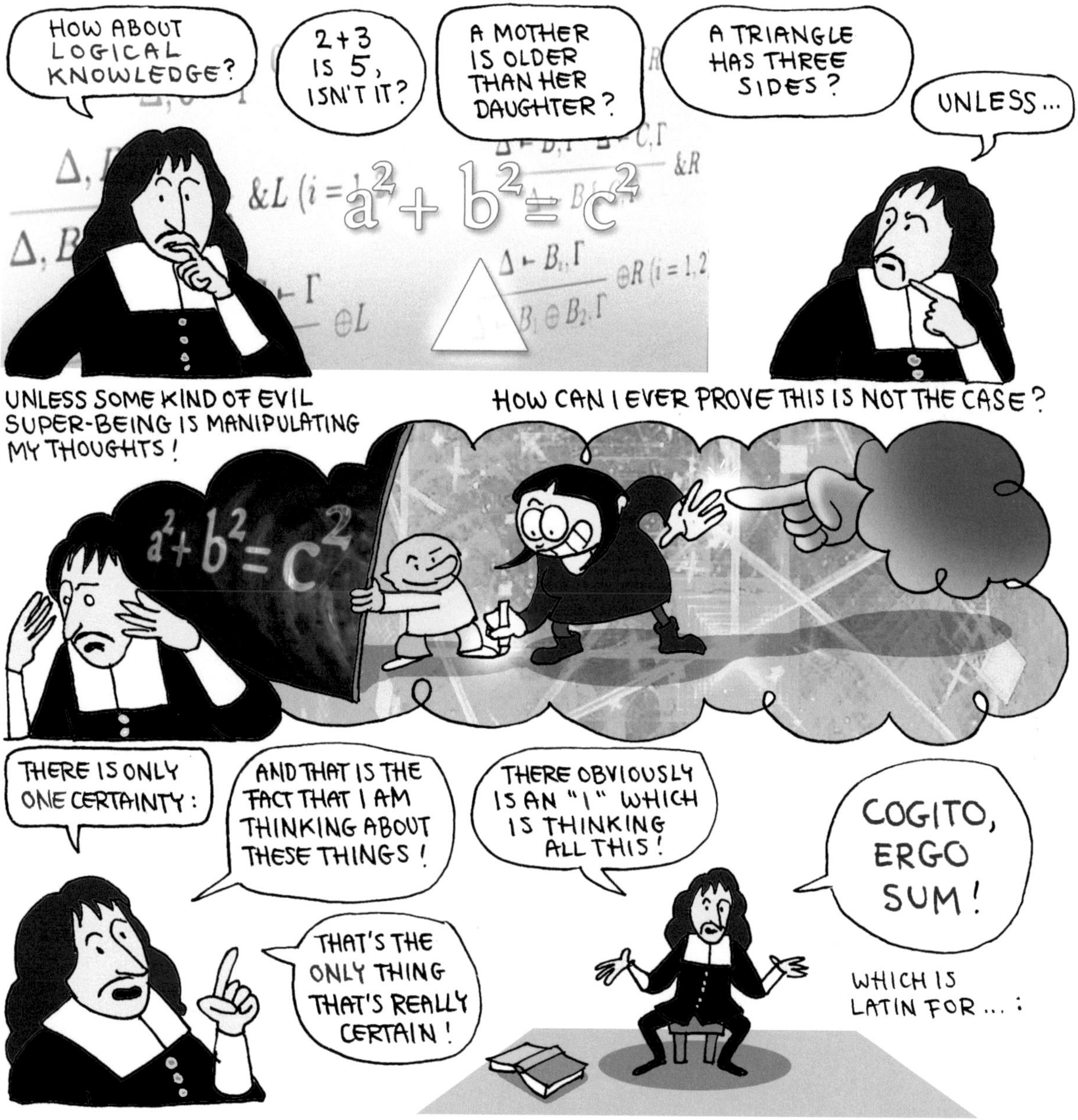
HOW ABOUT LOGICAL KNOWLEDGE?
2+3 IS 5, ISN'T IT?
A MOTHER IS OLDER THAN HER DAUGHTER?
A TRIANGLE HAS THREE SIDES?
UNLESS...
UNLESS SOME KIND OF EVIL SUPER-BEING IS MANIPULATING MY THOUGHTS!
HOW CAN I EVER PROVE THIS IS NOT THE CASE?
THERE IS ONLY ONE CERTAINTY:
AND THAT IS THE FACT THAT I AM THINKING ABOUT THESE THINGS!
THAT'S THE ONLY THING THAT'S REALLY CERTAIN!
THERE OBVIOUSLY IS AN "I" WHICH IS THINKING ALL THIS!
COGITO, ERGO SUM!
WHICH IS LATIN FOR... :

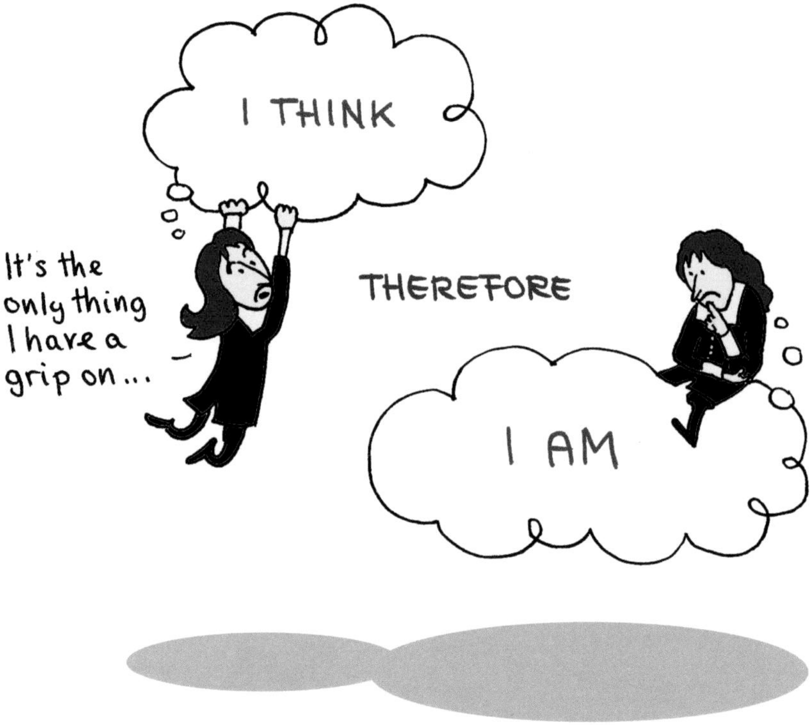
I THINK
It's the only thing I have a grip on...
THEREFORE
I AM

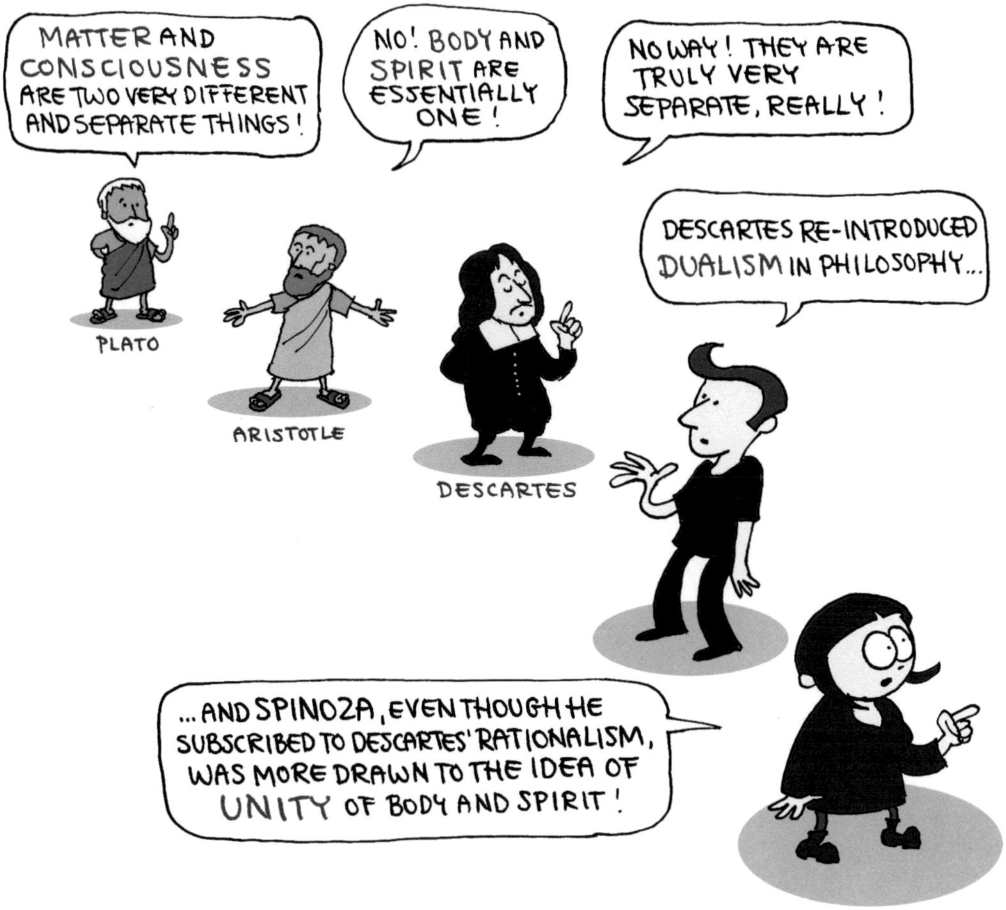
MATTER AND CONSCIOUSNESS ARE TWO VERY DIFFERENT AND SEPARATE THINGS!
PLATO
NO! BODY AND SPIRIT ARE ESSENTIALLY ONE!
ARISTOTLE
NO WAY! THEY ARE TRULY VERY SEPARATE, REALLY!
DESCARTES
DESCARTES RE-INTRODUCED DUALISM IN PHILOSOPHY...
...AND SPINOZA, EVEN THOUGH HE SUBSCRIBED TO DESCARTES' RATIONALISM, WAS MORE DRAWN TO THE IDEA OF UNITY OF BODY AND SPIRIT!

THE LIFE OF SPINOZA

NOV. 24, 1632 – FEB. 21, 1677

SPINOZA WAS BORN IN AMSTERDAM, TO JEWISH-PORTUGUESE PARENTS.

father Miguel merchant

mother Hanna died when Spinoza was 6 years old

Mirjam

Isaac

IN 1656, WHEN BARUCH DE SPINOZA WAS 23 YEARS OLD, HE WAS BANNED FROM THE JEWISH COMMUNITY.

BECAUSE YOU DON'T ABIDE BY OUR LAWS OF INHERITANCE!

OR BECAUSE OF YOUR CONTROVERSIAL IDEAS! WE DON'T WANT TO RISK AN ARGUMENT WITH THE CITY OF AMSTERDAM!

After all, we're Jews! — We always have to be careful!

FINE!

I'LL CALL MYSELF BENEDICTUS DE SPINOZA FROM NOW ON!

HE LIVED A SOBER LIFE AS A LENS GRINDER. HE WASN'T MARRIED BUT HE HAD MANY FRIENDS.

HIS LENSES ARE PERFECT!

HE WRITES WONDERFUL PIECES, ESPECIALLY ON THE FREEDOM OF SPEECH!

Constantijn Huygens

Mayor of Amsterdam

IN 1660 HE LEFT AMSTERDAM, TO FINALLY SETTLE IN THE CITY OF THE HAGUE.

I DON'T OWN MUCH, BUT I'M VERY ATTACHED TO MY PARENTS' FOUR-POSTER BED!

IN 1670 HE ANONYMOUSLY PUBLISHED THE TRACTATUS THEOLOGICO-POLITICUS.

TO HELL WITH FREEDOM OF SPEECH! IN A WAR CRISIS YOU CAN'T JUST SAY ANYTHING YOU WANT!

Who could it be?

Oops!

IN 1672 HE WITNESSED THE MURDER OF THE BROTHERS DE WITT, WHICH UPSET HIM VERY MUCH.

BARBARIANS! I WILL POST THIS PAMPHLET!

PLEASE BENTO, DON'T! IT'S MUCH TOO DANGEROUS!

ULTIMI BARBARORUM !!!

HE DIED IN 1677, 44 YEARS OLD, FROM LUNG DISEASE.

MUST'VE BEEN ALL THAT LENS DUST!

He always had a weak constitution!

THE SAME YEAR, HIS WRITINGS WERE PUBLISHED POSTHUMOUSLY.

B. D. S.
OPERA POSTHUMA,

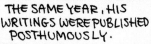

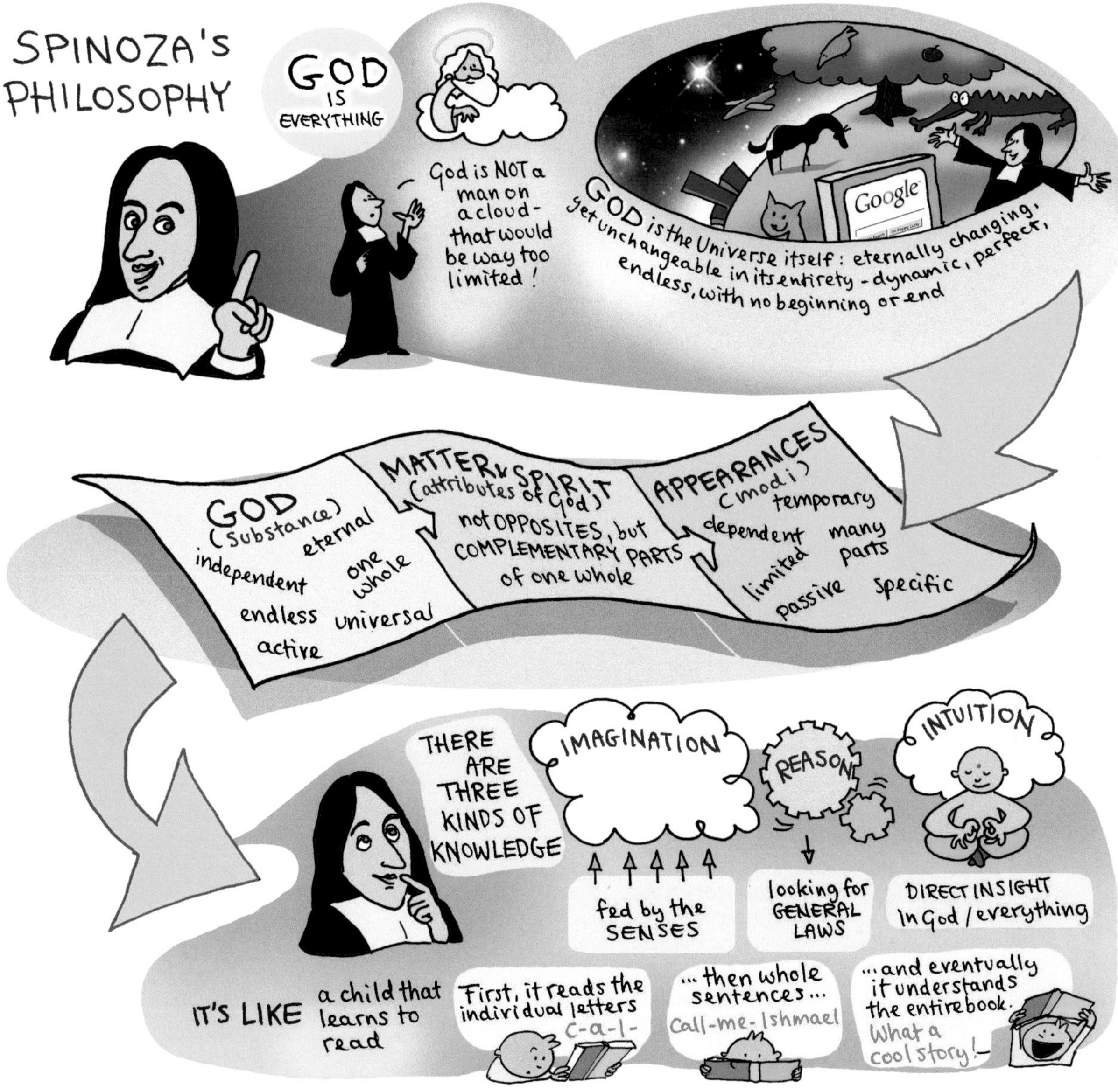
SPINOZA'S PHILOSOPHY
GOD IS EVERYTHING
God is NOT a man on a cloud - that would be way too limited!
Google
GOD is the Universe itself: eternally changing, yet unchangeable in its entirety - dynamic, perfect, endless, with no beginning or end
GOD (substance)
eternal
independent
one whole
endless
universal
active
MATTER & SPIRIT (attributes of God)
not OPPOSITES, but COMPLEMENTARY PARTS of one whole
APPEARANCES (modi)
temporary
dependent
many
limited
parts
passive
specific
THERE ARE THREE KINDS OF KNOWLEDGE
IMAGINATION
fed by the SENSES
REASON
looking for GENERAL LAWS
INTUITION
DIRECT INSIGHT In God / everything
IT'S LIKE
a child that learns to read
First, it reads the individual letters
c-a-l-
... then whole sentences...
Call-me-Ishmael
... and eventually it understands the entire book.
What a cool story!

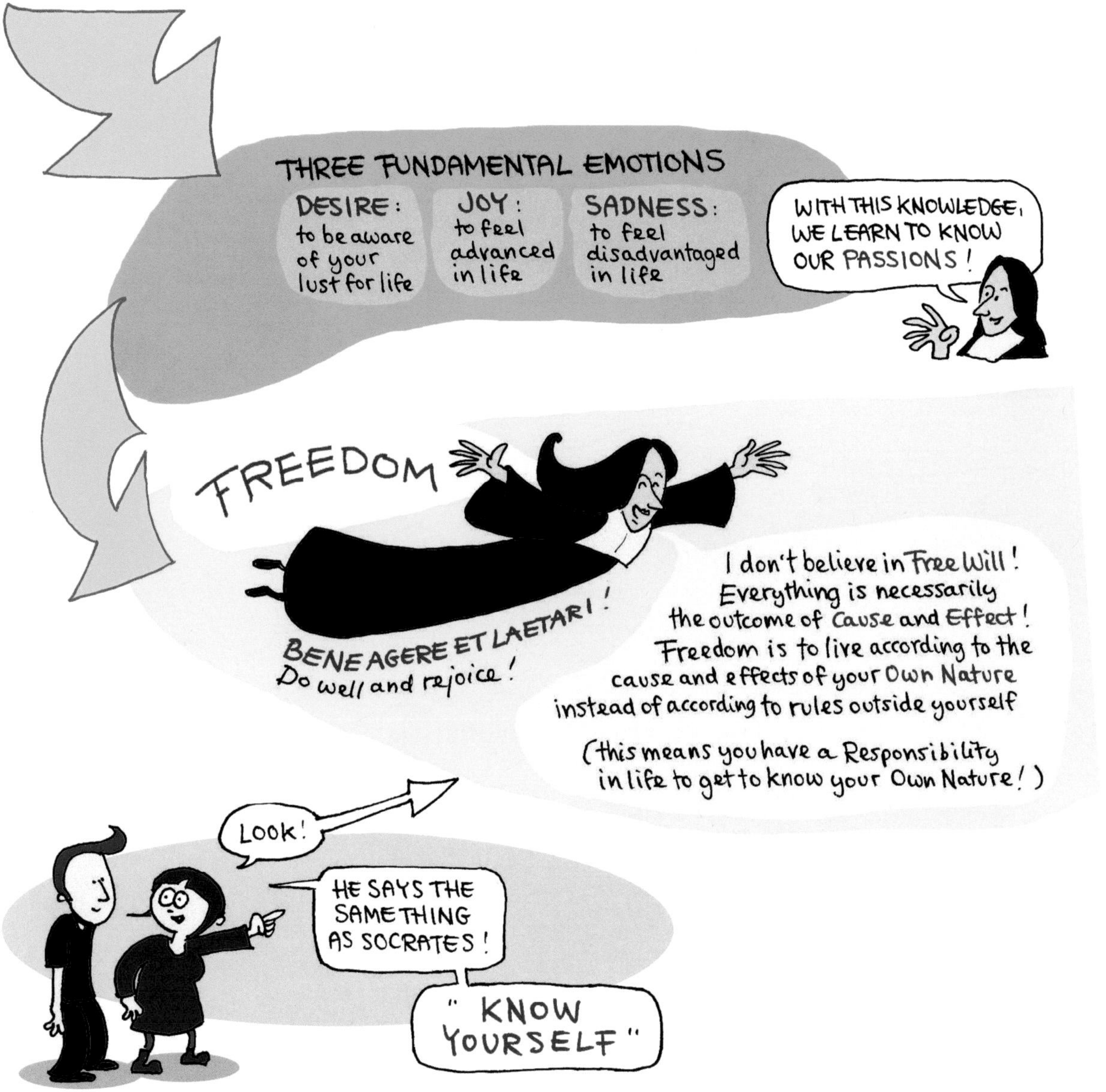
THREE FUNDAMENTAL EMOTIONS
DESIRE: to be aware of your lust for life
JOY: to feel advanced in life
SADNESS: to feel disadvantaged in life
WITH THIS KNOWLEDGE, WE LEARN TO KNOW OUR PASSIONS!
FREEDOM
BENE AGERE ET LAETARI!
Do well and rejoice!
I don't believe in Free Will! Everything is necessarily the outcome of Cause and Effect! Freedom is to live according to the cause and effects of your Own Nature instead of according to rules outside yourself
(this means you have a Responsibility in life to get to know your Own Nature!)
LOOK!
HE SAYS THE SAME THING AS SOCRATES!
"KNOW YOURSELF"

WHAT IS REALITY?

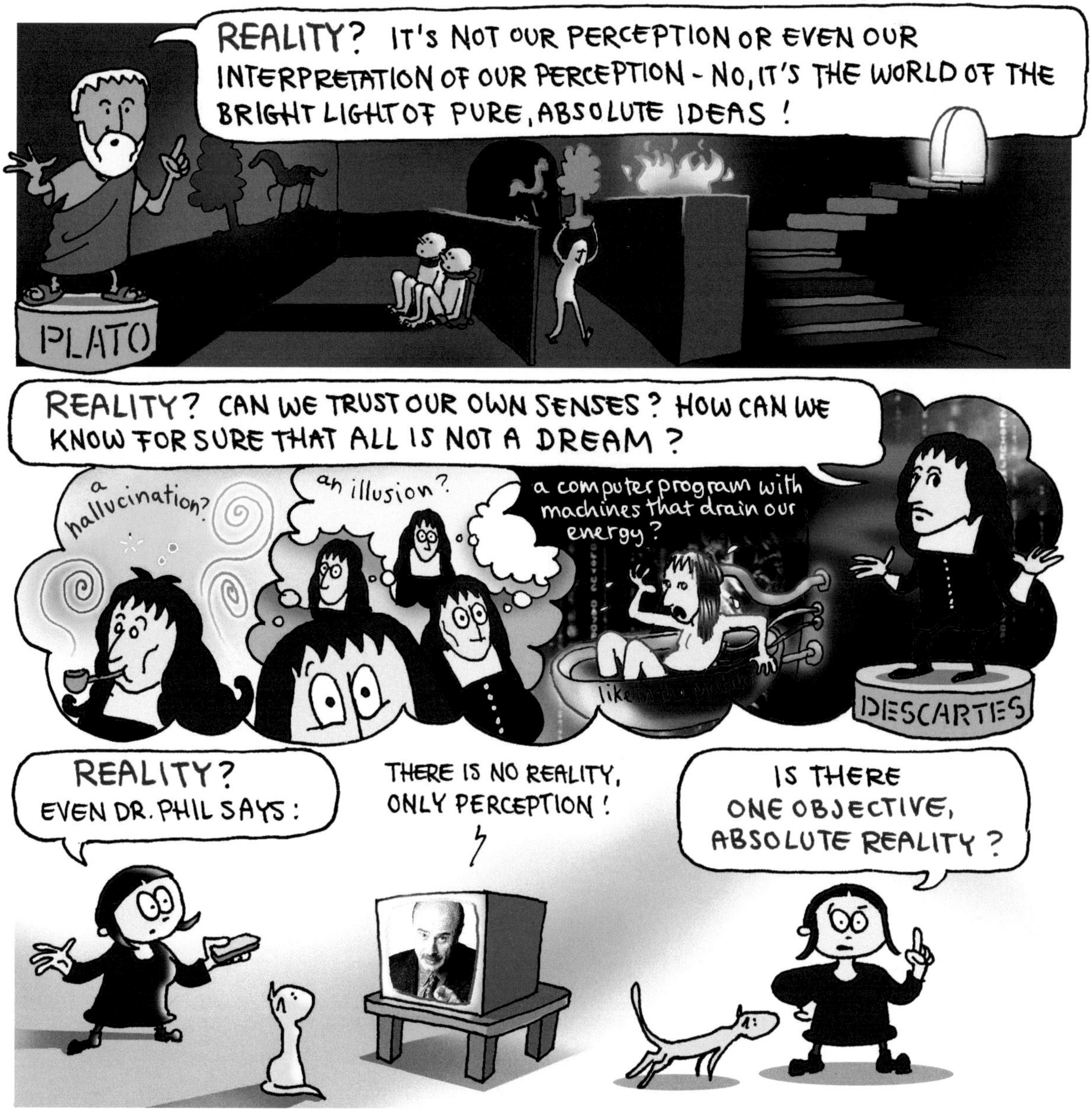
REALITY? IT'S NOT OUR PERCEPTION OR EVEN OUR INTERPRETATION OF OUR PERCEPTION - NO, IT'S THE WORLD OF THE BRIGHT LIGHT OF PURE, ABSOLUTE IDEAS !
PLATO
REALITY? CAN WE TRUST OUR OWN SENSES? HOW CAN WE KNOW FOR SURE THAT ALL IS NOT A DREAM ?
a hallucination?
an illusion?
a computer program with machines that drain our energy?
DESCARTES
REALITY? EVEN DR. PHIL SAYS:
THERE IS NO REALITY, ONLY PERCEPTION !
IS THERE ONE OBJECTIVE, ABSOLUTE REALITY ?

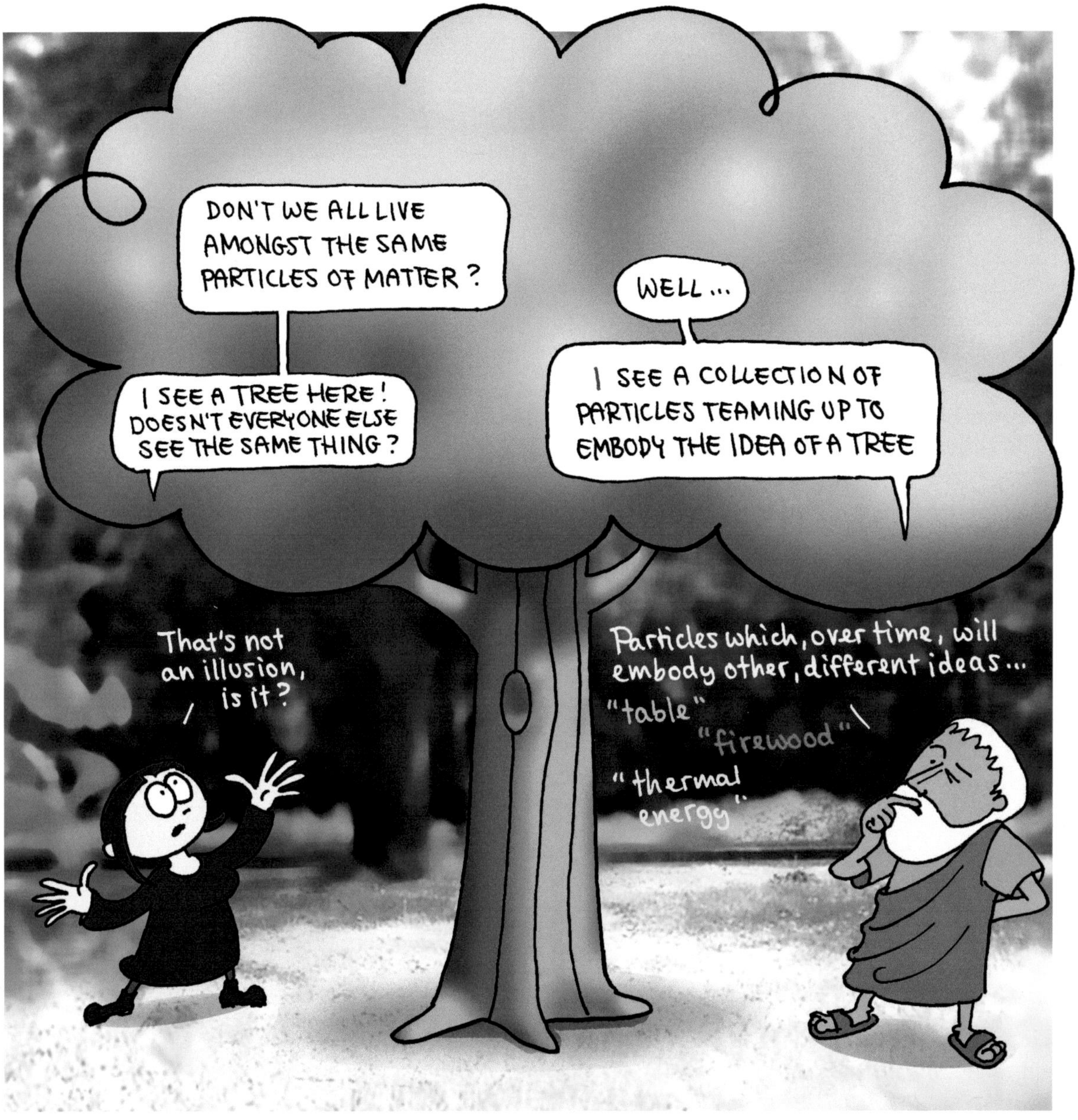
DON'T WE ALL LIVE AMONGST THE SAME PARTICLES OF MATTER?
I SEE A TREE HERE! DOESN'T EVERYONE ELSE SEE THE SAME THING?
WELL...
I SEE A COLLECTION OF PARTICLES TEAMING UP TO EMBODY THE IDEA OF A TREE
That's not an illusion, is it?
Particles which, over time, will embody other, different ideas...
"table"
"firewood"
"thermal energy"

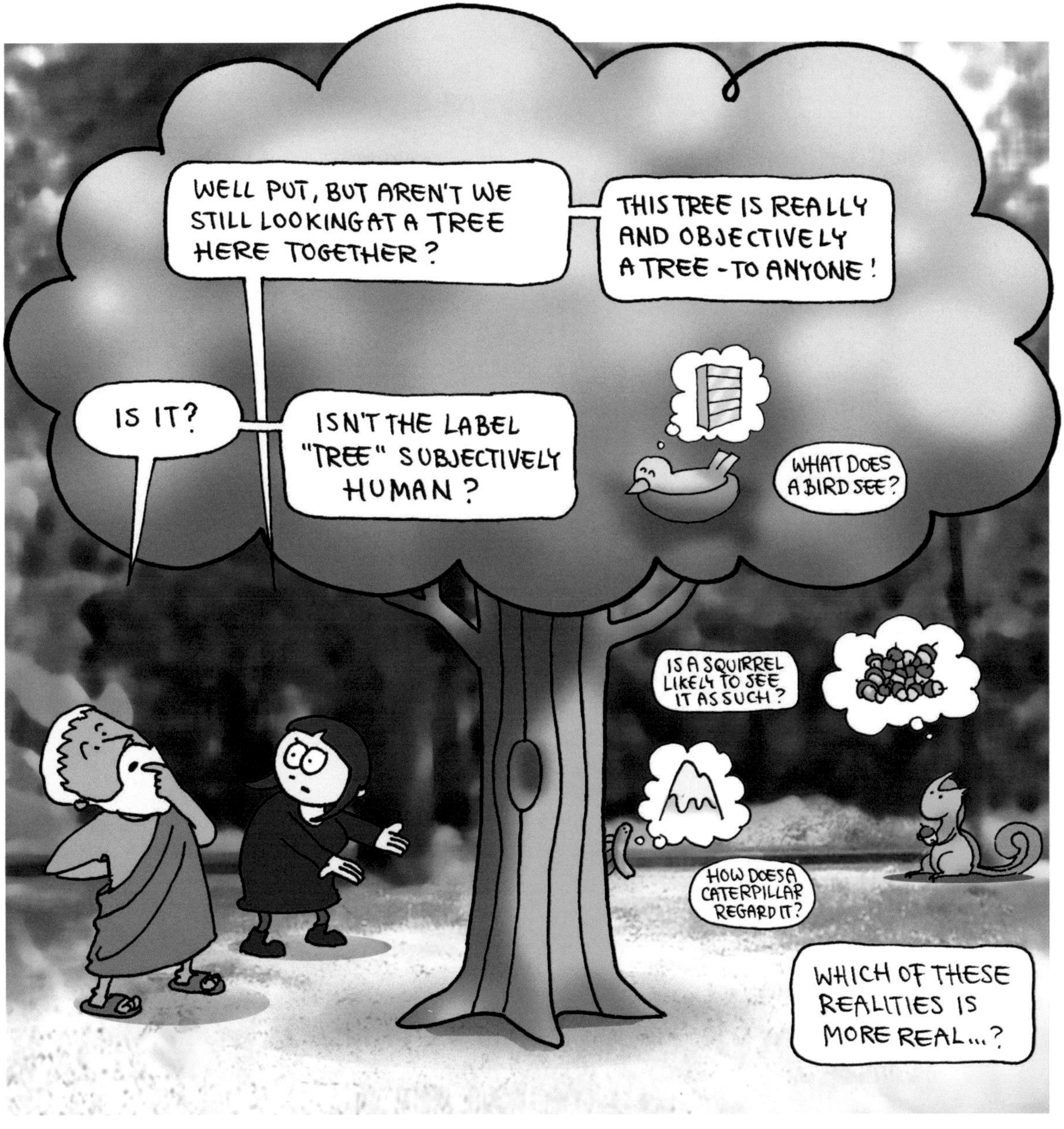
WELL PUT, BUT AREN'T WE STILL LOOKING AT A TREE HERE TOGETHER?
THIS TREE IS REALLY AND OBJECTIVELY A TREE - TO ANYONE!
IS IT?
ISN'T THE LABEL "TREE" SUBJECTIVELY HUMAN?
WHAT DOES A BIRD SEE?
IS A SQUIRREL LIKELY TO SEE IT AS SUCH?
HOW DOES A CATERPILLAR REGARD IT?
WHICH OF THESE REALITIES IS MORE REAL...?

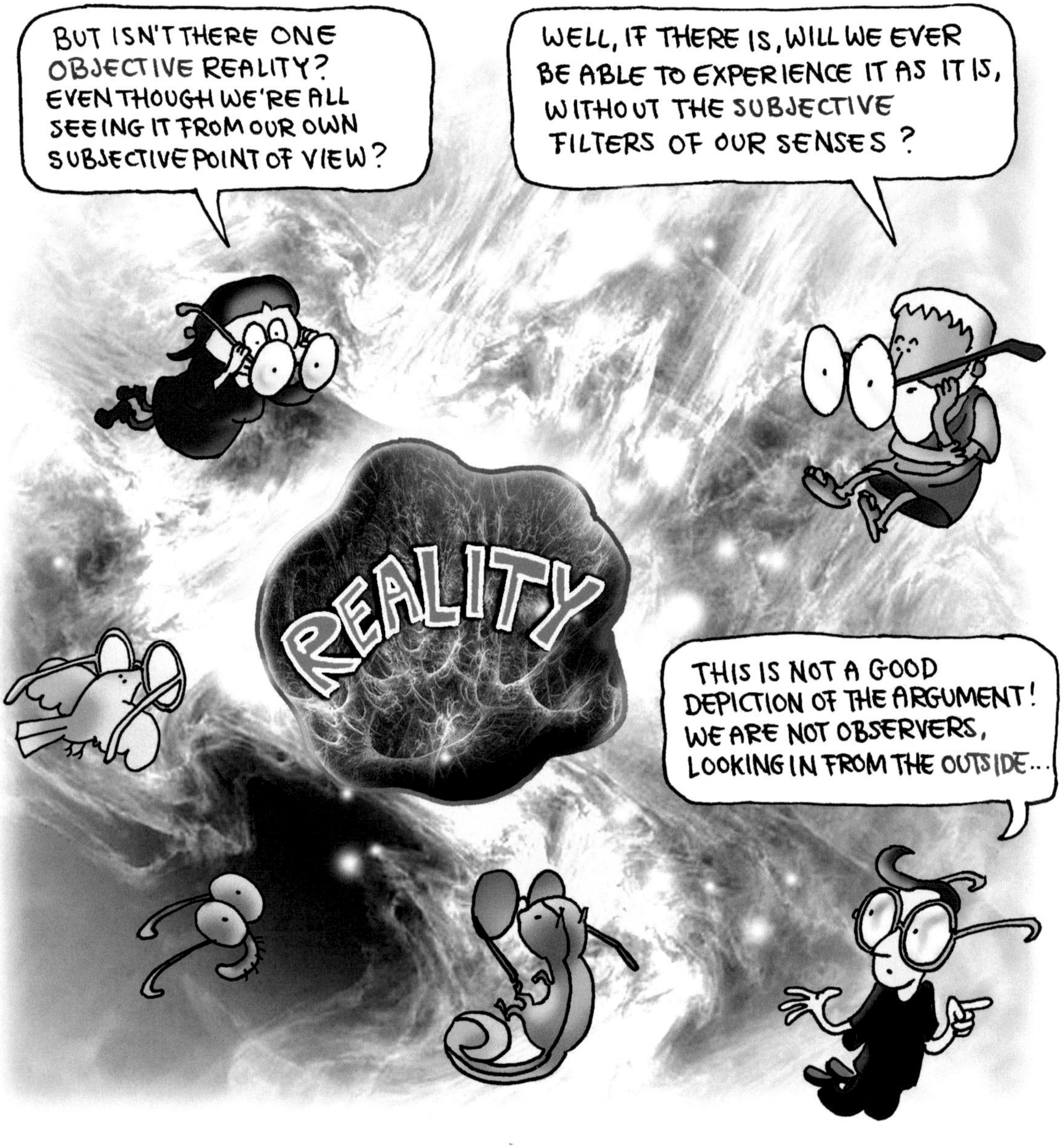
BUT ISN'T THERE ONE OBJECTIVE REALITY? EVEN THOUGH WE'RE ALL SEEING IT FROM OUR OWN SUBJECTIVE POINT OF VIEW?
WELL, IF THERE IS, WILL WE EVER BE ABLE TO EXPERIENCE IT AS IT IS, WITHOUT THE SUBJECTIVE FILTERS OF OUR SENSES?
REALITY
THIS IS NOT A GOOD DEPICTION OF THE ARGUMENT! WE ARE NOT OBSERVERS, LOOKING IN FROM THE OUTSIDE...

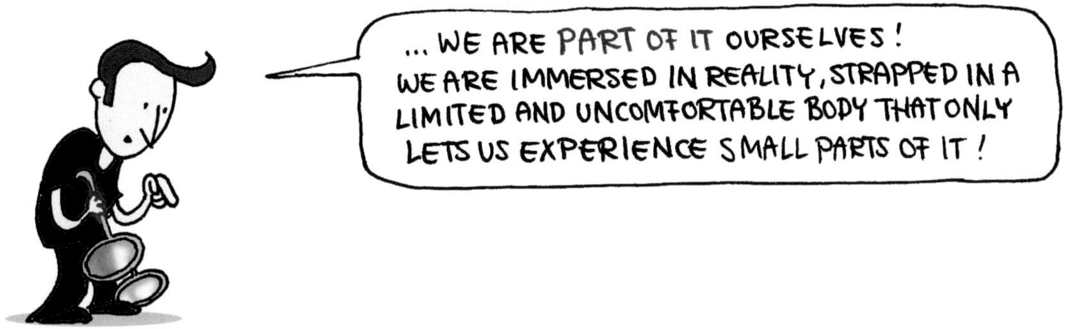
... WE ARE PART OF IT OURSELVES!
WE ARE IMMERSED IN REALITY, STRAPPED IN A LIMITED AND UNCOMFORTABLE BODY THAT ONLY LETS US EXPERIENCE SMALL PARTS OF IT!

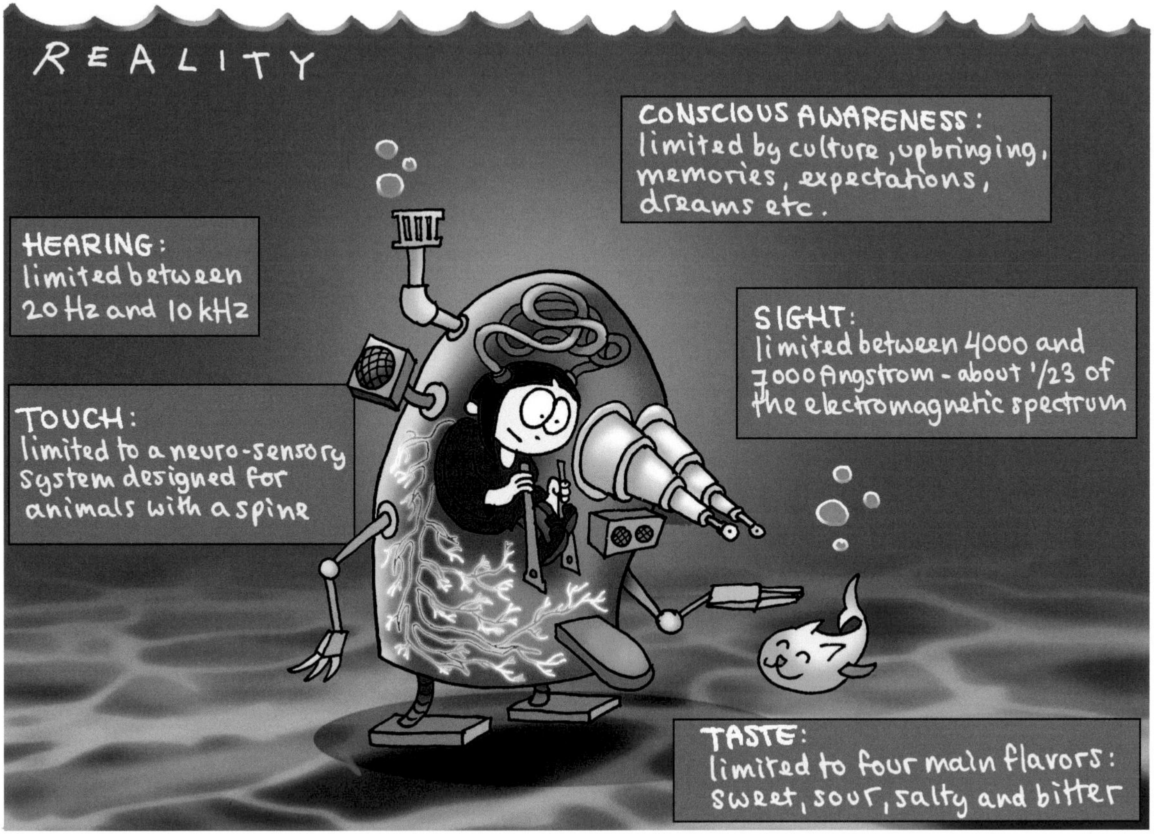
REALITY
CONSCIOUS AWARENESS: limited by culture, upbringing, memories, expectations, dreams etc.
HEARING: limited between 20 Hz and 10 kHz
SIGHT: limited between 4000 and 7000 Angstrom - about 1/23 of the electromagnetic spectrum
TOUCH: limited to a neuro-sensory system designed for animals with a spine
TASTE: limited to four main flavors: sweet, sour, salty and bitter

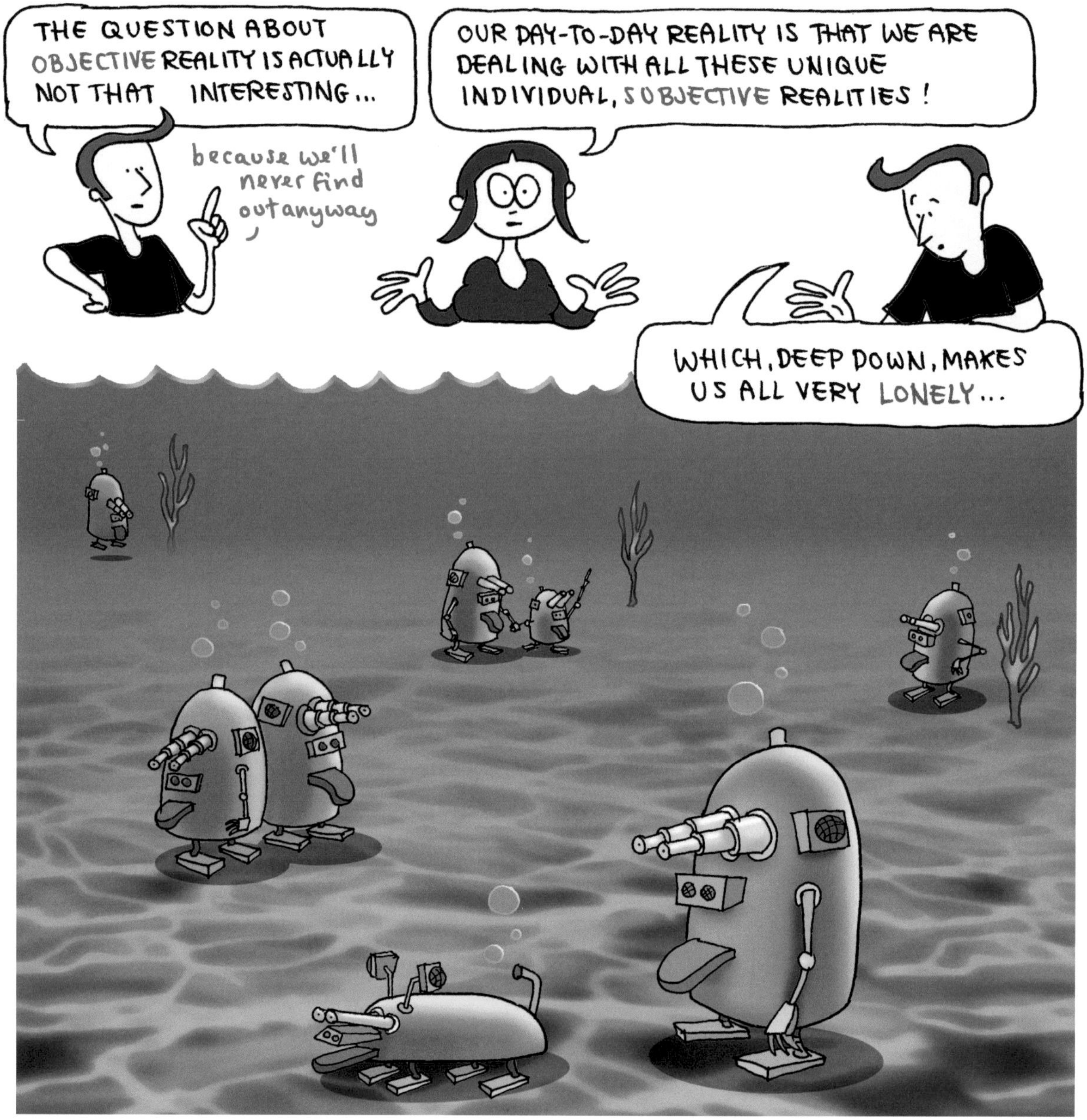
THE QUESTION ABOUT OBJECTIVE REALITY IS ACTUALLY NOT THAT INTERESTING...
because we'll never find out anyway
OUR DAY-TO-DAY REALITY IS THAT WE ARE DEALING WITH ALL THESE UNIQUE INDIVIDUAL, SUBJECTIVE REALITIES!
WHICH, DEEP DOWN, MAKES US ALL VERY LONELY...

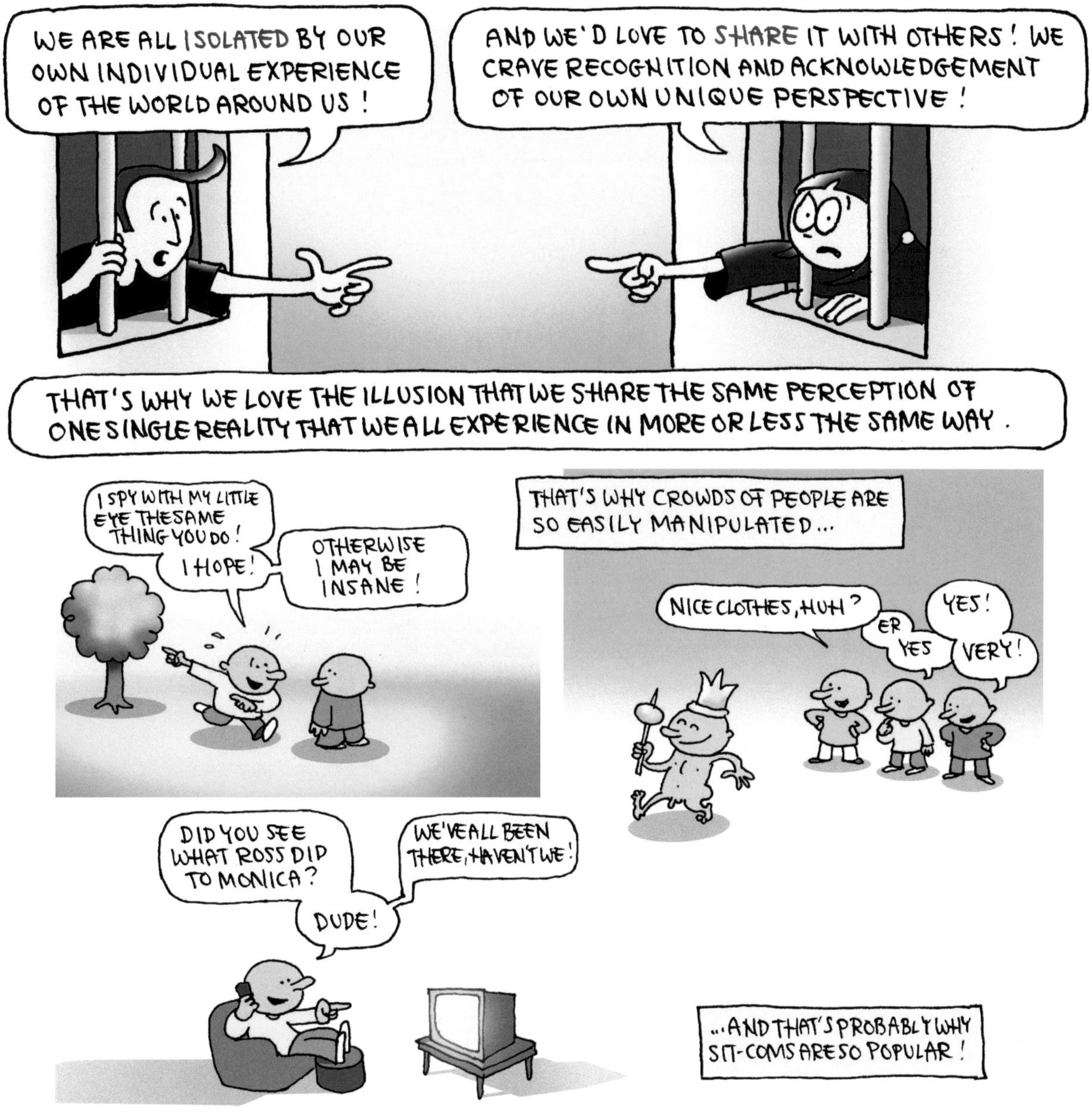
WE ARE ALL ISOLATED BY OUR OWN INDIVIDUAL EXPERIENCE OF THE WORLD AROUND US!
AND WE'D LOVE TO SHARE IT WITH OTHERS! WE CRAVE RECOGNITION AND ACKNOWLEDGEMENT OF OUR OWN UNIQUE PERSPECTIVE!
THAT'S WHY WE LOVE THE ILLUSION THAT WE SHARE THE SAME PERCEPTION OF ONE SINGLE REALITY THAT WE ALL EXPERIENCE IN MORE OR LESS THE SAME WAY.
I SPY WITH MY LITTLE EYE THE SAME THING YOU DO!
I HOPE!
OTHERWISE I MAY BE INSANE!
THAT'S WHY CROWDS OF PEOPLE ARE SO EASILY MANIPULATED...
NICE CLOTHES, HUH?
ER YES
YES!
VERY!
DID YOU SEE WHAT ROSS DID TO MONICA?
DUDE!
WE'VE ALL BEEN THERE, HAVEN'T WE!
...AND THAT'S PROBABLY WHY SIT-COMS ARE SO POPULAR!

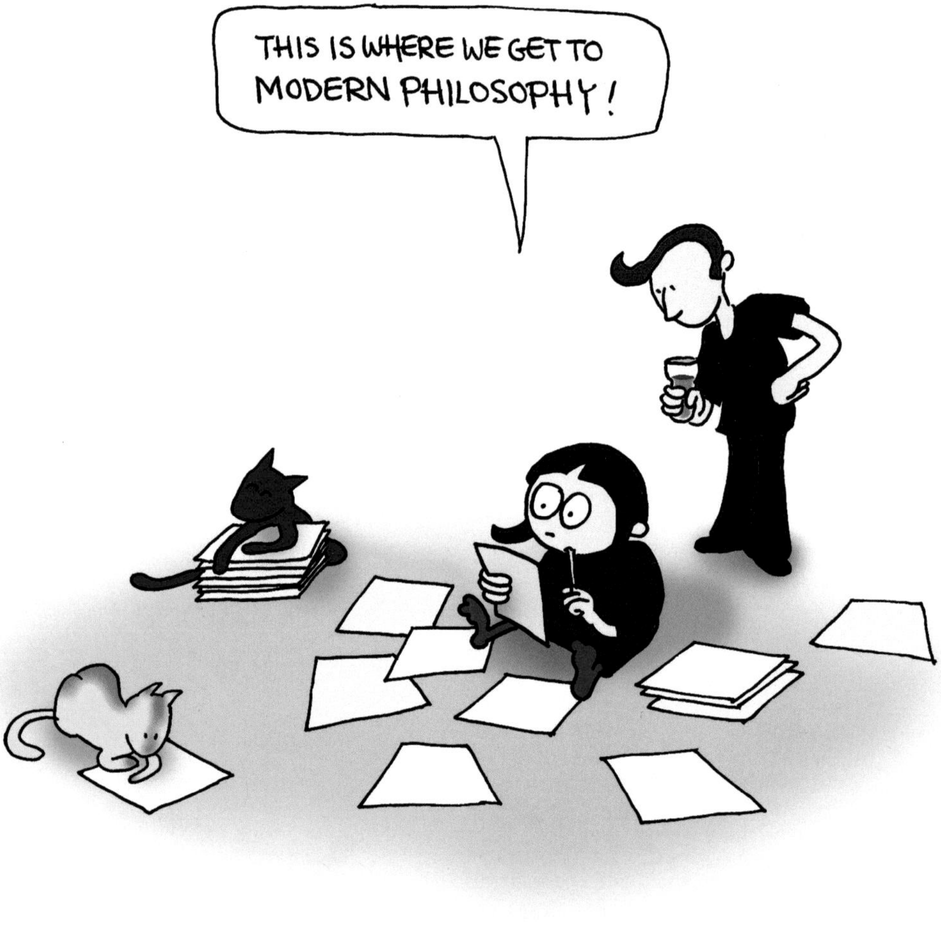
THIS IS WHERE WE GET TO MODERN PHILOSOPHY!

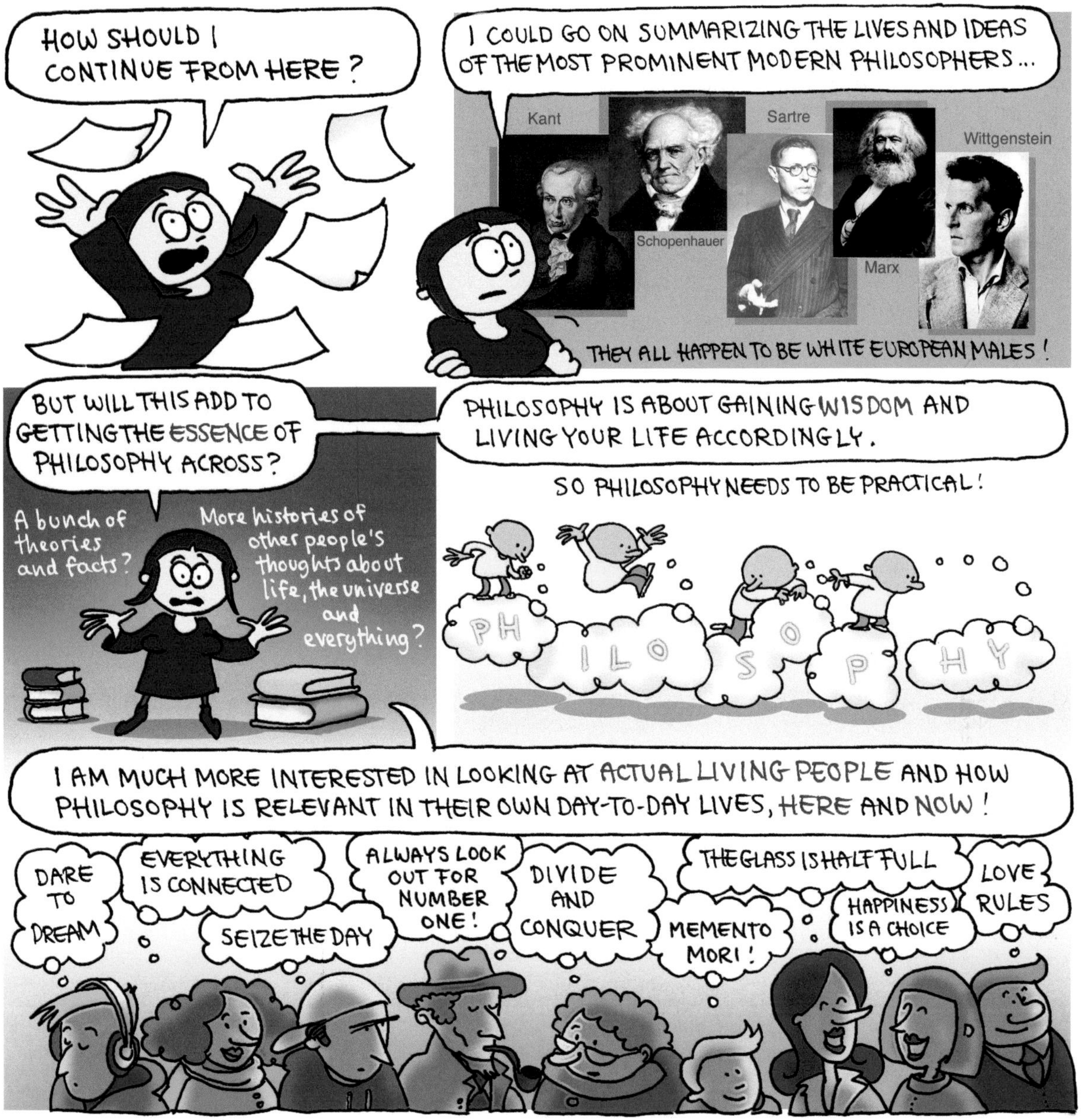
HOW SHOULD I CONTINUE FROM HERE?
I COULD GO ON SUMMARIZING THE LIVES AND IDEAS OF THE MOST PROMINENT MODERN PHILOSOPHERS...
Kant
Schopenhauer
Sartre
Marx
Wittgenstein
THEY ALL HAPPEN TO BE WHITE EUROPEAN MALES!
BUT WILL THIS ADD TO GETTING THE ESSENCE OF PHILOSOPHY ACROSS?
A bunch of theories and facts?
More histories of other people's thoughts about life, the universe and everything?
PHILOSOPHY IS ABOUT GAINING WISDOM AND LIVING YOUR LIFE ACCORDINGLY.
SO PHILOSOPHY NEEDS TO BE PRACTICAL!
PH ILO S O P HY
I AM MUCH MORE INTERESTED IN LOOKING AT ACTUAL LIVING PEOPLE AND HOW PHILOSOPHY IS RELEVANT IN THEIR OWN DAY-TO-DAY LIVES, HERE AND NOW!
DARE TO DREAM
EVERYTHING IS CONNECTED
SEIZE THE DAY
ALWAYS LOOK OUT FOR NUMBER ONE!
DIVIDE AND CONQUER
MEMENTO MORI!
THE GLASS IS HALF FULL
HAPPINESS IS A CHOICE
LOVE RULES

I'LL GO ASK A FEW PEOPLE I KNOW ABOUT THE PHILOSOPHIES THEY APPLY TO THEIR OWN LIVES !
WHICH THOUGHTS AND MOTTOS ARE EMPOWERING TO THEM ?
WHICH THINKERS INSPIRE THEM ?
PRESS
PAST
PRESENT

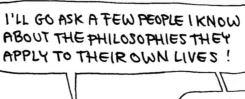

PERSONAL
PHILOSOPHIES

YIRI'S PHILOSOPHY

my husband! —

THERE ARE QUITE A FEW THINKERS WITH INSPIRING IDEAS...

... BUT IF I'D HAVE TO PICK ONE — UHM, GEORGE CARLIN!

THE LIFE OF GEORGE CARLIN

MAY 12, 1937 – JUNE 22, 2008

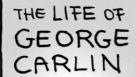

GEORGE CARLIN WAS BORN IN NEW YORK IN 1937, TO IRISH PARENTS.

father Patrick worked at the New York Sun

mother Mary, secretary

mother left father when George was little

HE HAD A DIFFICULT RELATION WITH HIS MOTHER AND RAN AWAY OFTEN.

HE BECAME A RADAR TECHNICIAN IN THE U.S. AIR FORCE, UNTIL HE GOT FIRED.

YOU, SIR, ARE AN UNPRODUCTIVE AIRMAN...!

zzzz

HE TEAMED UP WITH JACK BURNS TO FORM A COMIC DUO - TOGETHER THEY LEFT FOR CALIFORNIA IN 1960.

Burns   Carlin

CARLIN SOON APPEARED ON TV SHOWS LIKE THE ED SULLIVAN SHOW AND THE TONIGHT SHOW.

GEORGE CARLIN IS A STAND-UP COMEDIAN?!

YEAH, SO...?

100

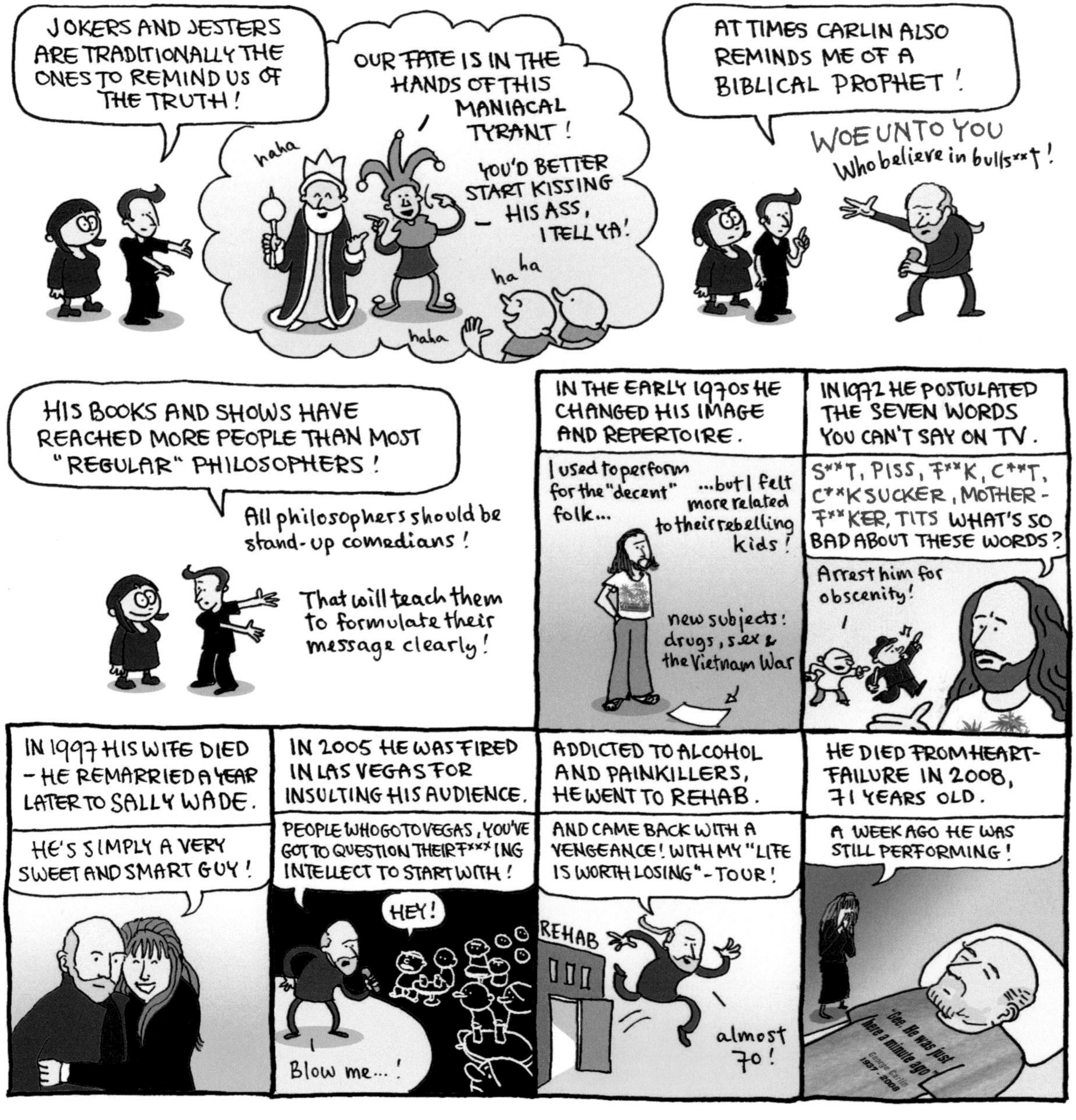

JOKERS AND JESTERS ARE TRADITIONALLY THE ONES TO REMIND US OF THE TRUTH!
haha
OUR FATE IS IN THE HANDS OF THIS MANIACAL TYRANT!
YOU'D BETTER START KISSING HIS ASS, I TELL YA!
ha ha
haha
AT TIMES CARLIN ALSO REMINDS ME OF A BIBLICAL PROPHET!
WOE UNTO YOU Who believe in bulls**t!
HIS BOOKS AND SHOWS HAVE REACHED MORE PEOPLE THAN MOST "REGULAR" PHILOSOPHERS!
All philosophers should be stand-up comedians!
That will teach them to formulate their message clearly!
IN THE EARLY 1970s HE CHANGED HIS IMAGE AND REPERTOIRE.
I used to perform for the "decent" folk...
...but I felt more related to their rebelling kids!
new subjects: drugs, sex & the Vietnam War
IN 1972 HE POSTULATED THE SEVEN WORDS YOU CAN'T SAY ON TV.
S**T, PISS, F**K, C**T, C**KSUCKER, MOTHER-F**KER, TITS WHAT'S SO BAD ABOUT THESE WORDS?
Arrest him for obscenity!
IN 1997 HIS WIFE DIED – HE REMARRIED A YEAR LATER TO SALLY WADE.
HE'S SIMPLY A VERY SWEET AND SMART GUY!
IN 2005 HE WAS FIRED IN LAS VEGAS FOR INSULTING HIS AUDIENCE.
PEOPLE WHO GO TO VEGAS, YOU'VE GOT TO QUESTION THEIR F***ING INTELLECT TO START WITH!
HEY!
Blow me...!
ADDICTED TO ALCOHOL AND PAINKILLERS, HE WENT TO REHAB.
AND CAME BACK WITH A VENGEANCE! WITH MY "LIFE IS WORTH LOSING"-TOUR!
REHAB
almost 70!
HE DIED FROM HEART-FAILURE IN 2008, 71 YEARS OLD.
A WEEK AGO HE WAS STILL PERFORMING!
"Gee, He was just here a minute ago"
George Carlin
1937 - 2008

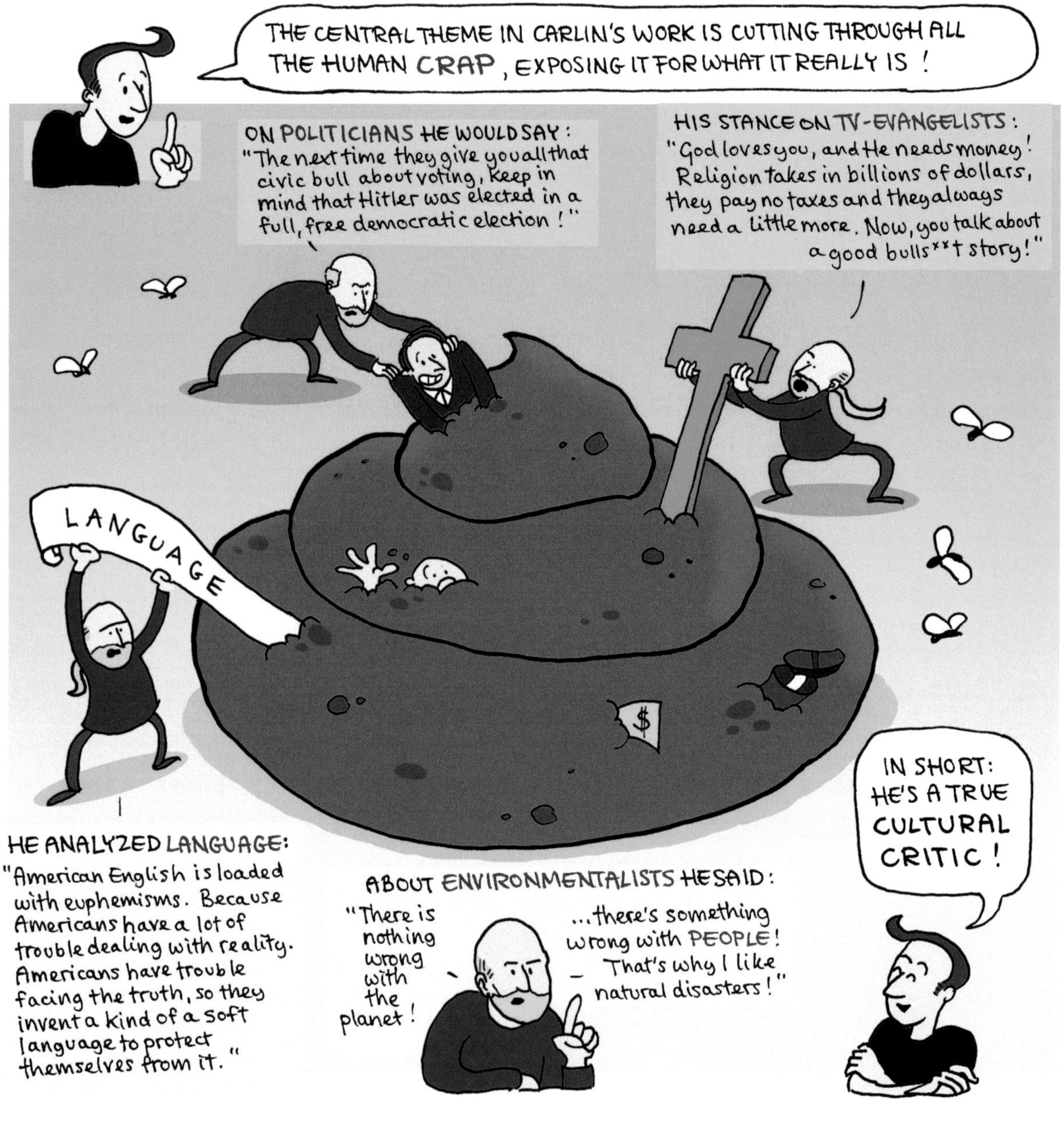
THE CENTRAL THEME IN CARLIN'S WORK IS CUTTING THROUGH ALL THE HUMAN CRAP, EXPOSING IT FOR WHAT IT REALLY IS !
ON POLITICIANS HE WOULD SAY: "The next time they give you all that civic bull about voting, keep in mind that Hitler was elected in a full, free democratic election!"
HIS STANCE ON TV-EVANGELISTS: "God loves you, and He needs money! Religion takes in billions of dollars, they pay no taxes and they always need a little more. Now, you talk about a good bulls**t story!"
LANGUAGE
$
HE ANALYZED LANGUAGE: "American English is loaded with euphemisms. Because Americans have a lot of trouble dealing with reality. Americans have trouble facing the truth, so they invent a kind of a soft language to protect themselves from it."
ABOUT ENVIRONMENTALISTS HE SAID:
"There is nothing wrong with the planet!
...there's something wrong with PEOPLE! That's why I like natural disasters!"
IN SHORT: HE'S A TRUE CULTURAL CRITIC!

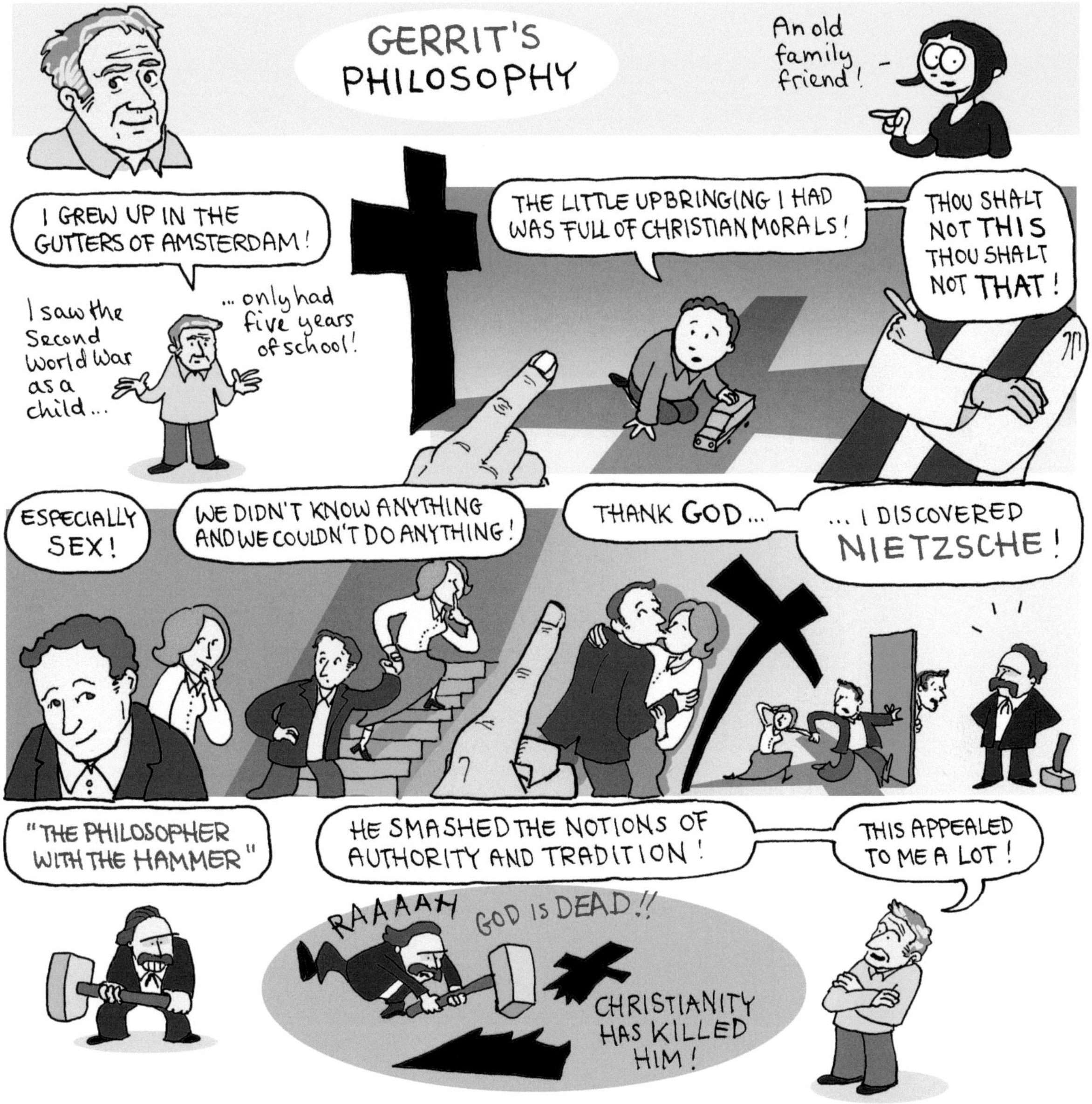

GERRIT'S PHILOSOPHY
An old family friend! -
I GREW UP IN THE GUTTERS OF AMSTERDAM!
I saw the Second World War as a child...
... only had five years of school!
THE LITTLE UPBRINGING I HAD WAS FULL OF CHRISTIAN MORALS!
THOU SHALT NOT THIS THOU SHALT NOT THAT!
ESPECIALLY SEX!
WE DIDN'T KNOW ANYTHING AND WE COULDN'T DO ANYTHING!
THANK GOD...
... I DISCOVERED NIETZSCHE!
"THE PHILOSOPHER WITH THE HAMMER"
HE SMASHED THE NOTIONS OF AUTHORITY AND TRADITION!
THIS APPEALED TO ME A LOT!
RAAAAH
GOD IS DEAD!!
CHRISTIANITY HAS KILLED HIM!

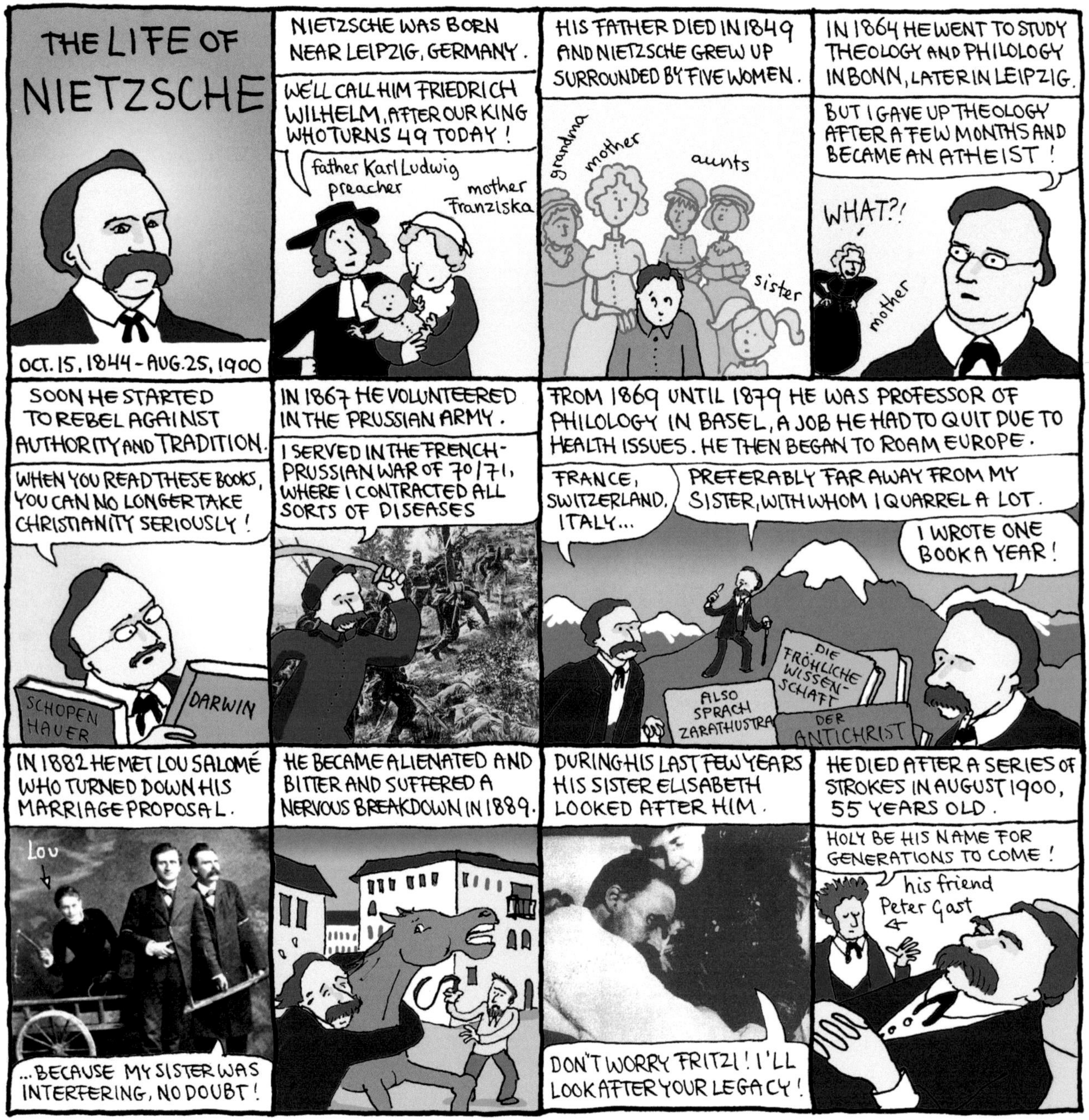
THE LIFE OF NIETZSCHE
OCT. 15, 1844 - AUG. 25, 1900
NIETZSCHE WAS BORN NEAR LEIPZIG, GERMANY.
WE'LL CALL HIM FRIEDRICH WILHELM, AFTER OUR KING WHO TURNS 49 TODAY!
father Karl Ludwig preacher
mother Franziska
HIS FATHER DIED IN 1849 AND NIETZSCHE GREW UP SURROUNDED BY FIVE WOMEN.
grandma
mother
aunts
sister
IN 1864 HE WENT TO STUDY THEOLOGY AND PHILOLOGY IN BONN, LATER IN LEIPZIG.
BUT I GAVE UP THEOLOGY AFTER A FEW MONTHS AND BECAME AN ATHEIST!
WHAT?!
mother
SOON HE STARTED TO REBEL AGAINST AUTHORITY AND TRADITION.
WHEN YOU READ THESE BOOKS, YOU CAN NO LONGER TAKE CHRISTIANITY SERIOUSLY!
SCHOPENHAUER
DARWIN
IN 1867 HE VOLUNTEERED IN THE PRUSSIAN ARMY.
I SERVED IN THE FRENCH-PRUSSIAN WAR OF 70/71, WHERE I CONTRACTED ALL SORTS OF DISEASES
FROM 1869 UNTIL 1879 HE WAS PROFESSOR OF PHILOLOGY IN BASEL, A JOB HE HAD TO QUIT DUE TO HEALTH ISSUES. HE THEN BEGAN TO ROAM EUROPE.
FRANCE, SWITZERLAND, ITALY...
PREFERABLY FAR AWAY FROM MY SISTER, WITH WHOM I QUARREL A LOT.
I WROTE ONE BOOK A YEAR!
DIE FRÖHLICHE WISSENSCHAFT
ALSO SPRACH ZARATHUSTRA
DER ANTICHRIST
IN 1882 HE MET LOU SALOMÉ WHO TURNED DOWN HIS MARRIAGE PROPOSAL.
Lou
...BECAUSE MY SISTER WAS INTERFERING, NO DOUBT!
HE BECAME ALIENATED AND BITTER AND SUFFERED A NERVOUS BREAKDOWN IN 1889.
DURING HIS LAST FEW YEARS HIS SISTER ELISABETH LOOKED AFTER HIM.
DON'T WORRY FRITZI! I'LL LOOK AFTER YOUR LEGACY!
HE DIED AFTER A SERIES OF STROKES IN AUGUST 1900, 55 YEARS OLD.
HOLY BE HIS NAME FOR GENERATIONS TO COME!
his friend Peter Gast

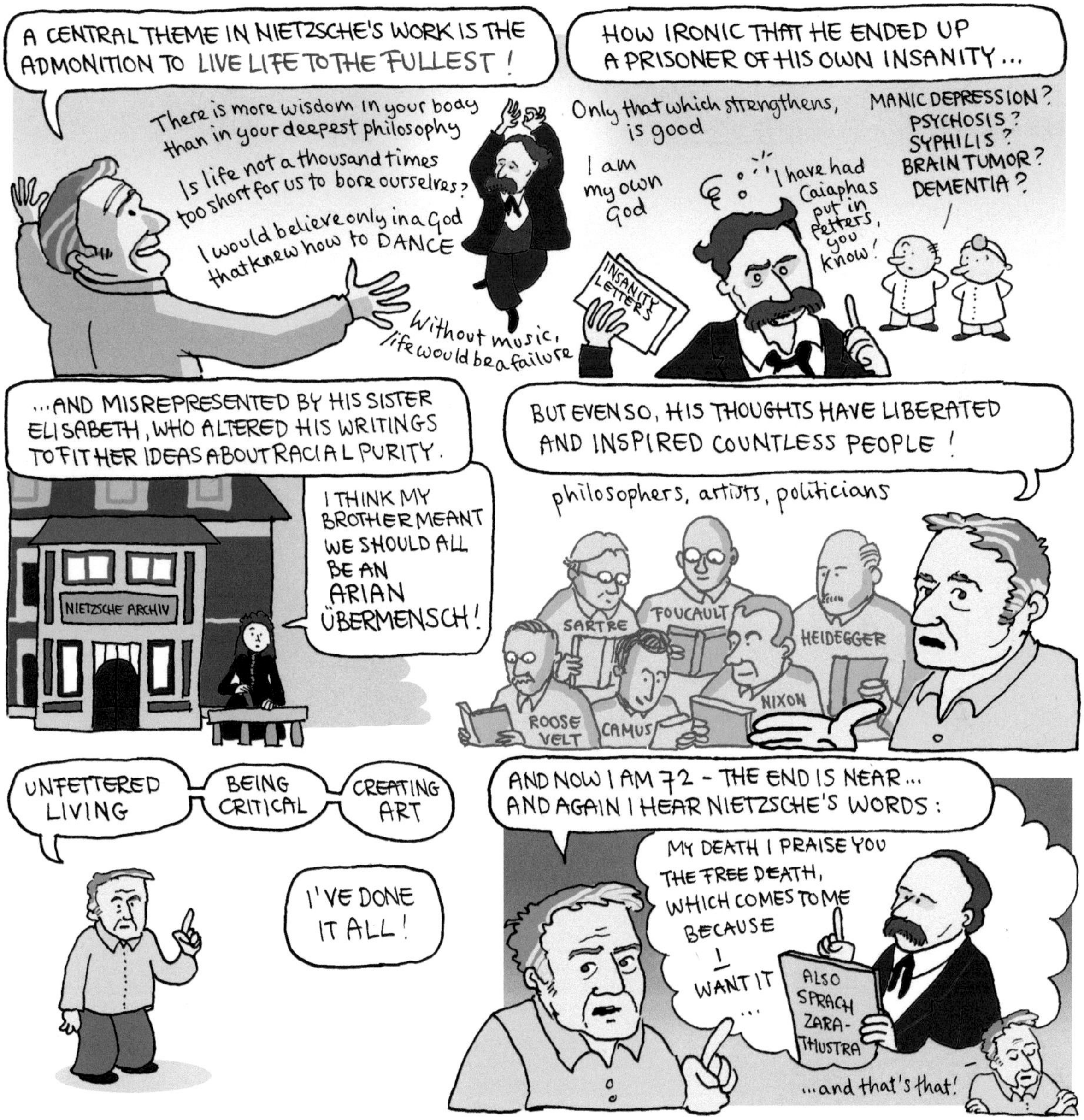
A CENTRAL THEME IN NIETZSCHE'S WORK IS THE ADMONITION TO LIVE LIFE TO THE FULLEST!
There is more wisdom in your body than in your deepest philosophy
Is life not a thousand times too short for us to bore ourselves?
I would believe only in a God that knew how to DANCE
Without music, life would be a failure
HOW IRONIC THAT HE ENDED UP A PRISONER OF HIS OWN INSANITY...
Only that which strengthens, is good
I am my own God
I have had Caiaphas put in fetters, you know!
INSANITY LETTERS
MANIC DEPRESSION? PSYCHOSIS? SYPHILIS? BRAIN TUMOR? DEMENTIA?
...AND MISREPRESENTED BY HIS SISTER ELISABETH, WHO ALTERED HIS WRITINGS TO FIT HER IDEAS ABOUT RACIAL PURITY.
NIETZSCHE ARCHIV
I THINK MY BROTHER MEANT WE SHOULD ALL BE AN ARIAN ÜBERMENSCH!
BUT EVEN SO, HIS THOUGHTS HAVE LIBERATED AND INSPIRED COUNTLESS PEOPLE!
philosophers, artists, politicians
SARTRE
FOUCAULT
HEIDEGGER
NIXON
ROOSEVELT
CAMUS
UNFETTERED LIVING
BEING CRITICAL
CREATING ART
I'VE DONE IT ALL!
AND NOW I AM 72 - THE END IS NEAR... AND AGAIN I HEAR NIETZSCHE'S WORDS:
MY DEATH I PRAISE YOU THE FREE DEATH, WHICH COMES TO ME BECAUSE I WANT IT ...
ALSO SPRACH ZARATHUSTRA
...and that's that!

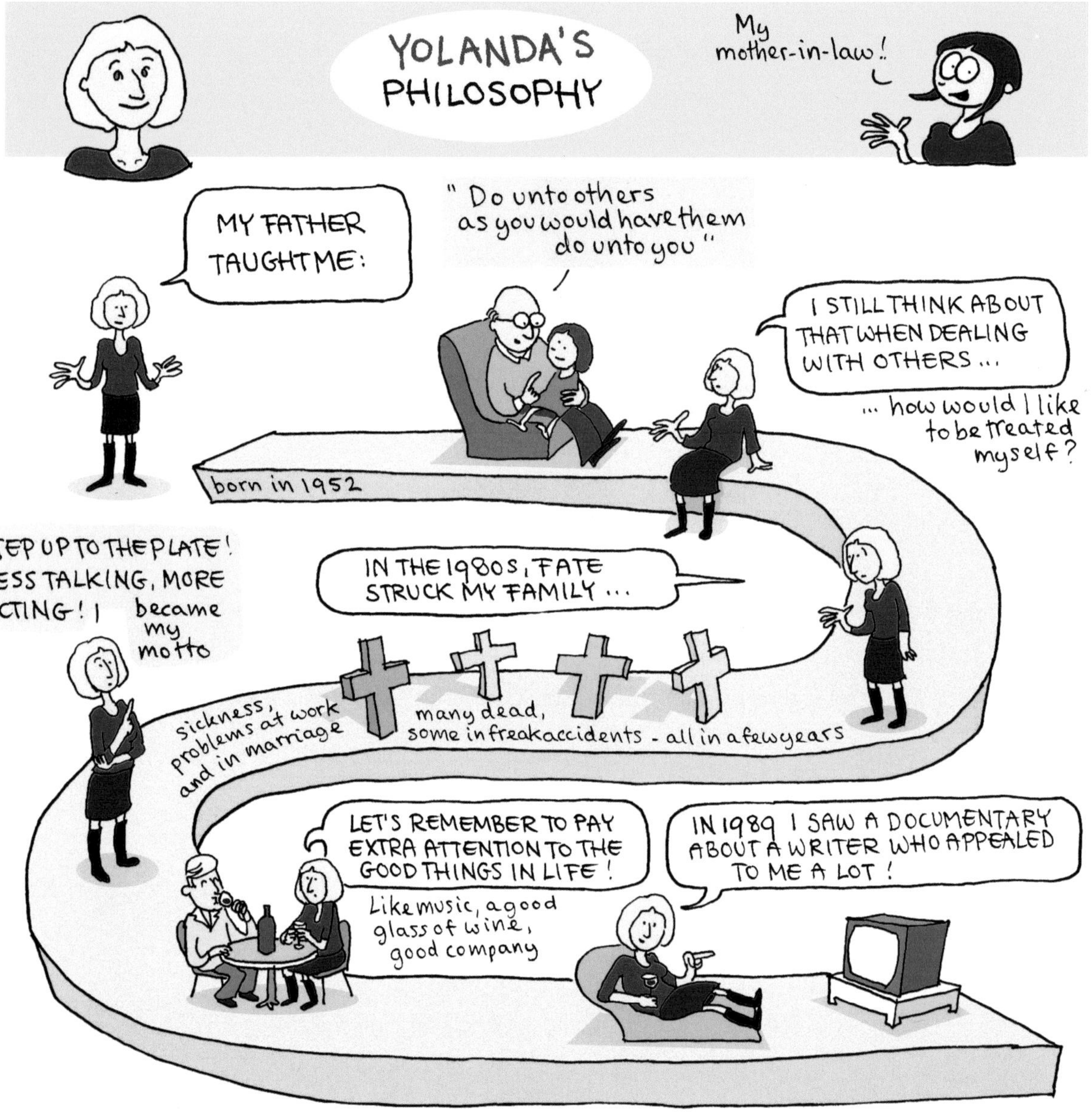
YOLANDA'S PHILOSOPHY
My mother-in-law!
MY FATHER TAUGHT ME:
" Do unto others as you would have them do unto you "
born in 1952
I STILL THINK ABOUT THAT WHEN DEALING WITH OTHERS ...
... how would I like to be treated myself?
IN THE 1980S, FATE STRUCK MY FAMILY ...
many dead, some in freak accidents - all in a few years
sickness, problems at work and in marriage
STEP UP TO THE PLATE! LESS TALKING, MORE ACTING! I became my motto
LET'S REMEMBER TO PAY EXTRA ATTENTION TO THE GOOD THINGS IN LIFE!
Like music, a good glass of wine, good company
IN 1989 I SAW A DOCUMENTARY ABOUT A WRITER WHO APPEALED TO ME A LOT!

THE LIFE OF GEORGE STEINER

STEINER'S PARENTS FLED VIENNA FOR PARIS IN 1924, DUE TO GROWING ANTI-SEMITISM.

father Frederick bank lawyer

mother Elise

ON APRIL 23, 1929, THEIR SON GEORGE WAS BORN.

sister Ruth

HE IS HANDICAPPED: HIS RIGHT ARM IS UNDER-DEVELOPED.

SELF-PITY MAKES ME SICK! YOU'LL LEARN TO TIE YOUR SHOES AND WRITE WITH YOUR RIGHT HAND JUST LIKE EVERYONE ELSE!

HIS PARENTS TAUGHT HIM THREE LANGUAGES AND RAISED HIM WITH THE CLASSICS.

FATHER, LESEN SIE DIE ILIAD WITH ME CE SOIR, S'IL VOUS PLAIT?

HOMERUS ILIAS

THE FAMILY FLED TO NEW YORK IN 1940, A MONTH BEFORE THE GERMANS TOOK PARIS.

HE STUDIED LITERATURE, MATH AND PHYSICS IN CHICAGO, HARVARD & OXFORD.

I'M MORE INTERESTED IN A BROAD EDUCATION THAN SPECIALIZATION!

IN 1955 HE MARRIED ZARA SHAKOW.

YOU OWE ME A TENNER! I TOLD YOU THEY WERE MADE FOR EACH OTHER!

Two such brilliant and dedicated students!

their professors

HE TAUGHT AT VARIOUS UNIVERSITIES IN EUROPE AND AMERICA.

I LOVE HOW HE TALKS ABOUT LITERATURE AND CULTURE!

HE'S A CRITIC, BUT NOT A PESSIMIST!

HE IS AN ESTEEMED CULTURE CRITIC, WITH SURVIVAL AS A CENTRAL THEME IN HIS THINKING.

MY LIFE IS ABOUT DEATH, REMEMBRANCE, THE HOLOCAUST...

TREES HAVE ROOTS AND I HAVE LEGS; I OWE MY LIFE TO THAT!

READ BOOKS, MEMORIZE THINGS — NO ONE CAN TAKE THAT AWAY FROM YOU!

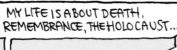

HE RETIRED IN 1994, BUT IS STILL GIVING LECTURES. HE LIVES IN CAMBRIDGE, ENGLAND

EVEN THOUGH I AM AMERICAN!

My father said: "If there is no one left in Europe with the name Steiner, Hitler will have won after all!"

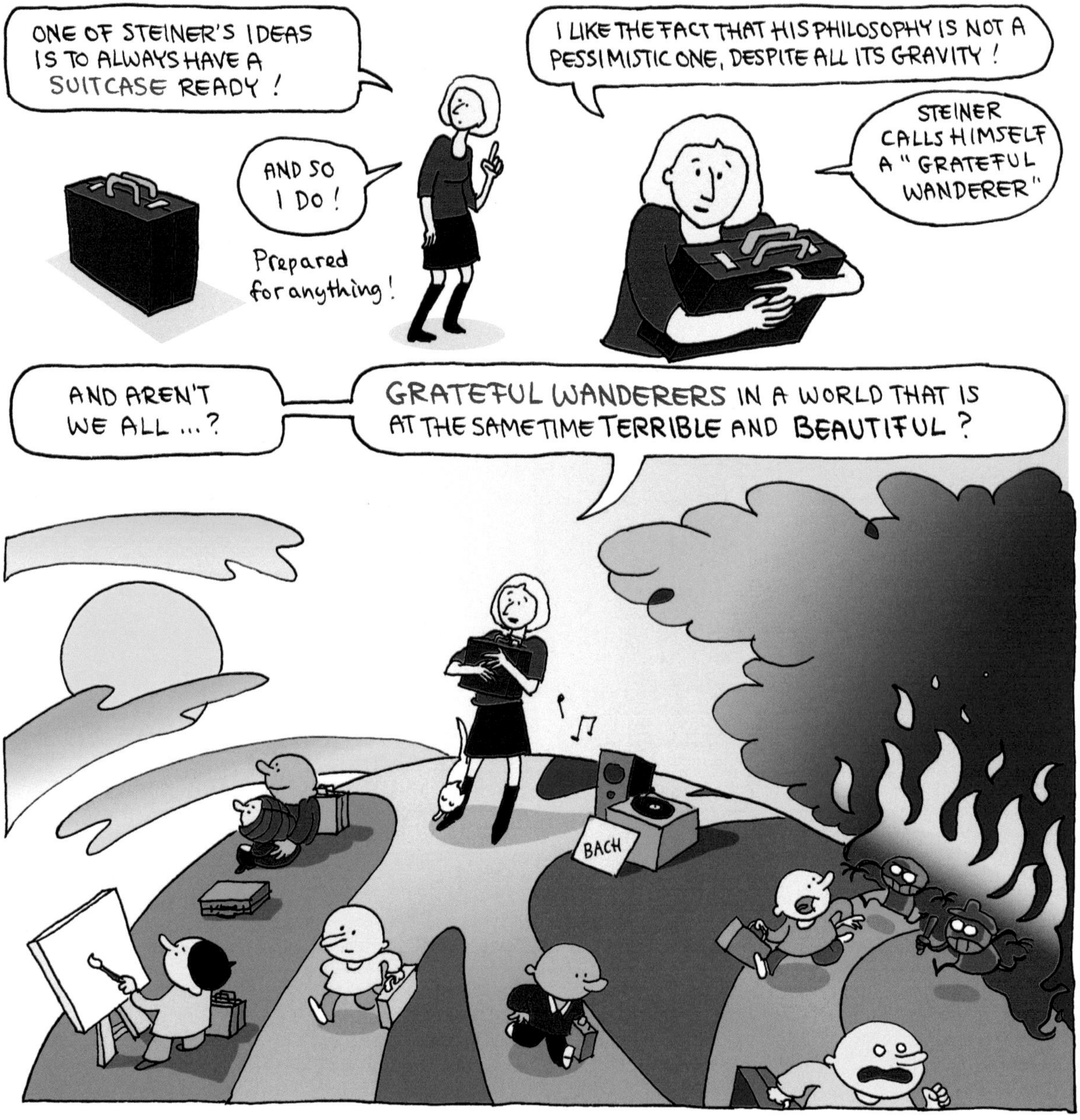
ONE OF STEINER'S IDEAS IS TO ALWAYS HAVE A SUITCASE READY !
AND SO I DO !
Prepared for anything !
I LIKE THE FACT THAT HIS PHILOSOPHY IS NOT A PESSIMISTIC ONE, DESPITE ALL ITS GRAVITY !
STEINER CALLS HIMSELF A "GRATEFUL WANDERER"
AND AREN'T WE ALL ... ?
GRATEFUL WANDERERS IN A WORLD THAT IS AT THE SAME TIME TERRIBLE AND BEAUTIFUL ?
BACH

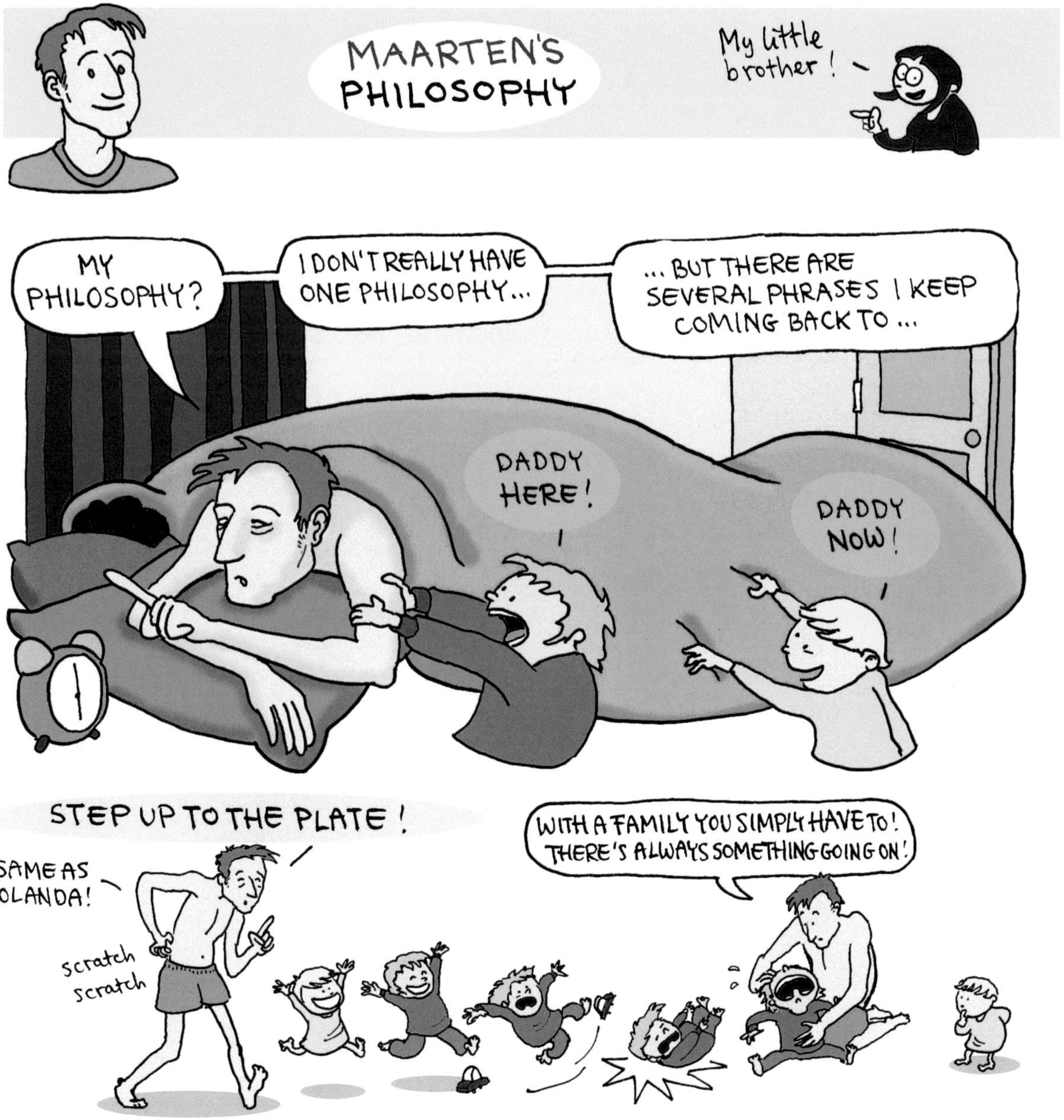
MAARTEN'S PHILOSOPHY
My little brother!
MY PHILOSOPHY?
I DON'T REALLY HAVE ONE PHILOSOPHY...
... BUT THERE ARE SEVERAL PHRASES I KEEP COMING BACK TO ...
DADDY HERE!
DADDY NOW!
STEP UP TO THE PLATE!
SAME AS YOLANDA!
scratch scratch
WITH A FAMILY YOU SIMPLY HAVE TO! THERE'S ALWAYS SOMETHING GOING ON!

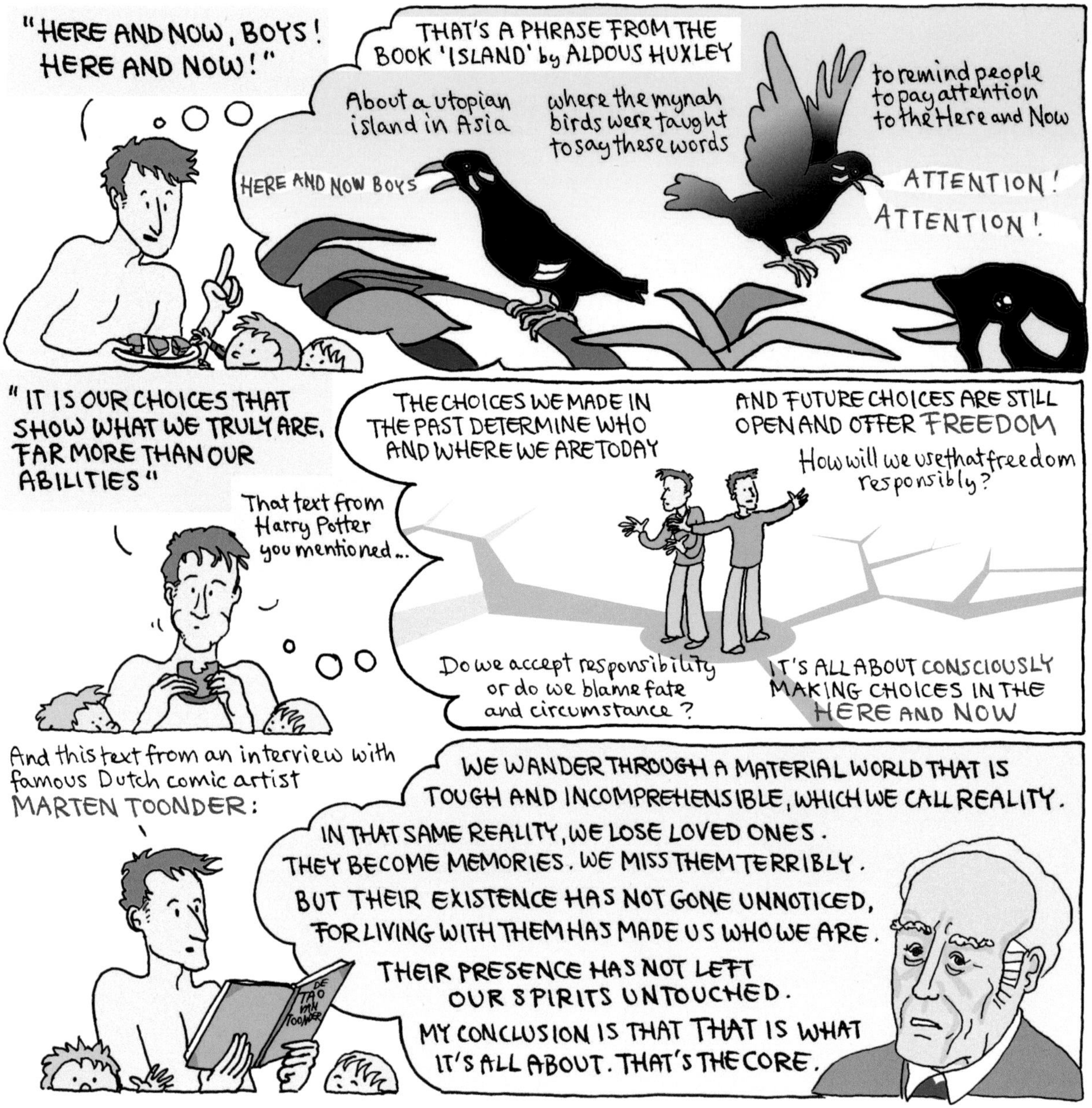
"HERE AND NOW, BOYS! HERE AND NOW!"
THAT'S A PHRASE FROM THE BOOK 'ISLAND' by ALDOUS HUXLEY
About a utopian island in Asia
where the mynah birds were taught to say these words
to remind people to pay attention to the Here and Now
HERE AND NOW BOYS
ATTENTION!
ATTENTION!
" IT IS OUR CHOICES THAT SHOW WHAT WE TRULY ARE, FAR MORE THAN OUR ABILITIES "
That text from Harry Potter you mentioned...
THE CHOICES WE MADE IN THE PAST DETERMINE WHO AND WHERE WE ARE TODAY
AND FUTURE CHOICES ARE STILL OPEN AND OFFER FREEDOM
How will we use that freedom responsibly?
Do we accept responsibility or do we blame fate and circumstance?
IT'S ALL ABOUT CONSCIOUSLY MAKING CHOICES IN THE HERE AND NOW
And this text from an interview with famous Dutch comic artist MARTEN TOONDER:
WE WANDER THROUGH A MATERIAL WORLD THAT IS TOUGH AND INCOMPREHENSIBLE, WHICH WE CALL REALITY.
IN THAT SAME REALITY, WE LOSE LOVED ONES.
THEY BECOME MEMORIES. WE MISS THEM TERRIBLY.
BUT THEIR EXISTENCE HAS NOT GONE UNNOTICED,
FOR LIVING WITH THEM HAS MADE US WHO WE ARE.
THEIR PRESENCE HAS NOT LEFT OUR SPIRITS UNTOUCHED.
MY CONCLUSION IS THAT THAT IS WHAT IT'S ALL ABOUT. THAT'S THE CORE.
DE TAO VAN TOONDER

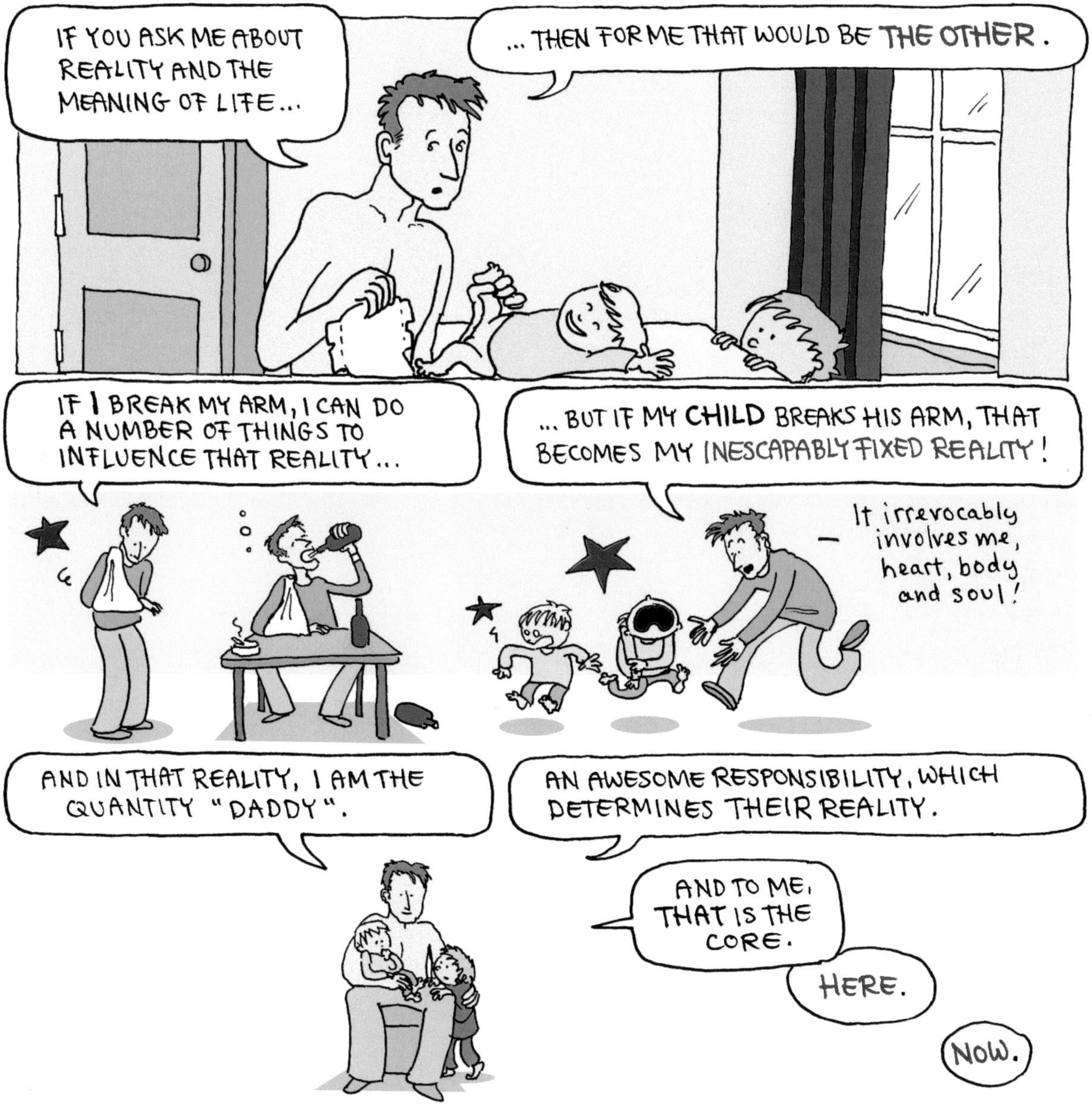
IF YOU ASK ME ABOUT REALITY AND THE MEANING OF LIFE...
... THEN FOR ME THAT WOULD BE THE OTHER.
IF I BREAK MY ARM, I CAN DO A NUMBER OF THINGS TO INFLUENCE THAT REALITY...
... BUT IF MY CHILD BREAKS HIS ARM, THAT BECOMES MY INESCAPABLY FIXED REALITY!
– It irrevocably involves me, heart, body and soul!
AND IN THAT REALITY, I AM THE QUANTITY "DADDY".
AN AWESOME RESPONSIBILITY, WHICH DETERMINES THEIR REALITY.
AND TO ME, THAT IS THE CORE.
HERE.
NOW.

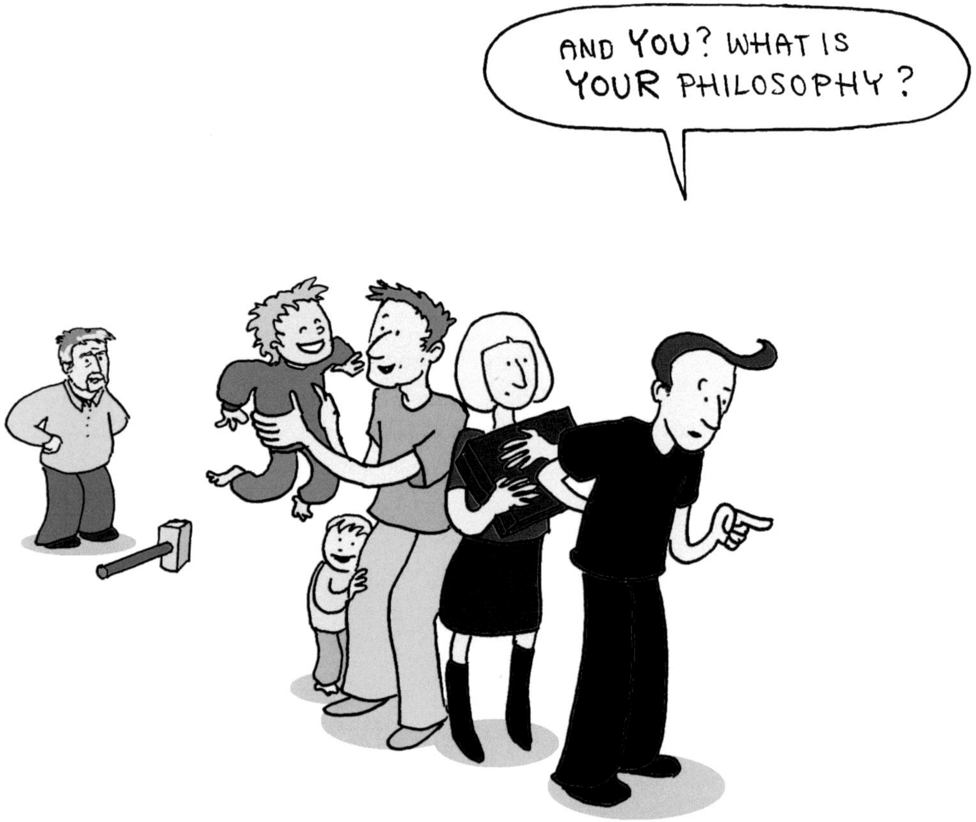
AND YOU? WHAT IS YOUR PHILOSOPHY?

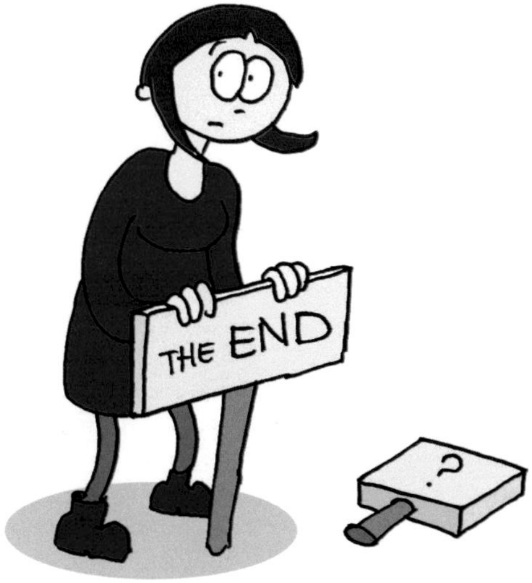
THE END
?

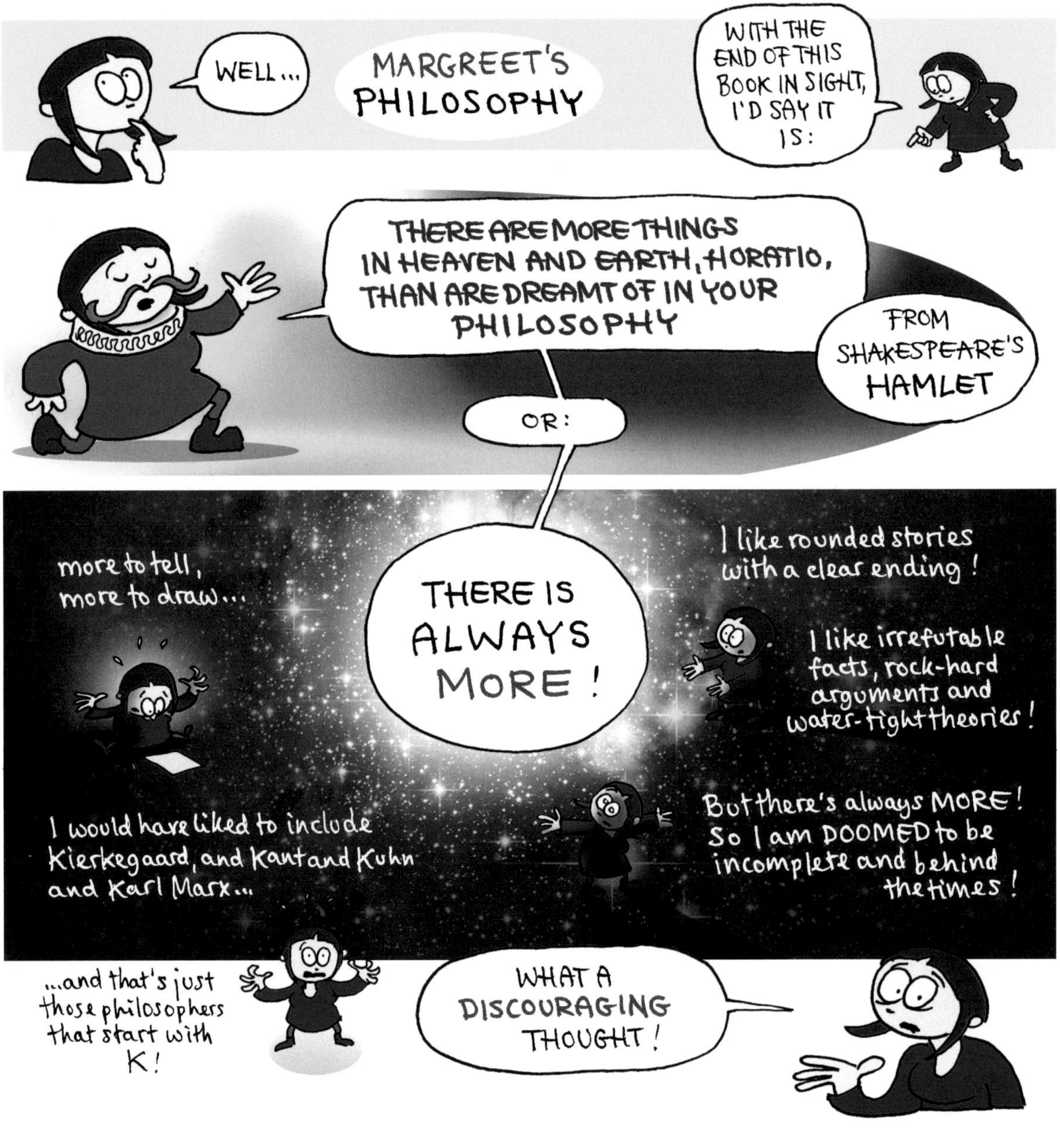
WELL...
MARGREET'S PHILOSOPHY
WITH THE END OF THIS BOOK IN SIGHT, I'D SAY IT IS:
THERE ARE MORE THINGS IN HEAVEN AND EARTH, HORATIO, THAN ARE DREAMT OF IN YOUR PHILOSOPHY
FROM SHAKESPEARE'S HAMLET
OR:
THERE IS ALWAYS MORE!
more to tell, more to draw...
I like rounded stories with a clear ending!
I like irrefutable facts, rock-hard arguments and water-tight theories!
I would have liked to include Kierkegaard, and Kant and Kuhn and Karl Marx...
But there's always MORE! So I am DOOMED to be incomplete and behind the times!
...and that's just those philosophers that start with K!
WHAT A DISCOURAGING THOUGHT!

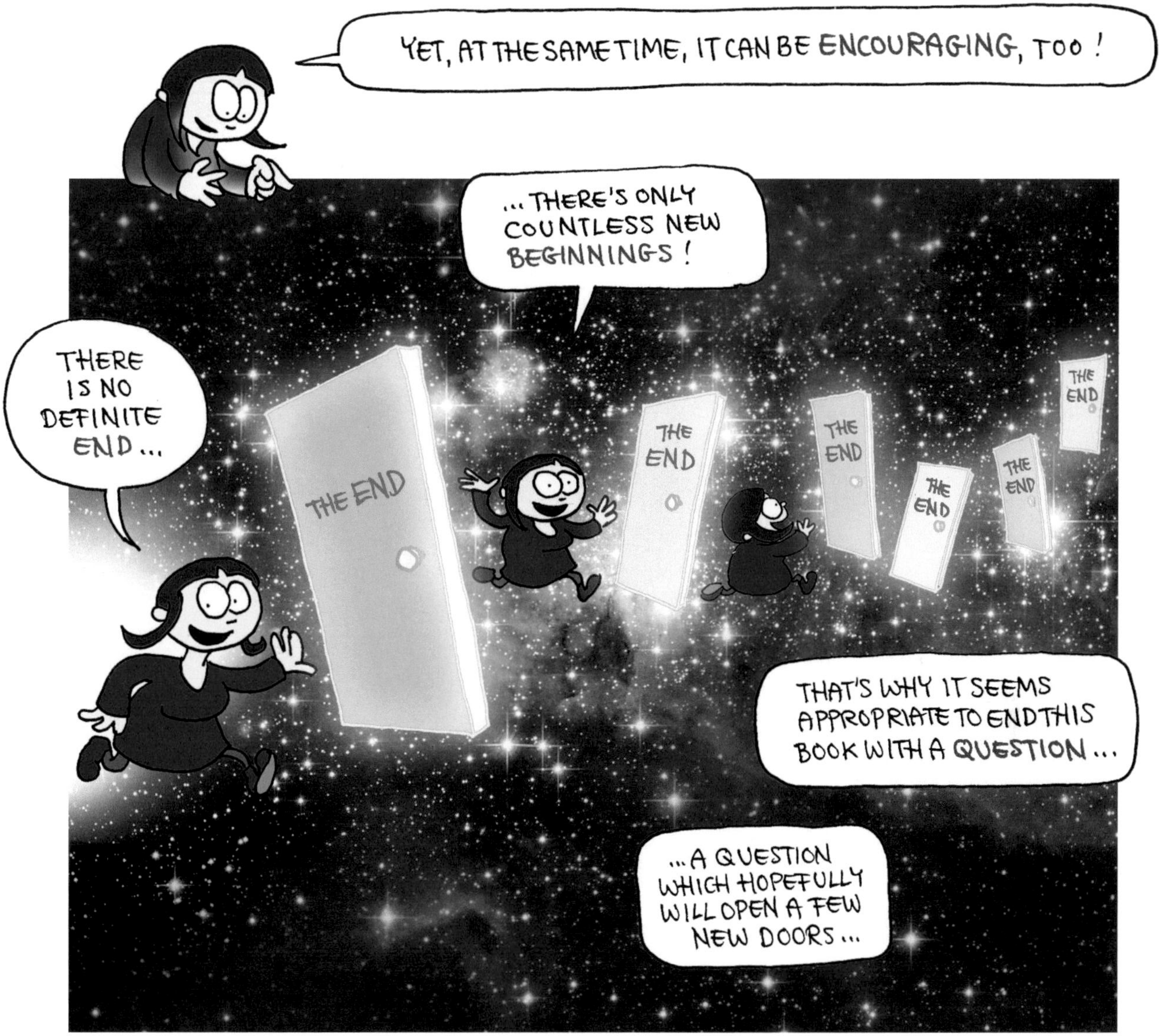
YET, AT THE SAME TIME, IT CAN BE ENCOURAGING, TOO!
THERE IS NO DEFINITE END...
...THERE'S ONLY COUNTLESS NEW BEGINNINGS!
THE END
THE END
THE END
THE END
THE END
THE END
THAT'S WHY IT SEEMS APPROPRIATE TO END THIS BOOK WITH A QUESTION...
...A QUESTION WHICH HOPEFULLY WILL OPEN A FEW NEW DOORS...

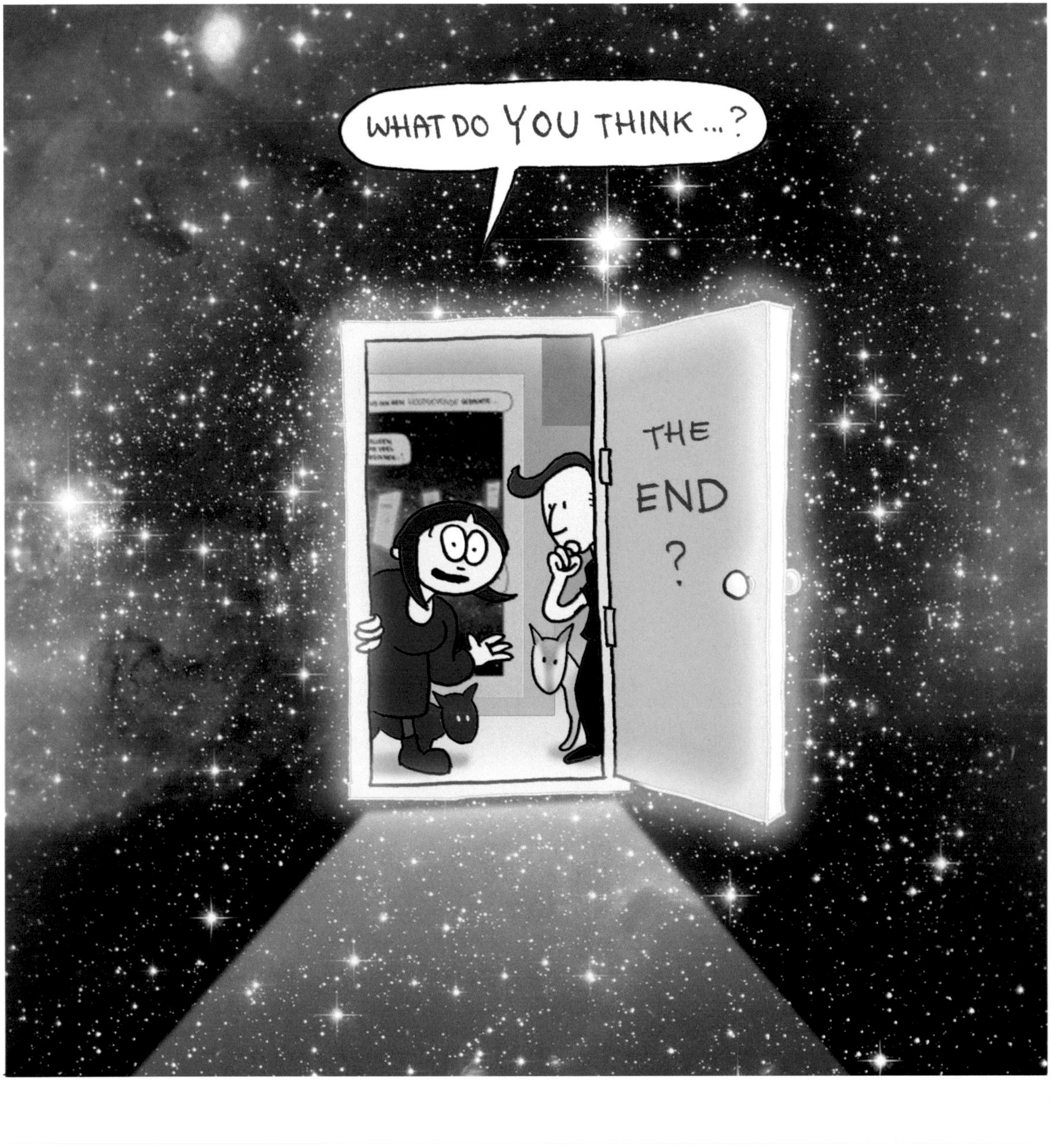
WHAT DO YOU THINK ...?
THE END ?

NOTES:
Sources for images and texts

This book could not have been made without the use of Google and Wikipedia

page 37:
Map of Mediterranean area circa 500 B.C.
from the *Historical Atlas* by Willliam R. Shepherd, 1926

page 38:
Painting of "The Allegory of the Cave", by Cornelis Corneliszoon van Haarlem,
in a print by Jan Saenredam, 1604

page 41:
Photo of Maik, by Mariette van Heyningen

page 57:
Picture from the book *Cosmographicus Liber*, by Petrus Apianus, 1524

page 58:
Cosmological world view of Ptolemaeus, from the atlas by Andreas Cellarius, 1660

Picture of the sphere of Sacrobosco, early 15th century

page 64:
Illustration of the seven liberal arts gathered around philosophy,
from the *Hortus Deliciarum*, by Herrad von Lansberg, 1180

page 74:
Map of the United Lowlands by Nicolaas Visscher I (1608-1679),
used with permission of the Koninklijke Bibliotheek, The Hague

Map of Europe about 1560, from William R. Shepherd's *Historical Atlas*, 1923

page 84:
"View of The Hague from the Delftse Vaart in the 17th century",
painted by Cornelis Springer and Kaspar Karsen, 1852

Print of "Le massacre de Messrs de Witte" (artist unknown)

page 100
Part of the album cover *George Carlin: Take-Offs and Put-Ons,
Recorded Live at the Roostertail, Detroit, Michigan*, from 1966

page 104:
Painting of the German-French war 1870/71: "Sturm auf den Spicherer Berg"
by Anton von Werner, 1880 (inverted image)

Photo of Lou Salomé driving Paul Rée and Friedrich Nietzsche.
Staged by Nietzsche after Salomé had turned down
proposals of marriage from both men, 1882

Photo from the series "Der kranke Nietzsche" by Hans Olde, 1899

Also available:

Taxes, The Tea Party, and those Revolting Rebels
A Comics History of the American Revolution by Stan Mack
$14.99

add $4 P&H.
See more with features and reviews at our website, including Margreet posting on our blog:
www.nbmpub.com

We have over 200 graphic novels available, write for a complete catalog:
NBM 160 Broadway, Ste. 700, East Wing
New York, NY 10038

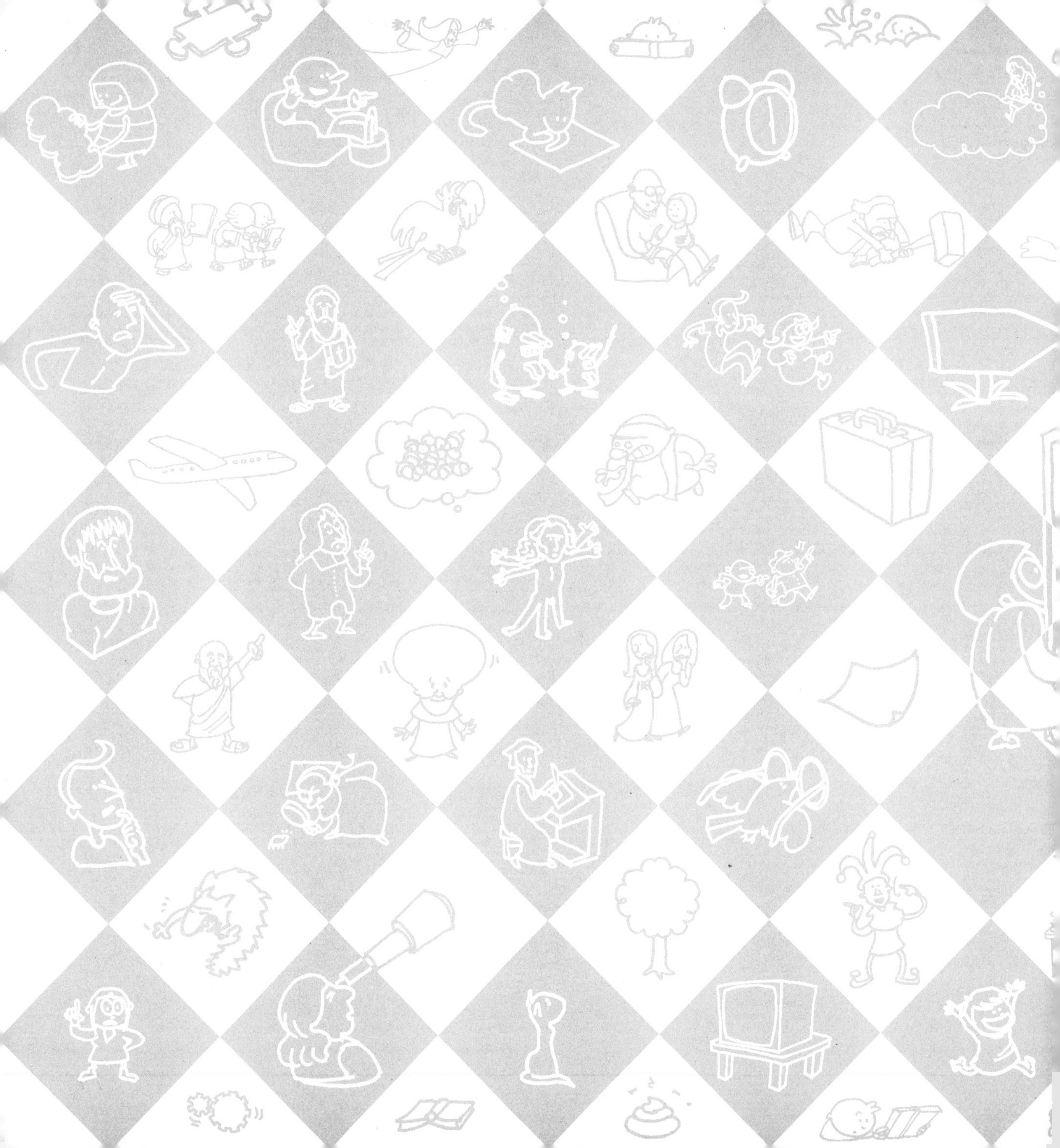